RITES *of* AUGUST FIRST

Antislavery, Abolition, and the Atlantic World
R. J. M. Blackett and James Brewer Stewart, Series Editors

RITES *of* AUGUST FIRST

Emancipation Day in the Black Atlantic World

J. R. KERR-RITCHIE

LOUISIANA STATE UNIVERSITY PRESS
Baton Rouge

Published by Louisiana State University Press
Copyright © 2007 by Louisiana State University Press
All rights reserved
Manufactured in the United States of America
Louisiana Paperback Edition, 2011

Designer: Tammi deGeneres
Typeface: Centaur MT
Typesetter: G&S Typesetters, Inc.

Library of Congress Cataloging-in-Publication Data

Kerr-Ritchie, Jeffrey R.
Rites of August First : Emancipation Day in the Black Atlantic world / J.R. Kerr-Ritchie.
p. cm. — (Antislavery, abolition, and the Atlantic world)
Includes bibliographical references and index.

1. Emancipation Day (British West Indies) 2. Slaves—Emancipation—West Indies, British.
3. Slaves—Emancipation—Ontario. I. title.
HT1031.K47 2007
326'.8—dc22
2006024849
ISBN 978-0-8071-4364-3 (pbk: alk. paper)—ISBN 978-0-8071-3570-9 (pdf)—ISBN 978-0-8071-4417-6 (epub)—ISBN 978-0-8071-4418-3 (mobi)

In memory of my grandmother Joyce French (1921–2005)

Contents

Tables

Acknowledgments

One of the pleasures of completing a book is the opportunity it provides to thank supporting institutions, colleagues, librarians, students, and friends.

I would like to begin by thanking Associate Director Robert P. Forbes and Director David B. Davis at the Gilder Lehrman Center for the Study of Slavery, Resistance and Abolition at Yale University. They awarded me a senior fellowship, together with a wonderful office and access to superb archival resources. The two major consequences were time to think about what exactly this book was going to be about, and an appreciation for the strengths and weaknesses of Anglo-American abolition. I would also like to thank secretary Mary Mahon for her help and good cheer.

Many thanks to Scholars Program Director Colin Palmer and Center Director Howard Dodson at the Schomburg Center for Research in Black Culture. They provided me with a six-month fellowship, access to a wonderful collection of archival materials, and serious scholarly exchange. Peter Hobbs was a fine research assistant: I hope he makes that independent movie one day! Troy Belle, Koreen Duncan, Genette McLaurin, Betty Odabashian, Michael Roudette, Donnalee Simon, Jatta Musa, and Pablo Jarama in General Research and Reference were unfailingly helpful in answering my questions. Miriam Jiminez Roman patiently steered the scholars through the logistics of the program. I cannot end without nods to the band of brothers: Ken Bilby, Frank Guridy, Winston Kennedy, and George Priestley. I trust the combination of serious discussion and easy conversation in the scholar's "closet" office improved their books; it certainly helped with this one.

If fellowships at Yale and the Schomburg helped in the research for this book, it was a fellowship at the National Humanities Center in Durham, North Carolina, which facilitated its writing. Deputy Director Kent Mulliken and Director Geoffrey Harpham provided constant financial support and encouragement for this project throughout 2003–4. Thanks to the library staff of Jean Houston, Betsy Dain, and Marianne Watson for their super efficiency and good grace to meet countless requests. I would also like to thank editor

Karen Carroll for her patience, Philip Barron and Joel Elliot for their assistance with computing, and Bernice Patterson and Virginia Guilfoile for their warm friendship. Thanks, too, to my fellow fellows for their intellectual support and fun company: Jordanna Bailkin, Lee Baker, Thomas Brothers, John Carson, Tom Cogswell, Lewis Erenberg, Sam Floyd, Gabrielle Foreman, Elizabeth Kennedy, James Peacock, Theda Purdue, and Brad Weiss.

The research for this book took me to archival collections and libraries at Cornell University, the National Library of Scotland and the New College Library in Edinburgh, the Ontario Archives in Toronto, the State University of New York at Binghamton, the University of North Carolina at Greensboro, the University of the West Indies at St. Augustine, Vaasar College, and Yale University. While I regrettably cannot name all those archivists, librarians, and individuals who assisted me, I can offer my sincerest appreciation and thanks to these hardworking and committed staff who make our historical research so rewarding.

Shukran to Ashraf Rushdy, Bob Engs, and Tom Dublin, all of whom constantly encouraged this project, through the tough as well as easy times.

Many thanks to the folks at Louisiana State University Press, including Antislavery, Abolition, and the Atlantic World series editors R. J. M. Blackett and James Brewer Stewart for insightful comments on an earlier draft, and acquisitions editor Rand Dotson for his efficiency. My thanks also to anonymous outside readers at Louisiana State University Press and the University of North Carolina Press.

I would especially like to give credit to numerous colleagues for comments on chapters, source suggestions, and post-presentation feedback over the years. They include Ken Bilby, Richard Blackett, Bridget Brereton, Jacqueline Glass Campbell, John Carson, Ira Dworkin, Bob Engs, Harold Forsythe, Steven Gregory, Josh Guild, Peter Hitchcock, Cindy Horan, Joel Kaye, Michelle Kuhl, Winston James, Steve Middleton, Colin Palmer, Tiffany Patterson, Dylan Penningroth, Ashraf Rushdy, Loren Schweninger, Kitty Sklar, Betsy Traube, and Carlton Wilson. The usual caveat of personal responsibility for errors applies.

Although much of this book was researched and written away from the classroom, the impact of students was ever-present. Shouts out to those who participated in my courses on Comparative Slavery, Comparative Emancipation, Black Protest Movements, Black Intellectuals, and African-American History at Wesleyan, SUNY-Binghamton, Columbia University, and UNC-Greensboro.

I would like to end by expressing my gratitude to nonacademic friends who supported this project. Bear, Nicolette, Clifford, and Leah Lowe-Davies in Oakville, Canada, provided evenings of fun after long days at the Ontario Archives. Kirk and Joe Ifill put up with me on two visits to Port-of-Spain, Trinidad and Tobago. Leah Gardiner and Barbara and Michael Jackson in Philadelphia have always believed in my work. Kidd and Jennifer Dorn were both supportive and fun during the fellowship year in New York City. A toast to the James Joyce crew in Durham for those relaxing moments.

Finally, my thanks to Elizabeth R. L. for her support, patience, and love. *Ventis secundis.*

Abbreviations

AA	*Anglo-African* (New York City)
ASB	*Anti-Slavery Bugle* (Salem, Ohio)
BAP	*Black Abolitionist Papers*
BDE	*Brooklyn Daily Eagle* (Brooklyn, New York)
BPP	*British Parliamentary Papers*
CA	*Colored American* (New York City)
CR	*Christian Recorder* (Philadelphia, Pennsylvania)
DG	*Daily Globe* (Toronto, Canada West)
E	*Emancipator* (New York City)
EAACH	*Encyclopedia of African-American Culture and History*
ER	*Evening Record* (Windsor, Ontario)
FDP	*Frederick Douglass' Paper* (Rochester, New York)
HF	*Herald of Freedom* (Concord, Massachusetts)
HS	*Hamilton Spectator* (Hamilton, Canada West)
L	*Liberator* (Boston, Massachusetts)
MRUPC	*Missionary Record of the United Presbyterian Church* (Edinburgh, Scotland)
NASS	*National Anti-Slavery Standard* (New York City)
ND	*Nashville Dispatch* (Nashville, Tennessee)
NE	*National Era* (Washington, D.C.)
NEQ	*New England Quarterly* (Boston, Massachusetts)
NS	*North Star* (Rochester, New York)
NYDT	*New York Daily Tribune* (New York City)
PE	*Poughkeepsie Eagle* (Poughkeepsie, New York)
PF	*Provincial Freeman* (Toronto, Chatham, Canada West)
PT	*Poughkeepsie Telegraph* (Poughkeepsie, New York)
VF	*Voice of the Fugitive* (Sandwich, Canada West)
WAA	*Weekly Anglo-African* (New York City)

1842   August First picnics begin in Massachusetts.
John Collins' *The Anti-Slavery Picnic* published.
U.S. Supreme Court decision in *Prigg v. Pennsylvania.*
Fugitive Nelson Hackett case.
New England Freedom Association founded in Boston.
Formation of Dawn Settlement in Canada West.
Webster-Ashburton Treaty.

1843   Abolition of slavery in British India by East India Company.
National Convention of Colored Citizens in Buffalo, N.Y.
James Phillippo's *Jamaica: Past and Present* published.

1844   U.S. Congress lifts Gag Rule.

1845   Henry Hammond's *Letter to an English Abolitionist* published.
F. Douglass's *Narrative of the Life of Frederick Douglass* published.

1846   Abolition of West Indies monopoly on sugar exports to the United Kingdom.

1847   National Convention of Colored People in Troy, N.Y.
Liberia declares national independence.

1848   Year of continental European revolutions.
Abolition of slavery in French Empire.
Abolition of slavery in Danish Empire.
Formation of Hannibal Guards, Brooklyn, N.Y.
National Convention of Colored People in Cleveland, Ohio.
David Walker's *Appeal to the Colored Citizens of the World* published.
Henry H. Garnet's *Address to the Slaves* published.

1849   Formation of Elgin Association Settlement in Canada West.
Thomas Carlyle's "Occasional Discourse on the Nigger" published.
Henry Bibb's *Narrative of Life and Adventures of Henry Bibb* published.

1850   Fugitive Slave Act passed in the United States.

1851   Antislavery Society of Canada founded in Toronto.
Fugitive armed defense at Christiana, Pa.
North American Convention in Toronto.
Voice of the Fugitive begins publication in Sandwich, Canada West.
Formation of Refugee Home Society in Sandwich.
The North Star issued under new title *Frederick Douglass' Paper*
Fugitive Jerry McHenry rescue in Syracuse, N.Y.
West India Association's *Case of the British West Indies Stated* published.

Abbreviations

AA	*Anglo-African* (NEW YORK CITY)
ASB	*Anti-Slavery Bugle* (SALEM, OHIO)
BAP	*Black Abolitionist Papers*
BDE	*Brooklyn Daily Eagle* (BROOKLYN, NEW YORK)
BPP	*British Parliamentary Papers*
CA	*Colored American* (NEW YORK CITY)
CR	*Christian Recorder* (PHILADELPHIA, PENNSYLVANIA)
DG	*Daily Globe* (TORONTO, CANADA WEST)
E	*Emancipator* (NEW YORK CITY)
EAACH	*Encyclopedia of African-American Culture and History*
ER	*Evening Record* (WINDSOR, ONTARIO)
FDP	*Frederick Douglass' Paper* (ROCHESTER, NEW YORK)
HF	*Herald of Freedom* (CONCORD, MASSACHUSETTS)
HS	*Hamilton Spectator* (HAMILTON, CANADA WEST)
L	*Liberator* (BOSTON, MASSACHUSETTS)
MRUPC	*Missionary Record of the United Presbyterian Church* (EDINBURGH, SCOTLAND)
NASS	*National Anti-Slavery Standard* (NEW YORK CITY)
ND	*Nashville Dispatch* (NASHVILLE, TENNESSEE)
NE	*National Era* (WASHINGTON, D.C.)
NEQ	*New England Quarterly* (BOSTON, MASSACHUSETTS)
NS	*North Star* (ROCHESTER, NEW YORK)
NYDT	*New York Daily Tribune* (NEW YORK CITY)
PE	*Poughkeepsie Eagle* (POUGHKEEPSIE, NEW YORK)
PF	*Provincial Freeman* (TORONTO, CHATHAM, CANADA WEST)
PT	*Poughkeepsie Telegraph* (POUGHKEEPSIE, NEW YORK)
VF	*Voice of the Fugitive* (SANDWICH, CANADA WEST)
WAA	*Weekly Anglo-African* (NEW YORK CITY)

Chronology

1831   *Liberator* begins publication in Boston.
Nat Turner's slave revolt in southern Virginia.
Sam Sharpe's slave revolt in western Jamaica.
Mary Prince's *The History of Mary Prince* published.

1832   British Parliament investigates colonial slavery.
Massachusetts Anti-Slavery Society founded in Boston.

1833   Abolition of Slavery Bill passed in Great Britain.
Glasgow Emancipation Society founded in Scotland.
American Anti-Slavery Society founded in Philadelphia.
Anglo-Canadian extradition law passed.
Philadelphia Committee of Vigilance founded.

1834   British Abolition of Slavery Bill implemented.

1835   New York Anti-Slavery Society founded.
New York Committee of Vigilance founded.
American Moral Reform Society founded in Philadelphia.

1836   U.S. Congress passes Gag Rule.

1837   Queen Victoria ascends the British throne.
William Lyon McKenzie's revolt in British Canada.
Fugitive Jesse Happy case.

1838   Thome and Kimball's *Emancipation in the West Indies* published.
Abolition of apprenticeship system in British West Indies.

1839   *Amistad* slave ship revolt.
Liberty Party founded in New York.

1840   World's Anti-Slavery Convention in London, England.
American and Foreign Anti-Slavery Society founded.

1841   *Creole* slave ship revolt.
J. W. C. Pennington's *Text Book of the Colored People* published.

1842   August First picnics begin in Massachusetts.
John Collins' *The Anti-Slavery Picnic* published.
U.S. Supreme Court decision in *Prigg v. Pennsylvania.*
Fugitive Nelson Hackett case.
New England Freedom Association founded in Boston.
Formation of Dawn Settlement in Canada West.
Webster-Ashburton Treaty.

1843   Abolition of slavery in British India by East India Company.
National Convention of Colored Citizens in Buffalo, N.Y.
James Phillippo's *Jamaica: Past and Present* published.

1844   U.S. Congress lifts Gag Rule.

1845   Henry Hammond's *Letter to an English Abolitionist* published.
F. Douglass's *Narrative of the Life of Frederick Douglass* published.

1846   Abolition of West Indies monopoly on sugar exports to the United Kingdom.

1847   National Convention of Colored People in Troy, N.Y.
Liberia declares national independence.

1848   Year of continental European revolutions.
Abolition of slavery in French Empire.
Abolition of slavery in Danish Empire.
Formation of Hannibal Guards, Brooklyn, N.Y.
National Convention of Colored People in Cleveland, Ohio.
David Walker's *Appeal to the Colored Citizens of the World* published.
Henry H. Garnet's *Address to the Slaves* published.

1849   Formation of Elgin Association Settlement in Canada West.
Thomas Carlyle's "Occasional Discourse on the Nigger" published.
Henry Bibb's *Narrative of Life and Adventures of Henry Bibb* published.

1850   Fugitive Slave Act passed in the United States.

1851   Antislavery Society of Canada founded in Toronto.
Fugitive armed defense at Christiana, Pa.
North American Convention in Toronto.
Voice of the Fugitive begins publication in Sandwich, Canada West.
Formation of Refugee Home Society in Sandwich.
The North Star issued under new title *Frederick Douglass' Paper*
Fugitive Jerry McHenry rescue in Syracuse, N.Y.
West India Association's *Case of the British West Indies Stated* published.

1852   Mary Shadd's *Notes of Canada West* published.
Antislavery Society of Windsor founded in Canada West.
Second Philadelphia Committee of Vigilance founded.

1853   National Convention of Colored People in Rochester, N.Y.
Henry Garnet's mission to Jamaica.
Henry Bleby's *The Death Struggles of Slavery* published.

1854   Formation of Manchester Anti-Slavery League in England.
Fugitive Anthony Burns returned to Virginia slavery.
Kansas-Nebraska Act passed.
Provincial Freeman begins publication in Toronto.
Henry Bibb's death.

1855   Samuel R. Ward's *Autobiography of a Fugitive Slave* published.
First Colored Convention meets in Sacramento, Calif.

1856   National Convention of Colored People in Cleveland, Ohio.
Sack of Lawrence, Kans.

1857   First Indian Uprising against British colonialism.
Parade of the Liberty Guard in Boston.
U.S. Supreme Court decision in *Dred Scott v. Sandford.*

1858   African Civilization Society founded.

1859   Twenty-fifth anniversary of West Indian Emancipation.
John Brown's revolt in Harper's Ferry, Va.
Anglo-African begins publication in New York City.

1860   Fugitive John Anderson case.
Ellen and William Craft's *Running a Thousand Miles to Freedom* published.

1862   Abolition of slavery in Washington, D.C.

1863   Lincoln's Emancipation Proclamation.

1865   Juneteenth.

1867   U.S. congressional Reconstruction Acts.
British Canada granted dominion status.

1884   Fiftieth anniversary of West Indian emancipation.

RITES *of* AUGUST FIRST

Introduction
Transnational Emancipation Day

On Friday, August 1, 1834, the Abolition of Slavery Bill passed by the British Parliament a year earlier came into effect. It legally abolished the centuries-old system of colonial slavery throughout the British Empire, but especially in the British West Indies. Colonial administrators, Christian missionaries, and former slaves celebrated the glorious event throughout the Caribbean. The "colored citizens" of Montreal, clergymen in Glasgow, Scotland, and abolitionists in the northern United States also joined in the celebrations. Over the next three decades, Emancipation Day, August First Day, or West India Day became one of the most important annual commemorative events among opponents of slavery in Canada West, the northern United States, the British Caribbean, and the United Kingdom. In particular, the public celebration of West India Day assumed special significance for people of African descent in the Anglo-Atlantic world. This book seeks to explain why this became so and the consequences for challenging American slavery.

This book focuses on public celebrations and representations of West Indian emancipation in the Atlantic world. Between 1834 and 1861, slavery became abolished in the British Empire but expanded in the United States. The connections between these processes were linked during annual commemorations on August First Day. This study investigates the historical role of ordinary people in forging these connections. In this sense, it is a social history with a focus on people, crowds, and their collective actions during commemorative events. But it is also a cultural history or social anthropology in its analysis of the social meaning of Emancipation Day parades, songs, objects, and images. In particular, this book seeks to unravel the cultural politics of West India Day—that set of social practices informed by public ritual, symbol, representation, and spectacle designed to elicit feelings of common identity. It further analyzes the events' ideological and cultural representations in print, oratory, and visual images. It examines how and why these commemorative events changed over a generation. It also analyzes the connections between local, regional, national, and international commemorations. Most important, it examines the contribution of commemoration toward antislavery mobilization. In short, it offers a social, cultural, and political history of a commemoration that was shaped by, as well as helped to shape, the Age of Anglo-American emancipation between the early 1830s and the 1860s.

Before outlining the book's organization, it is important to situate the topic in relation to recent historical literature on festive politics. A popular politics of public parades, commemorative celebrations, and public rituals has increasingly replaced an older political narrative of organized parties, great personalities, and competing ideologies. Rather than being excluded from the political process because they did not vote, or being mere passive spectators to whom politics was something done to them, people in the streets helped shape national political cultures especially during revolutionary and post-revolutionary eras.[1]

Much of this historical literature is helpful in detailing the expansion of politics beyond normative categories. The examination of festivals, parades, and participants has proven suggestive for understanding West India Day. Most useful has been working out the social meaning of events, symbols, and objects, together with critical analysis of print media in the construction of the cultural politics of emancipation. The contested nature of commemorative events, for instance, can be discerned by their familiar press depiction as orderly and decent rather than chaotic and unruly affairs.

But there are crucial differences between these events and West India Day. First, Emancipation Day did not help shape national political culture.

---

1. The scholarship is vast. The works I have found most helpful include Susan G. Davis, *Parades and Power: Street Theatre in Nineteenth-Century Philadelphia* (Philadelphia: Temple University Press, 1986); Orlando Figes and Boris Kolonitski, *Interpreting the Russian Revolution: The Language and Symbols of 1917* (New Haven: Yale University Press, 1999); Simon P. Newman, *Parades and the Politics of the Street: Festive Culture in the Early American Republic* (Philadelphia: University of Pennsylvania Press, 1997); Mona Ozouf, *Festivals and the French Revolution* (Cambridge, Mass.: Harvard University Press, 1988); Joao Jose Reiss, *Death is a Festival: Funeral Rites and Rebellion in Nineteenth-Century Brazil* (Chapel Hill: University of North Carolina Press, 2003); E. P. Thompson, *Customs in Common: Studies in Traditional Popular Culture* (New York: New Press, 1993); Len Travers, *Celebrating the Fourth: Independence Day and the Rites of Nationalism in the Early Republic* (Amherst: University of Massachusetts Press, 1997); David Waldstreicher, *In the Midst of Perpetual Fetes: The Making of American Nationalism, 1776–1820* (Chapel Hill: University of North Carolina Press, 1997).

Indeed, it was often in stated opposition. Second, oral culture played a vital role in the construction of political identities. One of the problems of nationalist historiography is its privileging of the written over the spoken word in the construction of imagined communities. Third, and most important, West India Day represented a transnational rather than national expression of festive politics. If festive politics help us to rethink how we understand political practice, August First Day should encourage us to think about how cultural politics interacts from the local through the international.

The new narratives of popular politics have also influenced African American historiography. An older tradition of elite African American studies focused on prominent institutions, intellectual history, and famous people. This has been challenged by social and cultural approaches to the African American past. One focus has been on freedom celebrations, especially during the nineteenth century, how these changed over time, and their political significance in the making of African American peoplehood. The most prominent of these commemorations included the abolition of the American slave trade (January 1), the abolition of state slavery in Massachusetts (July 14) and New York (July 5), British abolition (August 1), the presidential and constitutional abolition of American slavery (January 1, July 4), and the end of slavery in East Texas on June 19 (Juneteenth). Much of this festive scholarship has explored the secular, sacred, and cultural components of this commemorative tradition. It has also persuasively argued for the existence of a popular tradition of organization, commemoration, and mobilization among Americans of African descent during slavery and post-emancipation. The inescapable conclusion is that, as Mitch Kachun puts it, "collective memory matters."[2]

---

2. Geneviève Fabre, "African-American Commemorative Celebrations in the Nineteenth Century," in *History & Memory in African-American Culture*, ed. Geneviève Fabre and Robert O'Meally (New York: Oxford University Press, 1994), 72–91; Eddie S. Glaude, *Exodus: Religion, Race and Nation in Early 19th Century Black America* (Chicago: University of Chicago Press, 2000); William B. Gravely, "The Dialectic of Double-Consciousness in Black American Freedom Celebrations, 1808–1863," *Journal of Negro History* 67, no. 4 (Winter 1982): 302–17; Mitch Kachun, *Festivals of Freedom: Memory and Meaning in African American Emancipation Celebrations, 1808–1915* (Amherst: University of Massachusetts Press, 2003), quote on p. 14; Leonard Sweet, "The Fourth of July and Black Americans in the Nineteenth Century: Northern Leadership Opinion within the Context of the Black Experience," *Journal of Negro History* 61, no. 3 (July 1976): 256–75; William Wiggins Jr., *O Freedom! Afro-American Emancipation Celebrations* (Knoxville: University of Tennessee Press, 1987).

As with the scholarship on festive politics, this work on establishing the tradition of African American Emancipation Day celebrations has been of great help in writing this book. The expansion of normative political categories is especially important for African Americans. Otherwise, apart from a brief experience with the suffrage in some antebellum states, together with the eras of Reconstruction and post–civil rights, it can be falsely claimed that African Americans do not have a political history. Moreover, Emancipation Day celebrations provided separate and independent collective spaces for the construction of a nation within a nation, with contrasting ideological perspectives to the familiar narrative of America as the story of freedom.

But this African American festive scholarship also has its limitations. Although it pushes the social history agenda, it often ends as cultural history downplaying the hard work of archival research. Ritual replaces the historical experience of ordinary people. This is especially evident in the analysis of preachers, orations, and ideas at the expense of crowds, organizations, and political antislavery. Ironically, this represents a return to an elite intellectual history.[3]

Moreover, the construction of an African American national identity is *confined* to the development of American nationalism. As David Waldstreicher puts it, free blacks "used the tools of American nationalism to create black nationalism."[4] But such formulations ignore the international dimensions of emancipation and its commemoration: African enslavement in the New World; the abolition of the transoceanic slave trade; border state abolition in New York and Canada; and imperial abolition in the Anglo-Atlantic world. We must constantly question the utility of reducing the international dimensions of slavery and emancipation to nationalist constructions.

As we have seen, this scholarship on African American emancipation celebrations has noted August First Day as part of a commemorative tradition of popular politics. Scholars have noted the crowds, speakers, church sermons, and public parades. Despite some differences of emphasis, most of these treatments are in broad agreement concerning the significance of Emancipation Day celebrations. According to one of its most recent scholars, "Emancipation

3. Glaude, *Exodus*, 82–104; Gravely, "Dialectic of Double Consciousness."
4. Waldstreicher, *In the Midst of Perpetual Fetes*, 325.

in the West Indies was a pivotal event in the construction of African American historical consciousness and in the establishment of African American commemorative traditions." Also, it provided an opportunity for the black elite to assert its leadership and direction on the masses. Moreover, black orators used the event as an educational means of communication to provide an alternative historical interpretation of the American story of uplift and progress. Most important, August First Day served as the African American day of independence. As Benjamin Quarles put it over three decades ago: "Having no fourth of July the black man did the next best thing—he celebrated August I." This notion of the black Fourth has become the prevailing scholarly interpretation of the event.[5]

One of the ironies of this scholarship is that while scholars recognize the importance of West India Day, there has been little systematic analysis of its participants, social forms, and political significance. Even the best work ignores the spatial and temporal dimensions of this freedom festival. Thus, August First Day is treated as an unchanging event from the 1830s through the 1850s when in actuality its social forms, participants, and political significance underwent significant transformation. Furthermore, West India Day celebrations took on special meaning in various places and regions. These are easily overlooked when, in pursuit of an African American political tradition, the ritual is examined in terms of counting up the number of celebrations or collapsing all meetings into one geographical expression.

Moreover, the focus on commemorative celebrations as memory-work and the construction of a usable past has detracted from an emphasis on the political function of such commemorations in popular antislavery mobilization. Much of the scholarly work on *lieu de memoire* makes the point that emancipation was central to the historical consciousness of African Americans. This is indisputable, but it is also true that there was a political praxis to

5. The best social history accounts of August First Day are Benjamin Quarles, *Black Abolitionists* (New York: Oxford University Press, 1969), 116–42; and Kachun, *Festivals of Freedom*, 54–96. The quote is Kachun's on pp. 55–56. For studies of these commemorations as elite events, see Patrick Rael, *Black Identity and Black Protest in the Antebellum North* (Chapel Hill: University of North Carolina Press, 2002). For the black July Fourth, see R. J. M. Blackett, *Building an Antislavery Wall: Black Americans in the Atlantic Abolitionist Movement, 1830–1860* (Baton Rouge: Louisiana State University Press, 1983), 7–8; Sweet, "Fourth of July," 270.

this memory-work, especially at a time when millions of people of African descent continued to be enslaved. This makes the need to link up commemorative events with popular mobilization all the more urgent.

In addition, *lieu de memoire* has not always operated within the framework of the nation-state. August First Day scholars have operated primarily within national contexts: American nationalism, African American nation-building; British abolition, American slavery; American Republicanism, British monarchism; July Fourth, August First. In contrast, we examine the transnational dimensions of the abolition of British colonial slavery, its impact on anti-slavery mobilization, and its implications for international struggles against American slavery. Indeed, this project was fueled in part by my puzzlement as to why popular celebrations of West India emancipation in North America and elsewhere were treated primarily in national terms when the historical process was so clearly transnational.[6]

This book makes three major arguments. First, annual commemorations of slave emancipation illustrated how people of African descent constructed popular meanings of cultural identity around liberty and selfhood in opposition to prevalent structures of racial domination and subordination. Second, August First Day played an important role in the political mobilization of people, ideas, and actions against American slavery in the mid-nineteenth-century Atlantic world. Along with racial bonding and the construction of a usable past, these freedom festivals contributed to an international mobilization bringing with it an accompanying transnational consciousness. Third, West India Day commemorations reveal the conceptual limitations of nationalist narratives because of the connections among people of African descent, as well as the ways in which individuals, organizations, and ideas provide an alternative means for comparative analysis. Black protest in the North, for instance, ignores boundary crossings by fugitives, activists, and others to the Caribbean, Canada West, West Africa, and the United Kingdom.

---

6. My personal history might help explain this puzzlement. Born and raised in London to an English mother and Egyptian father, I was schooled in the wonders of British history until University, where I was drawn toward American, African, and Caribbean history. I have spent the last twenty years teaching and writing about American and African American history in U.S. academia from comparative and transnational perspectives. I can only surmise that such a background is not exactly conducive for doing nation-state histories!

This book is structured chronologically and spatially. Chapter 1 examines competing celebrations of the passage of British abolition by colonial officials, Christian missionaries, West Indian planters, and former slaves in the urban and rural environs of the British Caribbean, especially Jamaica and Trinidad, from the early 1830s through the 1850s. For officials, missionaries, and planters, celebrations were organized for didactic purposes of making new types of subjects—vassals, servants, and laborers—out of former slaves. Although former slaves participated in these celebrations, they also organized their own festivities—what Mona Ozouf usefully refers to as "other festivals"[7]—like Jonkonnu, Canboulay, and crop-over. The argument is that Emancipation Day celebrations represented an important arena of cultural politics revealing *both* similar and contrasting ideologies of freedom.

The second chapter switches from Caribbean emancipation to the struggle against American slavery. It examines West India Day celebrations organized by antislavery societies in the northern United States and elsewhere from the early 1830s through the late 1850s. The focus is on explaining the changing form of this celebration from thanksgiving church services to multiracial public gatherings. The purpose of this public picnic was to serve as an alternative to July Fourth celebrations, to proclaim immediate abolition, and to demonstrate the success of emancipation in the British West Indies. Over the next two decades, the antislavery picnic blossomed to become one of the most important public expressions of Garrisonian abolitionism. Apart from one brief extract published in 1944 and scattered references, this important commemoration, its various forms, and social meaning remain unexamined.[8]

These carefully scripted social gatherings of abolitionist supplication propagated a version of British abolition as a boon to be emulated in the United States. Supplication became increasingly symbolized by the famous image of the prostrate slave with outstretched hands begging for freedom. In reaction to this social control, black abolitionists developed their own autonomous commemorations and mobilizations. West India Day celebrations organized and participated in by Americans of African descent in the towns, villages, and cities of the northern United States from the early 1830s

---

7. Ozouf, *Festivals and the French Revolution,* 86.

8. Marian H. Studley, "An 'August First' in 1844," *New England Quarterly* 16 (December 1943): 567–77; Kachun, *Festivals of Freedom,* 67.

through the early 1860s are the subject of chapter 3, which examines church services, abolitionist picnics, and small public meetings by African Americans as important features of black institutional life and its politicization around issues of slavery and abolition.

The next two chapters explore the origins, nature, and consequences of West India Day celebrations among people of African descent in the British colonial province of Canada West (now Ontario) from the 1830s through the 1850s. In chapter 4, we examine these commemorations as public expressions of loyalty toward the British monarchy, especially among Afro-Canadians in the towns and cities of southern Lake Ontario. This patriotism was illustrated by support for the monarchy, the consumption of tea, membership in the established Anglican Church, and military service. The social forms of August First Day celebrations symbolized these aspects of black loyalty.

After the passage of the 1850 Fugitive Slave Act forced many African Americans into Canada West, however, we see a very different sort of August First Day celebration. This is the subject of chapter 5. Fugitives focused on the event less as a demonstration of patriotism but primarily as a means to mobilize for the destruction of American slavery. Their commemorations occurred several hundred miles westward in small all-black communities around southern Lake Erie. In these two chapters, I make two arguments. First, West India Day served as an important public display of political identities by black people in Canada. These identities ranged from patriotism, to liberation, through continental struggles over slavery and abolition. Second, the shifting social meaning of these events can only be understood within a transnational context of fugitive slaves, expanding American slavery, and racial tensions between fugitives and an older generation of black settlers in Canada. These chapters aim to provide the first scholarly analysis of these important annual commemorations and to situate them within a transnational context of imperial diplomacy, British colonial abolition, and the expansion of American slavery.

In chapter 6, we return to West India Day in the northern United States during the 1850s. The major concern is how the event changed over time, shifting from a politics of controlled respectability in black churches to more militant spectacles of public politics exemplified by outdoor parades, street marches, fiery speeches, and the rise of armed militias. In the face of the aggressive expansion of American slavery, the need for self-defense against the Fugitive Slave Act, and the obvious failure of moral persuasion, African Americans began to pursue a militant public politics of the street. The examination of people, parades, and mobilization against American slavery culminating in West India Day is the subject of this important chapter. The celebrations shifted from being commemorative to being *demonstrative*, and were concerned with the self-defense of black people and war on slavery. The catalyst was the 1850 Fugitive Slave Act, which fueled black emigration, transformed abolition, and facilitated the development of self-defense and armed struggle against American slavery. In other words, these August First Day events suggest that black communities were already at war with American slavery *before* the commencement of armed hostilities between the states in April 1861.

Having examined the origins, nature, and transformation of West India Day celebrations in the British Caribbean, the northern United States, and Canada West, we turn to the ideological content of the anniversary. Chapter 7 analyzes orations and writings by blacks in the Atlantic world arising from antislavery struggles. Although scholars have examined orators and their Emancipation Day speeches, their focus is usually on biblical content, the rights of man, and historical progress. In contrast, I argue that this Anglo-American Christian framework has silenced other significant political ideas concerning national liberation struggles, revolutionary emancipation, and the politics of African racial identity. Many orators celebrated West Indian emancipation as the liberation of fellow Africans in the New World. In particular, I show how the travels and writings of prominent black abolitionists like Samuel R. Ward, Henry Highland Garnet, and others resulted in a transnational reconfiguration of emancipation. This "other" black intellectual and political tradition is traced through scores of Emancipation Day orations delivered and published in the press and as separate pamphlets during the 1840s and 1850s. This chapter further explores the dialogic interaction between orators and crowds in search of a broader-based protest movement. Its most ambitious objective is to reveal a Pan-African consciousness based on slavery, abolition, and post-emancipation.

What happened to West India Day after the abolition of American slavery is briefly examined in the epilogue. The focus is on the contested nature of August First from the 1880s through the 1960s, and how its commemoration reflected older patterns as well as new liberation struggles in the black Atlantic world.

The research for this project has taken me to numerous archives throughout North America, the English-speaking Caribbean, and the United Kingdom. Much of the material for the British West Indies consists of official correspondence published in the voluminous *British Parliamentary Papers (BPP)*, Jamaican and Trinidad newspapers, stipendiary magistrates' accounts, missionary memoirs, and travel literature. The materials for West India Day in the United States and Canada West can be found in newspapers published by African Americans, antislavery societies, and the local press. There are two additional points worth mentioning about these documentary sources. In their republication of extracts from other published works on slavery, abolition, and emancipation, many of these records both established, as well as reflected, transnational links and connections. The *Liberator* is an underutilized resource for following the international dynamics of slavery, emancipation, and liberation movements. Furthermore, such sources must be read with a critical eye in order to retrieve the thoughts and feelings of people of African descent. As Woodville Marshall reminds us, "the direct evidence of the nature of blacks' hopes and expectations of emancipation hardly exists. They left no extended written records of their thoughts and feelings (memoirs, letters); oral history had not yet been invented; and contemporary commentators seldom bothered to interview them, no doubt convinced that they had little of importance to say or that whatever they might say was already obvious."[9] This method—what art critic Walter Benjamin once called reading against the grain—should be supplemented with a careful scrutiny of the existing evidence for all those scraps, grains, bits and pieces of direct evidence left by black people themselves.

This book has three major objectives. The primary aim is to provide the first major examination of an important black institution that has been relatively ignored compared to other popular celebrations like Pinkster and Juneteenth. Both the influential *Encyclopedia of African-American Culture and History*, published in 1996, and the abolitionist daily calendar produced by the Gilder Lehrman Center for 2002 do not have entries for West India Day.[10]

9. Woodville K. Marshall, "'We be wise to many more tings': Blacks' Hopes and Expectations of Emancipation," in *Caribbean Freedom: Society and Economy from Emancipation to the Present*, ed. Hilary Beckles and Verene Shepherd (Kingston: Ian Randle, 1993), 13.

10. Jack Salzman, David Lionel Smith, and Cornel West, eds., *Encyclopedia of African-American History and Culture* (New York: Macmillan Library Reference, 1996); 2002 Gilder Lehrman Center Calendar.

The second purpose of this book is to contribute to the study of emancipation and black Atlantic identity by examining the comparative dimensions of freedom festivals in the British Caribbean, the northern United States, Canada West, and the United Kingdom between the 1830s and the 1880s. This transnational approach challenges local and national narratives that have largely shaped previous investigations of these questions. Thus, we recover the international dimensions of antislavery activists and publications: the Boston *Liberator* on fugitives in Canada, Mexican antislavery, and the Indian Uprising of the late 1850s. This perspective also emphasizes the trans-hemispheric movement of people, ideas, and politics between the Caribbean colonies and North America, as well as across the Atlantic. This study is aligned with those works that insist on the need to think, research, and write in terms of hemispheric and transnational interconnections.[11]

The final aim is to contribute to contemporary debates on the politics of culture by demonstrating the historically specific ways in which Emancipation Day celebrations played a critical role in mobilizing for the abolition of slavery and providing alternative notions of freedom. Implicit in this objective is a rejection of a liberal integrationist framework for a popular politics of assembly, celebration, mobilization, and memory. The politics of this book demonstrate how culture and community were—and can be—political in contrast to our own time in which everything is claimed to be either cultural or political to the point of vacuity.

This book belongs to a trilogy of historical works examining the transition from slave to post-slave societies in the nineteenth-century world. The first study, *Freedpeople in the Tobacco South: Virginia, 1860–1900*, provides a materialist analysis of the neglected regional economy of the American Upper South within an international framework of emancipation, rural depression, and social protest. Some of the questions regarding political mobilization were insufficiently dealt with and are the subject of this book. Moreover, it covers an earlier time span, and is specifically comparative and transnational in scope. It

---

11. Paul Gilroy, *The Black Atlantic: Modernity and Double Consciousness* (Cambridge, Mass.: Harvard University Press, 1993); Robert Gregg, *Inside Out, Outside In: Essays in Comparative History* (London: St. Martin's Press, 2000); Peter Linebaugh and Marcus Rediker, *The Many-Headed Hydra: Sailors, Slaves, Commoners, and the Hidden History of the Revolutionary Atlantic* (Boston: Beacon, 2000).

was while researching this second work that I began to truly understand the historical importance of the international dimensions of slavery, abolition, and post-emancipation. The final project, *Century of Emancipation, 1791–1910,* provides a lucid narrative of the gradual shift from slavery toward emancipation in the New World from the 1790s (French St. Domingue) through the 1880s (Cuba, Brazil), and the reemergence of forms of unfree labor in Africa and elsewhere during the Age of Empire. It is my hope that this combination of regional, comparative, and international approaches will further demonstrate the vital significance of slave emancipation in the making of the modern world.

A word on the choice of terminology followed in this book. Although I sometimes use the word *international,* my preference is for *transnational* and *cross-national,* because these terms convey the sense of beyond, passing, carry over, transcending, and the like much more effectively. Furthermore, I prefer the terms *ante-emancipation* and *post-emancipation* rather than *antebellum* and *postbellum.* This is because our concern is with the transnational dimensions of slavery and antislavery, not the American Civil War and nationalist narratives. Finally, although I use the terms *Afro-Jamaican, African American, Afro-Canadian,* and the like, this is primarily for the sake of clarity for readers. My preference is for historically accurate terms—*apprentices, fugitives, colored,* and the like—and cross-national terms—*black loyalist, freed people, people of African descent,* and the like.

Chapter 1
August First in the British West Indies

*Great advantages would, I consider, be derived from this solemn
recognition of the Imperial Act for the Abolition of Slavery.*
Lionel Smith, July 2, 1834

On August 13, 1834, the Marquess of Sligo sat down and wrote a long letter
from King's House, Spanish Town, to the British colonial secretary Thomas
Spring Rice in London. The new governor of Jamaica was delighted to in-
form the new minister that the "transition from slavery to apprenticeship has
been effected in the most satisfactory manner." August 1, the day the law
abolishing colonial slavery came into effect, "was devoted in most parts of
the Island to devotional exercises." "Towards evening," reported the governor,
"the streets were crowded with parties of John Cause Men and their usual
noisy accompaniments." There were also nocturnal "fancy balls in which
the authorities of the Island, past and present, were represented." On rural
estates, proprietors had served special dinners for their apprentices together
with "usual holiday allowances of sugar, rum, and salt fish." On Sunday, the
chapels were once again full, "and the day passed in the most orderly and
quiet manner." The next day, wrote Governor Sligo, saw the return of apprentices to their agricultural duties except in the parish of St. Ann's, where there
had been some trouble.[1]

It is hard to determine what the colonial secretary's reaction was to this
report from his colonial governor. Secretary Spring Rice was probably relieved that the new abolition law had gone into effect with so little difficulty,
and that things appeared to be running smoothly, at least in Jamaica. From
our perspective, however, this dispatch raises some very interesting questions.
Why were sectarian chapels holding devotional services throughout the colony? Who were the John Cause men, what was so "usual" about their activities, and why were they parading on August First? What was the significance

1. Marquess of Sligo to Thomas Spring Rice, August 13, 1834, *BPP*, 1835, no. 17, p. 54.

of nighttime carnivals? Why were planters holding large estate dinners in festive fashion? What was going on in St. Anne's parish? And why does Governor Sligo sound positively relieved at the quiet state of affairs under his jurisdiction?

This chapter examines August First Day celebrations during the 1830s in the British West Indies colonies, especially Trinidad and Jamaica. These "new" and "old" colonies have been selected for their size, population, and better documentation of contemporary events. Also, Jamaica was of regional importance in imperial policy, and was often drawn upon to exemplify abolition's success or failure in transnational debates on the effects of emancipation. We focus on different organizations, expressions, and representations of August First Day celebrations and their contested social meanings, especially in 1834 and 1838. This chapter demonstrates how these freedom festivals evolved from rituals of white-sponsored historical events into rites confirming the same autonomy blacks were gradually securing in the post-emancipation decades—in particular, how official commemorations became increasingly transformed into former slaves' own shouts of freedom. These public rituals and community occasions demonstrate how conflict over emancipation—a much-studied political and economic process by historians—critically extended into cultural life. Finally, this chapter reveals the cultural politics of post-emancipation struggles in transnational terms through colonial policy, missionary evangelicalism, and freed people's communal events.[2]

In Jamaica, sugar and slavery took off under the protective mantle of British colonialism during the eighteenth century. In contrast, plantation slavery came relatively late to Trinidad, acquired as a result of the Napoleonic Wars. With the implementation of the abolition of British trade in African slaves in 1808, there were around 350,000 slaves in Jamaica compared to 21,000 slaves in Trinidad. By 1834, of the 665,000 slaves in the British West Indies, the

2. Barry Higman, "Slavery Remembered: The Celebration of Emancipation in Jamaica," *Journal of Caribbean History* 12 (1979): 55–74, and Bridget Brereton, "The Birthday of Our Race: A Social History of Emancipation Day in Trinidad, 1838–88," in *Trade, Government and Society in Caribbean History, 1700–1920*, ed. Barry Higman (Kingston, Jamaica: Heinemann, 1983), 69–83, examine freedom celebrations in Jamaica and Trinidad over 150- and 50-year periods respectively. While this chapter draws upon their pioneering work, its focus is short-term, comparative, and transnational.

largest number lived and worked in Jamaica. In contrast to the 90 percent slave population in Jamaica, around 56 percent of the population were enslaved in Trinidad. Moreover, much of the Afro-Creole slave population in Jamaica was concentrated in large plantation units. In 1834, almost half of Jamaica's enslaved population was held on estates with more than 150 slaves. It has also been estimated that the population of Trinidad was much more diverse than that of Jamaica. In 1834, around one-quarter of the slave population in Jamaica was African-born. After emancipation, Jamaica's predominantly African-descended population grew through natural increase with small additions of Asians. In contrast, Trinidad's Afro-Creole population was enhanced by a much larger influx of Asian peoples through the system of indentured servitude.[3]

The legal abolition of British colonial slavery cannot be understood outside the context of increased imperial power. There was a long history of West Indian slavery in which local powers were buttressed by the British government. This was to change as a result of the loss of the American colonies, a popular abolitionist campaign, and the amelioration of colonial slavery. The 1823 Amelioration Acts brought new regulations on slavery imposed by the British Colonial Office. By the late 1820s, the British government was reasserting its imperial power throughout the Caribbean colonies.[4]

This new authority was powerfully illustrated in response to both natural and human forces in the British West Indies. In August 1831, a violent hurricane hit the Leeward island colonies of St. Lucia, St. Vincent, and Barbados. Hundreds were killed, and thousands were injured. Property and sugar crops were destroyed. The colonial government provided a loan of 500,000 pounds sterling to hard-hit property owners. On the night of Tuesday, December 27,

---

3. Higman, "Slavery Remembered," 55–56; Brereton, "Birthday of Our Race," 69; Donald Wood, *Trinidad in Transition: The Years after Slavery* (London: Oxford University Press, 1968), 33; Robin Blackburn, *The Overthrow of Colonial Slavery, 1776–1848* (London: Verso, 1988), 16, 423–24; 88; Thomas C. Holt, *The Problem of Freedom: Race, Labor, and Politics in Jamaica and Britain, 1832–1938* (Baltimore: Johns Hopkins University Press, 1992), 88.

4. William A. Green, *British Slave Emancipation: The Sugar Colonies and the Great Experiment* (New York: Oxford University Press, 1976), 68; Blackburn, *Overthrow of Colonial Slavery*, 432; W. L. Burn, *Emancipation and Apprenticeship in the British West Indies* (London: J. Cape, 1937), 142–45; Michael Craton, *Testing the Chains: Resistance to Slavery in the British West Indies* (Ithaca: Cornell University Press, 1982), 295.

1831, slaves set alight the Kensington estate in western Jamaica. Over the next several days, the revolt spread over a radius of 750 square miles, eventually involving 60,000 slaves. (Subsequent investigations revealed that rumors of freedom granted but withheld by planters motivated many slaves to revolt.) The slave rebels routed local parish militias, but were no match for the combined might of the 84th West India Regiment, the British Royal Navy, and the resources of the colonial state. The total loss of life included 14 whites and 544 slaves, along with property damage to 207 estates worth over 1.1 million pounds sterling (over 50 million today). This military support in suppressing the Jamaican uprising further demonstrated the growing power of London in regulating imperial affairs.[5]

Despite its failure, bloody loss of life, and brutal suppression, the Jamaican uprising played a significant role in the advent of slave abolition in the British Empire.[6] On May 23, 1832, rebel leader Samuel Sharpe was executed; one week later, the British Parliament appointed a select committee to consider measures for abolition "compatible with the safety of all Classes in the Colonies." Between June 8 and August 11, dozens of witnesses were called to testify in London and hundreds of questions were asked by committee members. After months of debate, the "Act for the Abolition of Slavery" was passed by Parliament, receiving royal consent in late August 1833. Its chief provisions included the abolition of slavery throughout the British colonies, the full emancipation of slave children under age six and those born to slave mothers, and a system of apprenticeship. This system required agricultural laborers (praedials) to work for their former masters until August 1840, and nonagricultural laborers (non-praedials like domestics, craftsmen, etc.) to work for former owners until August 1838. Exactly one year later, the law came into effect throughout the British Empire of Canada, South Africa,

5. Craton, *Testing the Chains*, 291–321; Mary Reckord, "The Jamaica Slave Rebellion of 1831," *Past and Present* 40 (July 1968): 108–25; Mary Turner, *Slaves and Missionaries: The Disintegration of Jamaican Slave Society, 1787–1834* (Urbana: University of Illinois Press, 1982), chap. 6; Burn, *Emancipation and Apprenticeship*, 90–94.

6. "Endemic slave revolts," according to Walter Rodney, *A History of the Guyanese Working People, 1881–1905* (Baltimore: Johns Hopkins University Press, 1981), 31, "taught the lesson that slavery as a form of control over labor was proving uneconomical and unstable." For similar views, see Holt, *Problem of Freedom*, 14, 415; Green, *British Slave Emancipation*, 112–14, 124; Craton, *Testing the Chains*, 11, 323; Blackburn, *Overthrow of Colonial Slavery*, 451–59.

Mauritius, Ceylon, British Honduras, and the West Indies.[7] The Abolition Bill was ratified by representative assemblies in eleven legislative colonies, and imposed by Orders in Council in the three Crown colonies in the Caribbean. In two colonies, Antigua and Bermuda, the apprenticeship system was abrogated in favor of immediate legislative freedom for all slaves. Of the nearly 800,000 African slaves affected by the law in the British Empire, the vast majority lived and worked in the Caribbean.[8]

It is important to emphasize the links between increased imperial power, a history of slave revolts culminating in 1831 in western Jamaica, and the coming of legal abolition. The implementation of August First took place directly in the aftermath of the largest slave rebellion in the history of the British West Indies. The military force of the colonial state had successfully suppressed this revolt; it was on display again during the passage of emancipation with hundreds of extra troops drafted into Jamaica, while the Royal Navy patrolled the Caribbean ocean. The Colonial Office, however, sought to shape abolition in the image of the benevolent state. Nearly a century of imperial power in British India had taught London the effectiveness of seasonal ritual for social order. Ceremony and ritual were often much more effective than blood and bayonets in the battle for the hearts and minds of new subjects.[9]

In seeking to shape emancipation in their own image, numerous colonial administrators arranged for thanksgiving celebrations overseen by Christian missionaries. Chapels, churches, and places of worship were ordered to be open on Friday, August 1, 1834, as colonial governors sought to enlist Christian missionaries as agents of public order. Sir James Carmichael Smyth, lieutenant-governor of British Guiana, explained to one local minister that a

7. The law did not affect British India, which was controlled by the East India Company and fell outside of parliamentary jurisdiction. Slavery was abolished there in 1843.

8. Craton, *Testing the Chains*, 323, 379; Burn, *Emancipation and Apprenticeship*, 118. According to the speaker of the assembly in Antigua, immediate emancipation was adopted for psychological reasons: "it was better to meet the crisis at once, than to have it hanging over our heads for six years, with all the harassing doubts and anxieties." Thome and Kimball, *Emancipation in the West Indies*, 35. Burn, *Emancipation and Apprenticeship*, 169, offers a more obvious economic explanation: "the comparatively high development of the slaves and the difficulty which they would have in gaining a living beyond the bounds of the plantations."

9. For imperial power and social ritual, see Eric Hobsbawn and Terence Ranger, eds., *The Invention of Tradition* (Cambridge: Cambridge University Press, 1996).

"misconception on the part of the negro" about emancipation might "plunge the Colony into dreadful confusion." "I am therefore induced," he continued, "amongst other precautionary measures, to apply to you, as justly possessing considerable influence over your congregation for your aid and assistance upon the present occasion." Two weeks before abolition went into effect, Sir Smyth "command[ed] that all the churches, Chapels and places dedicated to the worship of Almighty God, in the province of British Guiana, shall be open on Friday the 1st of August, and that divine service shall be therein severally performed twice (at the least) on that day." Under advice from "His Majesty's Privy Council," the governor of the Leeward Islands, Sir Evan John Murray M'Gregor, issued a proclamation "that Friday the first day of August next be observed in all churches and chapels as a day of general thanksgiving for these mercies." In his July 2, 1834, message to the Barbados Council, Governor Sir Lionel Smith of the Windward Islands proposed "a day of thanksgiving, to commemorate in due form and solemnity the great change which commences that day." Great advantages, he added, would come from "solemn recognition" of this "Imperial Act." These official celebrations of abolition were being organized by colonial officials and supported by the Colonial Office with the express objective of making new subjects out of former slaves for purposes of social control.[10]

Watch night, or awaiting the final hours before abolition in dissenting chapels during the evening of Thursday, July 31, served as a particularly powerful expression of the didactic purpose of Emancipation Day celebrations. Nonconformist mission societies had been proselytizing in the British West Indies since the 1770s. By 1834, it has been estimated there were more than 150 missions claiming 47,000 communicant slave members and 96,000 "hearers or inquirers."[11] There had been longstanding social tensions associated with these missions, especially the Baptists because of their suspected

10. J. Carmichael Smyth to Reverend ? February 9, 1834, *BPP*, 1835, Enclosure C in no. 99, p. 261; Smyth, Proclamation, July 15, 1834, *BPP*, 1835, Enclosure 1 in no. 109, p. 276; Sir Evan John Murray M'Gregor, Proclamation, June 13, 1834, *BPP*, 1835, Enclosures in no. 160, p. 555; Sir Lionel Smith to Secretary Stanley, July 3, 1834, *BPP*, 1835, Enclosure in no. 68, p. 198; Burn, *Emancipation and Apprenticeship*, 146–47.

11. James Mursell Phillippo, *Jamaica: Its Past and Present State* (Philadelphia: J. M. Campbell & Co., 1843), 109; Craton, *Testing the Chains*, 247; Blackburn, *Overthrow of Colonial Slavery*, 426–27.

involvement in major slave rebellions in Demerara in 1823 and in Jamaica in 1831. The religious celebrations of emancipation, however, provided dissenters with an opportunity to both bond with colonial officialdom as well as proselytize abolition in God's image to the new apprentices of freedom.

The Baptist watch night in Jamaica was very well organized and attended. The dissenting chapels opened for religious business on Thursday evening, July 31, 1834. After the clock struck 12:00 ringing in abolition, prayer meetings were held early in the morning followed by sermons and daily services. These religious services were packed: 1,600 people showed up at Falmouth and 3,000 at Montego Bay. Similar religious services were held at Lucea and Savannah-la-Mar. From Kingston, it was reported that "the chapels in town were thronged," while in Spanish Town, the Reverend James Mursell Phillippo gleefully wrote: "the chapel in which I officiate was so crowded that I could scarcely find my way into the pulpit." "It is a remarkable feature in the progress of that transition," wrote Governor Sligo two weeks later, "that the 1st of August was devoted in most parts of the Island to devotional exercises. In the sectarian chapels the service was performed several times in the course of the day." [12]

The watch night in Antigua was equally well organized and enthusiastically attended. Reverend Mathew Banks reported joyous proceedings from the capital of St. John's. On Thursday evening, the Methodists "held watch-nights in all our chapels," where the "congregation of Negroes was very large; and though the people manifested strong feelings, yet it was solemn and devotional." Just before midnight, Rev. Banks asked the congregation to kneel: "The clock struck twelve, and I exclaimed: 'The first of August has arrived! You all are free!' At this the voice of weeping was heard and became general, mingled with subdued cries of 'Glory be to God!' and the like. We sang: 'Praise God, from whom all blessings flow,' offered up a solemn thanksgiving to the Author of all our mercies, and afterwards sang our own hymn for the King . . . That night will long be remembered by all who were present."

Around a thousand freed people attended a thanksgiving service at the Moravian Grace Hill Church. The memory of that day and night stayed with

---

12. Francis A. Cox, *History of the Baptist Missionary Society from 1792 to 1842*, vol. 2 (London: T. Ward, 1842), 252–55; *BAP*, 1:63; Marquess of Sligo to Thomas Spring Rice, August 13, 1834, *BPP*, 1835, no. 17, p. 54; Burn, *Emancipation and Apprenticeship*, 174.

the freed people. American antislavery visitors James A. Thome and J. Horace Kimball later reported a conversation with a boatman rowing them across St. John's harbor: "We inquired of him, what the negroes did on the first of August, 1834. He said they all went to church and chapel. 'Dare was more *religious* on dat day dan you could tink of.'" Other freed people informed the American travelers that they all went to church to "*tank God for make a we free.*"[13]

These reports and accounts suggest that abolition was a moment of genuine joy for dissenting ministers and supporters of emancipation. Such times also provided them with opportunities to shape emancipation in God's image and to do the state some service. That day also represented joyous times for former slaves, with the ending of slavery and expectations of freedom's promise. It would be foolish to deny that God was being thanked for abolition. But it would be just as foolish to ignore the personal significance to those formerly enslaved of the changed meaning of their conditions. This was particularly true in Antigua, where August First Day services represented celebrations of complete emancipation. Indeed, it was later reported from Antigua that "First of August" became the phrase by which the freed people always understood when slavery was abolished.[14]

After the watch night and daytime church services, former slaves in some colonies pursued "other" noisier public celebrations. One of the most striking alternative celebrations in Jamaica involved Jonkonnu (John Canoe, Junkanoo, John Kuner, John Cause, etc.). On public holidays, especially around Christmas, slaves would engage in Jonkonnu festive activities consisting of parading, serenading, dancing, singing, and reveling. These rural and street routines included mimes, dramatic performances, and the playing of musical and percussive instruments. Scholars have long debated Jonkonnu: the linguistic roots of its name; the function of white patronage; its secular versus religious components; its social license and inversion; and its longevity in the

13. G. G. Findlay and W. W. Holdsworth, *The History of the Wesleyan Methodist Missionary Society* (London: Epworth Press, 1922), 1:314–16; James A. Thome and Horace Kimball, *Emancipation in the West Indies. A Six Months' Tour in Antigua, Barbadoes, and Jamaica in the year 1837* (New York: American Anti-Slavery Society, 1838), 15–21; The National Museum of Antigua and Barbuda, Emancipation Panel, Grace Hill Church. When I visited in 2005, the church was in ruins; it sits next to Old Road village atop the glorious Carlisle Bay in southwest Antigua.

14. Thome and Kimball, *Emancipation in the West Indies*, 16.

Caribbean and elsewhere.[15] Less has been written about how Jonkonnu and related folk traditions were an integral part of a largely autonomous Afro-Creole cultural life on plantations and in towns that former slaves drew upon to celebrate the abolition of slavery. In particular, a traditional celebration from Christmas was adapted by former slaves to commemorate the passage of emancipation in August.[16]

Jonkonnu originated among Afro-Jamaican slaves sometime during the late seventeenth century. The English visitor to Jamaica, Sir Hans Sloane, is credited with the first report of the festival. In 1688, he witnessed feast days characterized by dance, song, drums, banjos, and costumed figures with "Cows Tails to their Rumps," and "other odd things to their bodies" that "gives them a very extraordinary appearance." English planter-politician Edward Long provided the earliest full account of Jonkonnu in his 1774 *History of Jamaica*:

> In the towns, during the Christmas holidays, they have several tall or robust fellows, dressed up in grotesque habits, and a pair of ox-horns on their head, sprouting from the top of a horrid sort of vizor, or mask, which about the mouth is rendered very terrific with large Boar tusks. The Masquerader, carrying a wooden sword in his hand, is followed with a numerous crowd of drunken women, who refresh him frequently with a cup of aniseed-water, whilst he dances at every door, bellowing out John Connu.

Even though this folk festival was to change with the increase of white patronage and new characters—such as teams of colorfully costumed "set girls"—the Jonkonnu tradition continued through abolition and the post-

15. The literature is large. Those works I have found most useful include Judith Bettelheim, "The Afro-Jamaican Jonkonnu Festival: Playing the Forces and Operating the Cloth"(Ph.D. diss., Princeton University, 1979); Robert Dirks, *The Black Saturnalia: Conflict and Its Ritual Expression on British West Indian Slave Plantations* (Gainesville: University of Florida Press, 1987); Kenneth Bilby, "Gumbay, Myal, and the Great House: New Evidence on the Religious Background of Jonkonnu in Jamaica," *African Caribbean Institute of Jamaica Research Review* 4 (1999): 47–70; Stuckey, *Slave Culture*, 68–73; Elizabeth A. Fenn, "'A Perfect Equality Seemed to Reign': Slave Society and Jonkonnu," *North Carolina Historical Review* 65, no. 2 (April 1988): 127–53.

16. I am indebted to Ken Bilby for helping me work through some of these connections.

emancipation years. In his book *Jamaica: Its Past and Present,* published in 1843, Baptist missionary James Mursell Phillippo provided a general account of Jonkonnu based on past accounts and personal observation. "On public holidays," wrote the minister,

> each of the African tribes upon the different estates formed itself into a distinct party, composed of men, women, and children. Each party had its King or Queen, who was distinguished by a mask of the most hideous appearance, and attired from head to foot in gaudy harlequin-like apparel. They paraded or gambolled in their respective neighbourhoods, dancing to the rude music, which was occasionally drowned by the most hideous yells from the whole party by way of chorus . . . In the towns, such processions were preceded by a tall, athletic man, attired in the same grotesque habiliments, in addition to which he wore a most hideous head-dress, surmounted by a pair of ox-horns, while from the lower part of the mask large boar-Tusks protruded . . . He bore in his hand a large wooden sword which he occasionally brandished, accompanying its evolutions by a thousand fantastic freaks. Several companions were associated with him as musicians, beating banjas and tomtoms, blowing cow-horns, shaking a hard round black seed, called Indian shot, in a calabash, and scraping the bones of animals together, which, added to the vociferations of the crowd, filled the air with the most discordant sounds. They were chiefly followed by children and disreputable women, the latter frequently supplying the performers with intoxicating drinks. Being generally encouraged, they paraded the streets, and exhibited themselves in private houses, for whole days and nights successively; and in consequence of the violent exercise, the drunken-ness, and other excesses in which they indulged, multitudes of them annually fell a prey to sickness and death.[17]

These British accounts by Sloane, Long, and Phillippo, together with the fieldwork of modern anthropologists, provide some useful insight into the

---

17. Fenn, "Perfect Equality," 127–28; Edward Lond, *The History of Jamaica, or, General survey of the ancient and modern state of that Island* (London: T. Lowndes, 1774), 423–26; Bilby, "Gumbay, Myal, and the Great House," 61–67.

nature of Jonkonnu. These celebrations occurred on Christmas every year. The leading figures were dressed in animal masks, including sizable headdresses. Several musicians played so-called rude music, primarily with percussive instruments. These included the gumbay drum, a small square wooden frame covered by a goat's skin, and a wooden plank beaten with two sticks. The procession was made up of women and children, many of whom encouraged the revelers through words, shouts, and song. Large amounts of "intoxicating drinks" appear to have been consumed on these occasions. This probably consisted of rum rations for the holiday as well as additional supplies. There is little doubt that the physical exertions and drinking took a heavy toll on some slaves, who found it hard to return to field labor once the holiday was over.[18]

There were several important components to the social meaning of Jonkonnu. First, this was an annual festival celebrated on the plantations and in the towns by Afro-Creole slaves. Second, although it appears to have attracted white patronage, especially the giving and receiving of alms, Jonkonnu remained an autonomous celebration. The Afro-Creole slave community had been shaped through large plantation units that facilitated the development of this cultural autonomy. Third, while Jonkonnu reflected improvisation and spontaneity, it was also planned, prepared, and rehearsed. Costumes had to be made; musical instruments were learned; and leaders, whether of the procession or monarchs, had to be appointed. Fourth, Jonkonnu represented rural and urban saturnalia far removed from more sober public and religious rituals of imperial power. The Afro-Jamaican people's rituals and customs took a very different form of social politicization than those of colonial officials and Christian missionaries. This helps to explain the barely concealed disdain—along with a sort of morbid fascination with the "other"—of white visitors who described such "depraved" celebrations. It might be added that sickness and death were more likely the result of the killing fields of plantation slavery rather than drinking binges and physical exertions at annual festivals.

On August 1, 1834, Afro-Jamaicans celebrated with Jonkonnu. Governor Sligo's reference to these festivities in his official dispatch opens this chapter. The "usual noisy accompaniments" to which he refers probably involved drumming, dancing, and singing. The nocturnal celebrations were no doubt enhanced by the addition of visiting former slaves from the plantations as well as "intoxicating drinks." Most important, the governor's usage of the term

18. Bilby, "Gumbay, Myal, and the Great House," 61–67.

usual suggests that these Jonkonnu revelers were probably less spontaneous and more rehearsed than the watch nights and chapel services. Moreover, in his 1837 publication, Italian traveler Isaac Mendes Belisario reported a song sung by the dancing set-girls bewailing the loss of a regimental soldier that ended: "Now pray my noble King, if you really love me so well, disband us from slavery, and set us at large." These lyrics clearly linked a Jonkonnu celebration with expectations of freedom. Finally, it has been pointed out that Jamaican planters objected to an original proposal to implement abolition on January 1, 1835, because this fell during the Christmas holidays. This was the "usual" Jonkonnu time; it was also the time of the Jamaican uprising. In sum, Jonkonnu represented an important folk festival whereby Afro-Jamaicans established distance from the subject-making strategies and social rituals of colonial officials and Christian missionaries.[19]

Along with Jonkonnu in Jamaica, Canboulay in Trinidad was adapted by Afro- Trinidadians for emancipation celebrations. Its origins came from the French *cannes brulées* (burned canes) during slavery. When an estate was burned (either accidentally or deliberately), slaves from surrounding estates were mustered by drivers blowing on conch-shell horns. Gangs were forced to cut and grind cane immediately before it spoiled. After abolition, former slaves paraded through the streets during early August bearing *flambeaux* (flaming torches) in commemoration of emancipation. According to some scholars, this torchlight procession was celebrated yearly by estate laborers on August First as their emancipation celebration.[20]

The crop-over festival was also adapted for the purposes of celebrating emancipation. This festival had its origins during slavery. At the harvest-end of sugar-making, gangs assembled around the boiling house receiving special rations of salt, fish, and rum. There was also dancing, singing, and reveling. One planter's wife provided a firsthand account of crop-over on the eve of abolition: "The male boys dress themselves in ribbons, and as there is generally a fiddler upon the estate, he leads the procession up to the proprietor's, or if absent, the manager's, who provides wherewithal to make them merry. The women, who are well dressed, dance before the door, singing their

19. Dirks, *Black Saturnalia*, 182; Higman, "Slavery Remembered," 56.

20. Susan Campbell, "Carnival, Calypso, and Class Struggle in Nineteenth Century Trinidad," *History Workshop Journal* 26 (1988): 10; Wood, *Trinidad in Transition*, 243; Gerard Aching, *Masking and Power: Carnival and Popular Culture in the Caribbean* (Minneapolis: University of Minnesota Press, 2002), 153.

wild choruses of joy at the last cane being cut. The evening is ended by a general dance."

According to Michael Craton, "the celebration of emancipation on August I replaced the yearly celebration of the ending of the crop" in Trinidad. But it was also the case that some planters organized crop-over festivals in Jamaica for very different purposes. Apprentices were given special rations of rum and beef on that Friday. "Several individuals in the towns," reported Governor Sligo, "had given dinners to their new apprentices on the previous day, and on very many of the estates steers were killed by the proprietors and given to the negroes, besides their usual holiday allowances of sugar, rum and salt fish." If former slaves appropriated Jonkonnu for their freedom celebrations, former masters sought to use crop-over as a means to subject apprentices to new forms of paternal management.[21]

Numerous colonial officials in the British West Indies recorded that the transition from slavery to apprenticeship had been a glorious success. William Rogers Isaacs, president of the Council of the Virgin Islands, wrote that the "1st of August has passed off very quietly." "There never was an occasion in this Island," noted the superintendent of police for Antigua, Henry Loving, "where a day was kept with such universal reverence and unbiased holiness." These reports of peaceable and orderly transition continued through the end of the year. William Miller, *custos* (justice of the peace) of Trelawney, Jamaica, noted that the "Christmas holidays passed over quietly." Special Justice Captain A. Dillon was pleased to report from St. Ann's that "there was not the least appearance of riot or disorderly conduct in the apprentices of my district during the Christmas." R. S. Cooper, special justice for St. Mary's, described the apprentices on the several estates he visited as being in "high spirits, and evidently too seriously bent on enjoying their little carnival, to spare even a passing thought on mischief." The Colonial Office in London must have been quite pleased with such reports.[22]

21. Dirks, *Black Saturnalia*, 147, 204–5; Higman, "Slavery Remembered," 56; Holt, *Problem of Freedom*, 56; Craton, *Testing the Chains*, 237; Sligo to Spring Rice, August 13, 1834, *BPP*, 1835, no. 17, p. 54; Burn, *Emancipation and Apprenticeship*, 174.

22. Isaac to Spring Rice, August 6, 1834, *BPP*, 1835, no. 238, p. 666; Loving to Murray M'Gregor, August 27, 1834, *BPP*, 1835, Enclosure in no. 163, p. 558; Miller, Extract of Letter, December 30, 1834, *BPP*, 1835, 119; Dillon, Extract of Letter, December 30, 1834, *BPP*, 1835, 119; Cooper, Extract of Letter, December 31, 1834, *BPP*, 1835, 119; Burn, *Emancipation and Apprenticeship*, 146.

Unlike colonial officials, however, we should be wary of the assignment of quiet and orderly corporate behavior to new apprentices and former slaves. While apprentices had joyfully participated in watch nights, public processions, and estate dinners, they had also pursued their own celebrations independent of colonial officialdom, planter paternalism, and missionary proselytism. Some of these celebrations were spontaneous acts; many drew from older festive traditions of momentary freedom carved out during colonial slavery. This "little carnival" represented an important cultural politics of emancipation.

The official record of order and sober proceedings notwithstanding, the implementation of the apprenticeship system wrought immediate tensions. The colonial authorities wanted to reshape masters and slaves into employers and employees whose social relations would be determined by the payment of wages for labor, regulation by legal contract, and the supply and demand of the marketplace. In contrast, planters sought to reshape the new system in ways reminiscent of former controls. As the historian W. L. Burn put it: "to many masters 'working for hire' meant working for what wages they cared to pay at such times as payment suited them." Planters and local employers also opposed legal encroachments of colonial power exemplified by an abolition process foisted upon them. In all the colonies, the new colonial system assumed local variations over the amount of work during the week by apprentices for former masters, the levels of compensation, and control over free time.[23]

As several historians have recently shown, in contrast to the old view that the transition from slavery to apprenticeship was quiet and orderly, many of the new apprentices proved quite troublesome in pursuit of their own "expectations of emancipation." They protested against the new system at several levels, including restrictions on freedom, working without compensation, the loss of customary privileges, and the length of the working day.[24] Lieuten-

23. Green, *British Slave Emancipation,* 124; Michael Craton, *Empire, Enslavement and Freedom in the Caribbean* (Kingston: Ian Randle Publishers, 1997), 380–81; Burn, *Emancipation and Apprenticeship,* 270, 166–95.

24. Marshall, "'We be wise to many more tings'"; Gad Heuman, "Riots and Resistance in the Caribbean at the Moment of Freedom," *Slavery and Abolition* 21 (September 2000); Holt, *Problem of Freedom,* 55–79.

ant Governor Sir C. M. Schomberg reported from the capital of Dominica that "an apparent sulky dislike to the apprenticeship system is quite manifest among the negroes, nor are there in Roseau, as yet any symptoms of rejoicing or satisfaction displayed." Hundreds of former slaves marched on Government House in Trinidad's capital city Port-of-Spain to express publicly their disapproval of the apprenticeship system. The governor tried to dissuade them from striking, but was met with abuse, laughter, and hooting. "Point de six ans, point de six ans" (no six years, no six years), they chanted, in clear opposition to the new apprenticeship system. Many were arrested and seventeen of the ringleaders were condemned to floggings and hard labor. Rather than disperse, the crowd followed those arrested to jail, calling for their release. After the reading of the Riot Act, troops moved in to break up the crowd, but former slaves still congregated. It was reported that freed women were especially vocal in vowing their opposition.[25]

One week after the passage of abolition, the great gang working the Adelphi estate in St. Vincent took strike action, believing they "had been worked beyond the time prescribed by law for their daily labour." Mr. Walker, legislative member for St. Ann and owner of the Shaw Park estate, Jamaica, informed Governor Sligo that "the apprentices on his estate and those around him had refused to work without payment, had threatened him with their own law, and shown the most insubordinate spirit." Receiving "several letters from that neighbourhood all to the same effect," and wishing to stop its spreading, the governor dispatched troops to the trouble spots. Although "the effect produced by their sudden apparition was very great," he wrote, "strange to say, even with that effect it became necessary to punish a vast number of the negroes, as well by flogging as confinement in the workhouse." On the Belvedere estate, apprentices staged a slowdown. After some arrests, the seventy-year-old midwife of the estate urged crowd protection because three of her children had been arrested. The police were surrounded and a sugarcane trash house was set ablaze. This incident was clearly a local event with its own set of specific conditions. But it also had wider spatial and temporal

---

25. Lt.-Gvr. Sir C. M. Scomberg to Spring Rice, August 1, 1834, *BPP*, 1835, no. 245, p. 673; Green, *British Slave Emancipation*, 131; Campbell, "Carnival, Calypso, and Class Struggle in Nineteenth Century Trinidad," 4; Eric Williams, *History of the People of Trinidad and Tobago* (Port of Spain, Trinidad: PNM Publishing, 1962), 88; Wood, *Trinidad in Transition*, 46.

ripples. Apprentices on several adjoining estates had protested in similar ways. It had been the setting alight of sugar cane trash at Belvedere and several surrounding estates that sparked the Jamaican slave revolt the night of December 27, 1831.[26] It was out of these economic differences between apprentice former masters and former slaves, together with political tensions between the Colonial Office and legislative assemblies, that the new labor system was terminated on August 1, 1838, two years earlier than originally mandated by the 1833 Act of Abolition.[27]

In the words of one colonial official, August 1, 1838, was marked "with good order, decorum and gratitude." According to W. L. Burn, the day "was observed in Jamaica by the negroes as the same day had been observed in 1834." And it is true that Emancipation Day celebrations were similar in a number of ways. Colonial officials, Christian missionaries, and estate planters organized celebrations in the towns and countryside. Former apprentices attended these official events en masse; they also organized and participated in "other" celebrations beyond the ken of the white authorities. But the 1838 festivities were also very different. The early termination of the apprenticeship system provided an additional opportunity for colonial officials to portray emancipation as the gift of a benevolent state. In other words, abolition had been the kind act of a young new monarch, seventeen-year-old Queen Victoria, who had mounted the British throne a year earlier. This is the clear message of the image on the book's dust jacket. Moreover, abolitionists, missionaries, and former slaves could now celebrate the clear and unequivocal termination of a centuries-old colonial slave system whose last vestiges were buried with the end of apprenticeship. Broken whips and chains symbolized not just the end of slavery, apprenticeship, and coercion, but a new promise of freedom. Meanwhile, planters saw paternal management as especially important since the apprenticeship system opened them up to the vagaries

26. Edward Cox, "From Slavery to Freedom: Emancipation and Apprenticeship in Grenada and St. Vincent, 1834–1838," in *Crossing Boundaries: Comparative History of Black People in the Diaspora*, ed. Darlene Clark Hine and Jacqueline McLeod (Bloomington: Indiana University Press, 1999), 372; Sligo to Spring Rice, August 13, 1834, *BPP*, 1835, no. 17, p. 54; Holt, *Problem of Freedom*, 13, 61–62; Craton, *Testing the Chains*, 303.

27. Craton, *Empire, Enslavement*, 380–81; Burn, *Emancipation and Apprenticeship*, 357–58.

of free market competition in which former slaves could be enticed to work elsewhere or simply desert the sugar estates altogether.[28]

On the night of July 31, 1838, missionaries organized watch nights in local chapels throughout Jamaica. Large congregations met at the Baptist chapels of Salter's Hill, Bethtephil, and Brown's Town. The next day, 2,500 freed people assembled at Salter's Hill for an address by the pastor. Mr. Denby quoted from Nehemiah 12:42, 43, where the "singers sang loud, with Jezrahiah, their overseer" and they, together with wives and children, "rejoiced, so that the joy of Jerusalem was heard even far off." Mr. Denby further exhorted the freed people to remember their new position and "not [to] disappoint the expectations of their friends." Mr. Pickton addressed the congregation at Bethtephil quoting the Israelites on being released from Babylon: "The Lord hath done great things for us, whereof we are glad." Rev. Clarke conducted the watch night at Brown's Town. After hymns and prayers, he sketched the rise and fall of West Indian slavery. "Just before the midnight hour," reported Rev. Cox, "the large assemblage knelt down, and in solemn silence supplicated the blessing of God on the freedom they anticipated. A few minutes after twelve, all arose and lifted up their voices in a song of praise to him who had broken the chain of slavery." The next day, Mr. Clarke preached from Psalm 113:25, while an address to the governor was read and adopted. Afterward, the congregation resolved to build an extension to the chapel funded with "the first fruits of their free labor," to accommodate all those unable to attend the service.[29]

Missionaries made freed children central to this religious rite of emancipation. On August 2, 1838, Mr. Russell organized the children in Jamaica's Bethtephil congregation to spread along the road to the Chatham intersection bearing the banners "August the first, 1838," "This is the day of Jubilee," "Ethiopia shall stretch out her hands unto God," and "Freedom." At Brown's Town on the same day, the Sabbath-school children had a "commemorative festival," each one being presented with a book (bible?) from the London Religious Tract Society. Numerous Baptist chapels organized children to cel-

---

28. Burn, *Emancipation and Apprenticeship*, 359. Because Higman and Brereton begin their studies of Emancipation Day in 1838 rather than 1834, they miss this important contrast.

29. Cox, *Baptist Missionary Society*, 266–67.

ebrate abolition. These youthful festivities not only advertised the joys of freedom; they also sought the social politicization of freed children. Emancipation had been God's work, in exchange for which, they were expected to be obedient, dutiful, and respectful. The visual signs were easy to read; Bibles provided powerful memories; and the events were fun.[30]

Although these religious rites involving children were carefully scripted, they did not always go according to plan. On August 3, 1838, 552 children gathered at Salter's Hill in Jamaica for a commemoration. Rev. Cox provided a detailed account that deserves full quotation:

> The chapel was tastefully decorated with branches of palm-trees, fruits, and flowers. A hymn being sung, preparations were made for the burial of slavery. The whip, the chain, and the shackle, were separately produced, and the question asked, "What is to be done with the old slave-whip?" "Cut it up," was the reply. It was done. "What with the chain?" "Break it." This was also done. "What with the shackle?" "To be destroyed." After each was exhibited, three enthusiastic cheers were given, that they were no longer liable to the evils of slavery, but released from its terrors. The question being asked, what was to be done with the remains of slavery, "Bury them, bury them," was the universal cry. "Where?" "On Salter's Hill?" "No!"—"Yes!" "No; we will not have the remains of Slavery so near us." However, this was overruled by its being remarked, that Salter's Hill would be the most appropriate place, as its grave could be watched, so as to prevent it's rising again. The emblems were carried to the hole dug for them, and consigned for ever to the dust.

There were several revealing aspects to this ceremony. The decorated chapel evoked a biblical setting. The brutal emblems of slavery were displayed, destroyed, and solemnly buried. There was shared agreement over the destruction of the emblems of slavery, while the monster slavery was cheered

---

30. Ibid. Former slave children in the district of Parham, Antigua, had been given bibles on the cover of each was stamped in large capitals: "PRESENTED BY THE BRITISH AND FOREIGN BIBLE SOCIETY, IN COMMEMORATION OF THE FIRST OF AUGUST, 1834." Thome and Kimball, *Emancipation in the West Indies*, 30.

to death. But dissent emerged over the burial of these emblems. While all agreed to burial, some freed children did not want the emblems buried near them. These would serve as close reminders of the cruelties of the old system. They were overruled and the emblems were buried in the chapel graveyard. Moreover, what appears to have begun as a somber burial ceremony became transformed into an enthusiastic freedom celebration that was also marked by some dissent. It was the youth who were responsible for this change.[31]

Such actions recalled spontaneous youthful displays after the Act of Abolition. Having described the success of Baptist thanksgiving services in the chapels of Kingston in 1834, Rev. Tinson reported: "In the evening, there were a few joyous groups about the streets; one passed our house, chiefly young persons and children, adorned with green leaves and flowers, and carrying branches in their hands, dancing and singing, 'Tankee, Massa, fus a' Augus! Hurra! hurra! fus a' Augus come! Fus a' Augus for eber! We da 'prentice now, God bless de King! Hurra! Hurra! fus a' Augus for eber!'" The youngsters were clearly grateful to the authorities for their changed condition. The late hour and spontaneity of this nocturnal street parade, however, stood in marked contrast to the order and control of religious events, and probably caused Rev. Cox some concern.[32]

One of the most elaborate religious commemorations was organized in Falmouth, Jamaica. Contemporary accounts reveal the didactic purpose as well as contested nature of the event. On the evening of July 31, 1838, several hundred people from the surrounding countryside descended upon the coastal town to attend thanksgiving services. The dissenting chapels were specially illuminated for the occasion. At the Baptist chapel, long-serving minister William Knibb commenced to say a few words to the assembly a few minutes before the clock struck 12:00. Although "perfect silence reigned," Rev. Knibb "begged" the congregation of more than two thousand "to listen— *'The hour is at hand,'* said he, *'the monster is dying!'* As the twelfth peal vibrated, he exclaimed—'THE MONSTER IS DEAD! THE NEGRO IS FREE! THREE CHEERS FOR THE QUEEN!'" Instead of three cheers, however, the large congregation "broke out into one loud and long-continued burst of exultation and joy." About 5:30 the next morning, a large assemblage gathered

31. Cox, *Baptist Missionary Society*, 266.
32. Ibid., 253.

at the Suffield schoolroom to bury a coffin filled with a chain, handcuffs, and an iron collar. On one side of the coffin was painted "Cornwall Courier," on the other, "Jamaica Standard"; on the plate, "Colonial Slavery died July 31st, 1838, aged 276 years," and on the bottom, "Sir John Hawkins"—Queen Elizabeth's famous seadog and slave captain of the 1560s. During the burial, the assembly of former apprentices and missionaries sang: "Now *Slavery* we lay thy vile form in the dust, and buried for ever, there let it remain; and rotted, and covered with infamy's rust, be every man-whip, and fetter, and chain." A Union Jack was hoisted and a liberty tree planted, this time accompanied by three cheers.[33]

After various services in the town, a large public meeting was held at the Baptist chapel. Mr. Knibb chaired the meeting, whose purpose was to express thanks to God for "the boon of freedom" as well as to provide an "expression of gratitude" to those who were the "instruments" of God's will. Thirteen speakers, all of whom were described as "descendants of Africans," followed Rev. Knibb. Their speeches successfully addressed the meeting's purpose. Just to take two examples: Mr. William Gibson urged that "we must thank the people of England for freedom," while Mr. M'Laughlin blessed God "that he had sent us ministers to preach the gospel to us."[34]

According to Catherine Hall, these speeches demonstrated the "upright and responsible character of freed Black men." This is no doubt true. The publication of edited speeches in an official Baptist history propagating a particular presentation of emancipation as God's boon left little room for dissenting voices or irresponsible freedmen. But a careful look at the edited speeches implies a richer vision of freedom by former apprentices than simply the politics of respectability. This freedom festival, for instance, provided a reminder of the horrors of slavery to Afro-Jamaican people. William Kerr insisted: "Let we remember that we been on sugar estate from sunrise a-morning till eight o'clock at night; the rain falling, the sun shining, we was in it all. Many of we own color behind we, and many before; we get whip, our wives get beat like a dog, before we face, and if we speak we get the same; they put we in shackles." Edward Barrett recalled: "We have been made to stand up and see our wives flogged, and we could not help them." Moreover, other

33. Ibid., 267.
34. Ibid., 268–70.

speakers described the importance of emancipation. William Smithson called on the crowd to "pray for better freedom, for that good part which shall never be taken from us." Thomas Gardner rejoiced: "I am slave no more, and you are slaves no more—Jamaica is slave no more." Furthermore, some of these speakers knew the difference between 1834 and 1838. Edward Barrett blessed Queen Victoria: "kings [William IV] did sit on the throne, but kings did not make we free; no, that was left for a woman to do; when kings could not do it, Victoria did." Finally, some speakers referred to international solidarity. After thanking God and the English people for freedom, William Gibson asked the crowd: "Let us pray that our brothers and sisters in other lands may be made free and let us look for better freedom."[35]

At the same meeting, James Wallace urged the assembly "to train up ourselves and our children to good conduct." On the next day, the town of Falmouth was "thronged with hundreds of youth." Around 10:00 A.M., "a thousand scholars" began a processional led by a carriage pulled by two horses "caparisoned" with the mottoes "LIBERTY TO THE SLAVE" and "THE DAY OF JUBILEE." The children bore four banners: "The chain is broken," "Africa is free, August, 1838," "Holy Bible," and "Infant School." The chapel was "tastefully decorated with branches of trees, with flowers, and with the pictures of Clarkson, Wilberforce, Buxton, &c." A crowded chapel, with teary-eyed "parents and friends," listened to Mr. Knibb's address, after which the children returned to the schoolroom with portraits of the queen and Clarkson "placed in the most conspicuous situations, the flag of freedom waving over all." The children's fete ended with an "ample banquet." This festival was clearly designed to impress the youth with the godly and paternal nature of emancipation.[36]

Much like the dissenting chapels, the established church of Great Britain held special thanksgiving services in its Caribbean colonies. Although the Anglican Church had not been as prevalent as nonconformist missions in the

35. Catherine Hall, *Civilizing Subjects: Metropole and Colony in the English Imagination 1830–1867* (Chicago: University of Chicago Press, 2002), 117–19; Cox, *Baptist Missionary Society,* 268–70.

36. Hall's *Civilizing Subjects* makes a persuasive case for the transnational construction of imperial identities through the dual mission of English Baptist ministers to remake themselves and Jamaican former slaves in the image of God. The book is less successful in demonstrating the ways in which former slaves resisted such agendas, especially through Afro-Creole communal and cultural forms.

British West Indies during slavery, this began to change in the years leading up to abolition. Two dioceses were established with bishops at Barbados and Jamaica as a consequence of the 1823 Amelioration Acts, while the number of Anglican clergymen rose by 60 percent between 1825 and 1834.[37] The private diary entry of Special Magistrate John Bowen Colhurst of St. Vincent in the Windward Islands provides a rare glimpse of an Emancipation Day ceremony organized by the established church:

> As the police magistrate of the district, I was present all day in the town of Barrouallie, inspected the police and issued such orders as I considered necessary in case of any ebullition of popular feeling. All, however, was order and, I must add, solemn tranquility even far beyond anything I had reason to expect from the uniform good conduct of the apprentices of the entire district since I became their Special Magistrate. I attended service at the Protestant church which was crowded to excess with now, thank Heaven, a free people . . . The service throughout was appropriate, and the sermon preached by the Rev. Mr. Brathwaite extremely to the purpose. It embraced the captivity of the Jews by the Egyptians, how they became the chosen people of God, etc. etc., how they rebelled against him, and the consequences. He compared the slavery of the Africans in the West Indies with the captivity of the Jews, with the great difference in the period of its continuance, etc. etc., and finally explained to his hearers their duties to God, their Queen, their County, and to each other, and terminated his discourse pathetically and solemnly, so much so that few dry eyes were to be found in the church, my own among the many.

Much like other colonial officials, Colhurst expected emancipation to be met with some social disorder. The enthusiasm of former slaves for the ending of apprenticeship and the start of full emancipation was evident by their packing the Protestant church. (We should not forget that the Anglican Church was far less popular with slaves and apprentices than the dissenting chapels.) The clergyman's sermon was a deliberately chosen piece comparing slavery with

37. Green, *British Slave Emancipation*, 327, 335–36, 411.

freedom and the dire consequences of rebelling against God. (The reverend, along with the magistrate, was quite anxious about the behavior of the former apprentices.) The sentimental ending should not blind us to the didactic purpose of making subjects by tightly wrapping the flag of patriotism around the Bible of liberation.[38]

The most elaborate freedom festival was organized in the heart of Jamaica's capital city. After thanksgiving services, some seven thousand adults, together with two thousand children, paraded through the streets of Spanish Town. The order of procession consisted of teachers, children, the pastor, and singers, followed by the "mass." The marchers bore fifteen flags and banners proclaiming emancipation to be a moral process: "Education, social order, and religion," "Wisdom and knowledge the stability of the times," and "Knowledge is power." The advent of abolition was portrayed as a state boon with "silk flags" naming the primary protagonists: the British monarch Victoria; colonial officials Sir Lionel Smith, the Earl of Mulgrave, and the Marquis of Sligo; and abolitionists Joseph Sturge and Henry Brougham. Small flags with inscriptions were handed out en route to the observers. Some identified the former apprentices as God's subjects: "Am I not a man and a brother?" "Ethiopia bends her knee to God and give him glory," "Philanthropy, patriotism, and religion, have under God, achieved for us this glorious triumph," and "path to heaven." Other flags proclaimed exceptional English liberty: "England, land of liberty, of light, of life," "Freedom shall henceforth for ever be enjoyed throughout the British empire," and "Equal rights and privileges." Abolition had been and was to be a conflict-free process: "Emancipation in peace, in harmony, in safety, and acquiescence, on all sides." And abolition was never to be forgotten: "The day of our freedom," and "The Ist of August, I838, never to be forgotten through all generations."[39]

The parade eventually arrived at King's Square. This imposing space had been built up during the eighteenth century as an architectural expression of colonial power. To the west was the governor's residence, King's House, with its ionic columns of Portland stone, white marble portico, and royal arms. To the east was the two-storied Doric column building housing the assembly and

---

38. Woodville K. Marshall, ed., *The Colhurst Journal: Journal of a Special Magistrate in the Islands of Barbados and St. Vincent* (Millwood, N.Y.: KTO Press, 1977), 226–27.

39. Phillipo, *Jamaica*, 71.

supreme court. To the south was the old courthouse. On the north side, there was a crescent-shaped colonnade of white stone, with a temple in the middle, and two wings used as military barracks. Having arrived, the former apprentices were addressed by the governor, who read out the official proclamation of freedom, offered his congratulations, and "was greeted by reiterated and enthusiastic cheering." The lord bishop, whose diocese was based in Jamaica, also spoke, taking the opportunity to explain the responsibilities of freedom to the former slaves. After one hour of this ceremony, three cheers were given to the queen and the governor. The assembly then followed the pastor to the Baptist mission. This construction of emancipation as a state boon continued the following day. In the evening, a "charitable bazaar" opened at the decorated schoolrooms. Some four thousand people gathered in the presence of the governor, chief justice, council and assembly members, several military officials, and prominent citizens. This freedom festival in the capital city represented a theater of colonial power: its major actors were kind English people; its scenery, imposing neo-classical architecture; and its audience, grateful and orderly former apprentices. The supporting cast consisted of military units housed in the nearby barracks.[40]

In the countryside, plantation proprietors organized crop-overs, feasts, and festivities to celebrate the end of emancipation and their own paternal management. At the Oxford estate in Trelawny parish, a dinner was held for 450 "guests" with toasts to the queen, success to the friends of freedom, and happiness to Jamaica. Banners inscribed with "FREEDOM" hung from the trees. On August 3, 1838, six hundred children with parents and friends "seated on the green sward, under the wide branches of a tamarind tree," listened to an address by Baptist preacher Mr. Ward. (Mr. Ward had also been one of the speakers at Falmouth.) After a brief ceremony, the children returned to the aptly named Wilberforce station "making the welkin [sky] ring' with their loud huzzas and cheers."[41]

40. Ibid.; Burn, *Emancipation and Apprenticeship,* 17; Higman, "Slavery Remembered," 57; Green, *British Slave Emancipation,* 160. There is an illustration of this August First in Phillippo, *Jamaica,* 174.

41. Higman, "Slavery Remembered," 58; Cox, *Baptist Missionary Society,* 268, 270. Cox's book was published in 1842. In the June 24, 1842, issue of the *Liberator,* Rev. Samuel J. May used almost identical language in his call for American abolitionists to celebrate West Indian Emancipation to make "the welkin ring [with] long and loud huzzas."

Lord Carrington's Farm Pen estate was the scene of a particularly elaborate crop-over celebration. People from the adjacent estate of Lord Seaford as well as the governor and various dignitaries were invited. A great deal of preparation—no doubt by the former apprentices—went into the making of the "rustic saloon."

> The tables were stretched out along a beautiful lawn between the great house and the negro village, and were enclosed in their whole extent, which could not have been less than 200 feet, by a beautiful and highly-finished fabric of evergreens, adorned with chaplets and festoons of flowers. The exterior presented to the eye, at a distance, the appearance of a spacious arcade in the Gothic style—the graceful cocoa-nut branch tastefully woven, forming the numerous arches and columns. The inside was fitted up in a style still more chaste and elegant, being, in addition to the ornaments culled from nature's garden, supplied with various articles of household furniture, and adorned with flags of different colours, on which were inscribed the names of the illustrious living characters who, under God, had achieved the glorious triumph they were met to celebrate.

The theme of thanksgiving was quite clear: the supper arrangements; the evergreens in the cathedral-like arcade stretching heavenward; and the instruments of God's will on prominent display. After the blessing, the banquet began, followed by the songs. Toasts were raised to the queen, followed by a verse of the national anthem, and to the governor with one "enthusiastic shout of applause." The choir struck up: "Joy, for every yoke is broken, And the oppressed all go free." Speeches, toasts, and cheers followed. The celebration ended with "each individual going peacefully and joyfully to his home."[42]

According to Rev. Phillippo, these were among "the last of the entertainments." There was nothing "Bacchanalian" in the repasts with "no dancing, no noisy mirth, [and] no carousing." In their account of West Indian emancipation, Thome and Kimball made a similar point about the 1834 celebrations in Antigua: "There were no riotous assemblies, no drunken carousals." It is

---

42. Phillippo, *Jamaica*, 72–73. There is an illustration of an estate dinner at Dawkins Caymanas, Jamaica, in Holt, *Problem of Freedom*, 57.

clear, however, that this was not the whole story. After long protesting the limitations of the apprenticeship system in St. Kitts, it was reported that the laborers greeted its abolition "more joyfully than the first." John Anderson, special magistrate in St. Vincent, provided detailed descriptions of crop-over celebrations and coffee dances held on the sugar estates. From Kingstown, he reported "dances are held . . . which are resorted to, from far and near; the wearied assistants making their way back to their estates in time next morning for the six o'c. bell;—but in reality . . . incapable of work." (Anderson's objections anticipated Rev. Phillippo's concerns about the exhausting nature of Jonkonnu celebrations in Jamaica.) A Presbyterian minister reported from Jamaica that one sugar estate apprentice organized a "ball" and gathered some local people, "whose singing, and drumming, and dancing, disturbed the neighbourhood." When the missionary complained, the former slave

> furiously threatened, that if I should come that way again to spoil his meeting, I should not leave the negro town in a whole skin. I had no right, he said, to come to his yard; for he might do what he liked in his own place, and have what company he pleased. Because he had a black face and I a white one, made me do so. But when the first of August arrived, he would see who would meddle with him or his dance. He would be as good as me then, and would split my skull if I came into his yard again.

Former slaves attended official celebrations. They should have then gone home peacefully and joyfully. Instead, they often organized independent celebrations.[43]

The abolition of slavery and apprenticeship affected other parts of the British Empire besides the West Indies colonies. In South Africa, the Dutch East India Company had opened the slave trade and chattel slavery from the mid-1600s onward. The majority of slaves were held in Cape Town, where they labored as domestic servants and artisans, as well as in the southwestern regions of Stellenbosch and Drakenstein, where they worked on wheat and

43. Ibid., 184; Thome and Kimball, *West Indian Emancipation*, 37, 42; Roderick A. Mc-Donald, "The Transition from Slavery to Freedom in the British West Indies: The Journal of John Anderson, St. Vincent Special Magistrate, 1836–1839," unpublished manuscript, 26; Higman, "Slavery Remembered," 59.

wine farms. The advent of British occupation in 1795 did not end the system of slavery, but it did inaugurate some important changes. In 1807, the Abolition of the Slave Trade Act effectively ended the legal importation of slaves into South Africa after 1808. Thereafter, slaves owned by the Dutch East India Company dwindled in size and importance, eventually gaining their freedom in 1827. Two years earlier, a slave named Galant attempted an uprising in Koue Bokkeveld, only to be crushed by a local militia. In the words of the leading scholars of Cape slavery: "Although there were no massive slave revolts of the kind that took place in the Caribbean, Cape slave owners were considerably alarmed by the Bokkeveld uprising of 1825 and the spectre of violent resistance which it evoked." The 1833 Abolition Act legally transformed the Cape's 36,169 slaves into apprentices as in the British West Indies. The system of apprenticeship was finally terminated on December 1, 1838.[44]

Much like the West Indies, the new day was celebrated in religious services and private ceremonies. The *South Africa Commercial Advertiser* reported: "On Saturday the places of Public Worship open to them [freed people] in the forenoon and evening, were filled to the doors by most orderly and attentive congregations." The missionary chapel at Stellenbosch "was crowded to excess at three different services during the day and many who could not gain admittance, remained outside, near the door, and windows endeavouring to catch some portion of the service." Missionary G. A. Zahn reported from Tulbagh that "the old and the young, known and unknown, could be seen with joy on their faces." From Worcester, the local magistrate wrote: "New Epoch in Colony, slavery abolished, all Apprentices this day emancipated. Happy event for the future generation." Much like their formerly enslaved brethren in the British Caribbean, freed people in South Africa were glad to be free and gave expression to this feeling through attendance at public places. The official record is mute, however, on "other" festivities by former apprentices that probably occurred as a consequence of such joyous and glad feelings.[45]

44. James C. Armstrong and Nigel A. Worden, "The Slaves, 1652–1834," in *The Shaping of South African Society, 1652–1840*, ed. Richard Elphick and Hermann Giliomee (Middletown, Conn.: Wesleyan University Press, 1989), 109–83.

45. Pamela Scully, *Liberating the Family? Gender and British Slave Emancipation in the Rural Western Cape, South Africa, 1823–1853* (Portsmouth, N.H.: Heinemann, 1997), 64. For freed people's attendance at Moravian commemorations and *winti* dances on Emancipation Day in Dutch Suriname, see Alex Van Stipriaan, "July 1, Emancipation Day in Suriname: A Contested *Lieu de Memoire*, 1863–2003," *New West Indian Guide* 78 (2004): 272.

What happened to August First Day in the immediate decades after the abolition of the imperial apprenticeship system in 1838? Most obviously, celebrations of emancipation continued to be held and contested, albeit in very different ways. The colonial government expanded its imperial power but seems to have taken less interest in sponsoring its role as giver of freedom. While Christian missionaries continued to proselytize around freedom celebrations, the chapels underwent a major decline in power and influence. In contrast, Emancipation Day celebrations continued to evolve from white-sponsored historical events into communal rituals confirming the same autonomy that freed people were gradually winning in the post-emancipation decades. A particularly striking feature of this evolution was its transnational configuration.

The expansion of British imperial power begun in the late 1820s continued into the post-emancipation decades. The passage of laws abolishing protective duties on corn and sugar production in 1846 inaugurated a free trade policy, undermining a two-century-old system of imperial protectionism. Many West Indian planters denounced this new ruinous policy, especially coming as it did only a decade after abolition. Emancipation had allowed many former slaves to seek alternative ways of living besides sugar estate and family household labor for planters. This estate labor withdrawal by freed people promoted the development of a new system of indentured servitude, transporting laborers from coastal China and India to the sugar plantations of the British Caribbean, especially the new colonies of Trinidad and Guyana. Between 1834 and 1865, it has been estimated that 96,580 Asian indentured laborers were imported to the British Caribbean. This trade in indentured servants was not independent but regulated by the colonial authorities. This enhanced economic control of colonial life was buttressed by increased political power, especially during the 1850s and 1860s. Both the 1857 uprising in British India, as well as the 1865 Morant Bay revolt in Jamaica, resulted in new imperial control in South Asia as well as the replacement of assembly government by Crown colony rule in Jamaica.[46]

While metropolitan power advanced, Christian missionaries and their dissenting places of worship underwent a major decline in the post-emancipation

46. Green, *British Slave Emancipation*, chaps. 8, 9; Blackburn, *Overthrow of Colonial Slavery*, 464; Dennis Judd, *Empire: The British Imperial Experience from 1765 to the Present* (London: Fontana Press, 1997), chap. 8; Holt, *Problem of Freedom*, chap. 8.

decades. Missionary reports of "crowded" chapels became less evident from the early 1840s onward. Methodist and Baptist congregations slowly declined; missions were reported to be in a sad state of disrepair; schools often closed; and teachers spoke of hard times. According to William Green, "the moral force of European missionaries was spent, their energies sapped, [and] their influence abated" by mid-century. Rev. Phillippo's Baptist chapel in Spanish Town, home to spectacular Emancipation Day celebrations in 1838 and 1839, was twice the scene of sectarian violence—in March 1845 and July 1851. On the latter occasion, his house was burgled, his wife beaten, and his own life spared due to the timely arrival of the local militia. Although the planter press in Trinidad continued to urge the efficacy of church services as a safe way of social celebration by former slaves, these services were becoming less popular. Church attendance in Port-of-Spain in August 1839 was reported as "select rather than numerous." By the late 1840s, there were even fewer services and churches no longer used August First Day for didactic purposes.[47]

Correspondence by Christian missionaries published in the *Missionary Record of the United Presbyterian Church* located in the National Archives of Scotland provide firsthand accounts of the decline in the chapel life of Jamaica. Between 1847 and 1854, several August First Day commemorations were held. Although an "immense assemblage" showed up at New Broughton in 1847, "only 150 came out" in 1853. Two-thirds of the congregation showed up the following year at Mount Olivet, earning a rebuke from Rev. Strang: "I am never satisfied with the attendance on these occasions." Moreover, there appears to have been some concern over the changing memories of enslavement and emancipation. In 1834 and 1838, emancipation was heralded as an important and universal theme that was always to be remembered; by the late 1840s, some missionaries expressed their concern that former slaves needed to be reminded of why they should be grateful. One of Reverend A. G. Hogg's "black elders" spoke "of some who disliked to be reminded that they were once in slavery." Some of the speeches delivered at the 1853 commemoration contained "anecdotes to show the young what things their fathers and mothers endured in slavery time, and how great were their privileges now."[48]

47. Green, *British Slave Emancipation*, 340–45; Brereton, "Birthday of Our Race," 72–73.
48. *MRUPC*, December 1847, 195; November 1851, 180–82; October 1854, 165–67.

One of the reasons for this social decline in Christian missionary work was the rise of independent black preachers together with Afro-Caribbean spiritualism. As early as 1842, a revival of West African–derived Myalism had infiltrated Christian churches and proved too pervasive for even the most seasoned proselytizers. Rev. Phillippo's discussion of this revivalism could not escape the implications of this new proselytism. "The more effectually to delude the multitude," wrote the minister,

> the priests of this deadly art, now that religion has become general, have incorporated with it a religious phraseology, together with some of the religious observances of the most popular denominations, and thus have in some instances succeeded in imposing on the credulity and fears of many of whom better things had been expected. These circumstances have aroused the energies of the missionaries to an exposure of the system; as also the civil authorities to the punishment of the offenders when convicted of a violation of the law; so that in a very short period it may be hoped but few vestiges of the superstition will remain.

As Robert Stewart and Dianne Austin-Broos have recently demonstrated, this missionary failure led to a shift toward more negative racist views of the "Afro-Jamaican character," in contrast to earlier, more positive views. These latter views were associated with missionary-led celebrations of emancipation in the past rather than independent expressions of liberation by freedom's first generation in the present.[49]

Some of these independent expressions played an important role in reshaping ongoing racial politics of state and society in the post-emancipation decades. In 1840–41, political power struggles in the Kingston Common Council resulted in confrontations between drummers and dancers and the police over the traditional Christmas Jonkonnu celebrations. In one showdown, some of the crowd told officials and police that the drummers and

49. Phillippo, *Jamaica*, 263–64; Robert Stewart, "A Slandered People—Views on 'Negro Character' in the Mainstream Christian Churches in Post-Emancipation Jamaica," in *Crossing Boundaries: Comparative History of Black People in the Diaspora*, ed. Darlene Clark Hine and Jacqueline McLeod (Bloomington: Indiana University Press, 1999), 179–201; Diane J. Austin-Broos, "Redefining the Moral Order: Interpretations of Christianity in Postemancipation Jamaica," in *Meaning*, ed. Drescher, 221–43.

their supporters had a right to parade since "they were free and would not be made slaves of." The attempts to ban these Jonkonnu celebrations in Kingston ended in riots. In 1843, a proclamation banning street parades went into effect and limited the urban marches. In 1843, fines were imposed in Kingston for loud noises, kite flying, and the use of firearms and fireworks. Such regulations, however, were less enforceable in the countryside. In August 1847, a parish magistrate tried to halt ten days of "John-canoeing, and licentious dancing," and was assaulted for his efforts. It was reported from Trelawny parish that laborers moved "from one estate to another, drumming, fifing, dancing, and john-cannooing, in the demi-savage spirit of the olden time."[50]

August First Day celebrations continued to be contested in the Crown colony of Trinidad. In the years following 1838, an educated Afro-Creole elite together with European-born radicals came together every August First to celebrate the anniversary of abolition. Lavish public dinners were organized by the Trinidad Auxiliary Anti-Slavery Society (TAASS) in the major cities of Port-of-Spain and San Fernando. Toasts were drunk to the regeneration of Africa, the press, the governor and queen, and the abolition of slavery wherever it still existed (i.e., the United States, Brazil, etc.). The primary purpose of these celebrations was to promote the civic incorporation of this Afro-Creole elite through the pursuit of a politics of respectability. These people had never been enslaved, owned property, and deserved the rights of colonial citizenship. Their bourgeois kin on the North American mainland likewise sought to use Emancipation Day celebrations as a means for civic incorporation, although it is important to stress that they were also still fighting for abolition.[51]

These TAASS celebrations were never designed to include former slaves and other working-class people in Trinidad. In contrast to respectable banquets, estate laborers pursued alternative means of celebrating emancipation. Their primary means was through the appropriation of Carnival. During colonial slavery, the celebration of Carnival between Christmas and Ash Wednesday, with its grand costumes, serenading, and public dancing, was confined to the slaveholding class. Slaves took little part in this annual festival, although

50. Swithin Wilmot, "The Politics of Protest in Free Jamaica—The Kingston John Canoe Christmas Riots, 1840 and 1841," *Caribbean Quarterly* 26, nos. 3 and 4 (December 1990): 65–75; Green, *British Slave Emancipation*, 318; Bettleheim, "Jonkonnu," 3; Higman, "Slavery Remembered," 59–61.

51. Wood, *Trinidad in Transition*, 44, 238; Blackburn, *Overthrow of Colonial Slavery*, 424; Brereton, "Birthday of Our Race," 7; Higman, "Slavery Remembered," 62.

they were very much involved in celebrating Canboulay. After abolition, former slaves in Trinidad began to celebrate August First with Canboulay in ways similar to Jonkonnu festivities in Jamaica. Sometime during the 1840s, Canboulay shifted again to provide the opening for Carnival. The important points here are twofold: the African, Creole, and European elite withdrew from public participation in Carnival; and Canboulay, Carnival, and celebrations of emancipation became inextricably interconnected. Two festivals held in Port-of-Spain illustrate this process.[52]

In March 1847, Charles W. Day witnessed Carnival in Trinidad's capital city. "The maskers," the English visitor wrote,

> parade the street in gangs of from ten to twenty, occasionally joining forces in procession. The primitives were negroes, as nearly naked as might be, bedaubed with a black varnish. One of this gang had a long chain and padlock attached to his leg, which chain the others pulled. What this typified, I was unable to learn; but, as the chained one was occasionally thrown down on the ground, and treated with mock bastinadoing [*sic*] it probably represented slavery.

There was much more to Day's account of Carnival, including the bearing of weapons, colorful costumes, masking, character impersonations, and loud "bands of execrable music." In this brief extract, however, we can discern some of the ways in which Carnival represented the memory of slavery and the advent of emancipation. The street gangs might well have been based on sugar estate labor units. The chained individual personified slavery, while the rest of the gang members acted out physical brutality. Though unsure, even Day thought this was an enactment of the slave past.[53]

Such representations were still evident a decade later. In 1858, a journalist noted that Canboulay had become an established part of Carnival. "In our towns," this correspondent noted, "commencing with the orgies on Sunday night, we have the fearful howling of a parcel of semi-savages emerging from

---

52. Andrew Pearse, "Carnival in Nineteenth Century Trinidad." *Caribbean Quarterly* 4 (1956): 176–93; Campbell, "Carnival," 10; Wood, *Trinidad in Transition,* 242–43; Brereton, "Birthday of our Race," 73–74.

53. Pearse, "Carnival," 185; Charles W. Day, *Five Years' Residence in the West Indies* (London: Colburn & Co., 1852); Campbell, "Carnival," 9–10; Aching, *Masking,* 16–17.

God knows where from, exhibiting hellish scenes and the most demoniacal representations of the days of slavery as they were 40 years ago." In subsequent years, these representations would be taken over by the *jamette* class of "singers, drummers, dancers, stickmen, prostitutes, matadors, bad-johns, dunois, makos and corner-boys." Moreover, there was evidence of scenes of amusement and temptation at celebrations. An anonymous policeman denounced August First Day as "a chaos of impudent, insolent, drunken freedom run mad, and radical spouting." One speaker at a Baptist celebration in Savanna Grande bemoaned those thousands who were celebrating emancipation "in a far less rational and becoming manner."[54]

In sum, the post-emancipation decades witnessed the transformation of an old elite festival into a popular celebration by the freed people with memories of slavery and emancipation. More broadly, post-emancipation generations shifted emancipation celebrations *timewise* much like Jonkonnu and crop-over. Former slaves drew upon "the olden time" to remake emancipation in their own image. They ended up appropriating emancipation celebrations for their own purposes. They celebrated emancipation in different ways, places, and times, sharing a politics of cultural identity centered on expectations of freedom. Freedom festivals were organized and celebrated where and when the opportunity arose. Perhaps this was the ultimate collective expression of freedom in a post-slave society.[55]

In the aftermath of legal abolition, Emancipation Day celebrations in the British West Indies took on transnational dimensions. Colonial officials followed imperial directives; they also made certain decisions on the ground according to local circumstances. Christian missionaries sought to spread the word of God throughout the Empire in South Africa and the British Caribbean. God's

---

54. Pearse, "Carnival," 187–92; Brereton, "Birthday of our Race," 71, 73. According to Brereton, "there is absolutely no evidence, for the post-1838 years, of any popular celebrations by the ex-slaves on August First." Additional local and oral research, however, might well turn up evidence of such celebrations overlooked by a hostile bourgeois press. For instance, Amelia Benn recalled annual August First Day celebrations at Blankenburg, British Guyana, from the early 1840s onward featuring church services along with African-derived dancing and drumming. See Barbara P. Josiah, "After Emancipation: Aspects of Village Life in Guyana, 1869–1911," *Journal of Negro History* 82, no. 1 (Winter 1997): 112.

55. Marshall, "We be wise to many more tings," 16.

children belonged to all nations and races. The official investigation into the Jamaican slave uprising revealed that many slaves were prompted to revolt because they thought that emancipation had already come from the colonial government overseas but was being suppressed by planters and local assemblies. Moreover, former slaves celebrated the abolition of slavery and apprenticeship drawing upon both African and Creole cultural traditions. Finally, the abolition of British slavery had a wider impact on colonial slavery in the Caribbean. Two visiting American abolitionists "were informed that the eagerness of the French negroes to taste the sweets of liberty, which they hear to exist in the surrounding English islands, is so great, that notwithstanding all the vigilance by land and sea, they are escaping in vast numbers." [56]

Let us conclude with a cross-national connection that is rarely explored by scholars: the thoughts and feelings of emancipated people in the British West Indies toward their enslaved brethren in the United States. The evidence is scant; it is also located in missionary memoirs and travel reports whose authors often acted as self-appointed spokesmen and interpreters for former slaves. Despite these limitations, however, some sources contain fragments of freed people's thoughts and feelings regarding slavery and freedom in an international context.

One of the central components of Emancipation Day celebrations was the common identity formed by West Indians of African descent around the experience of enslavement. In 1850, a Baptist minister named Cowen organized an August First celebration near the New Grand estate in Savanna Grande in southern Trinidad. This region had been settled by the descendants of an earlier generation of American ex-slave soldiers. Many of them, we are told, stayed away from the meeting because they identified as free men before 1838 and were not "fuss augus niggers.'" But others did attend the event. After Cowen read some extracts from the recently published *Narrative of the Life of Frederick Douglass*, some of the assembly recalled "experiences in the United States, and the horrors they escaped by aid of the British fleet." At the anniversary of the Bible Society held in a Moravian schoolroom, two visiting American abolitionists to Antigua explained the horrors of slavery to the assembled crowd of freed people. "The state of feeling produced by this reference to slavery," James Thome and Joseph Kimball reported, "was such

56. Thome and Kimball, *West Indian Emancipation*, 53.

as might be anticipated in an audience, a portion of which were once slaves, and still remembered freshly the horrors of their late condition." Earlier on, Thome and Kimball had interviewed "Grandfather Jacob," who was a former estate laborer and helper in the Moravian church. The American visitors "asked him whether it was not better to be a slave if he could get food and clothing, than to be free and not have enough. He darted his quick eye at us and said 'rader be free *still.*'" When told about slaves in America, Jacob exclaimed, "Ah, de Savior make we free, and he will make dem fre too. He come to Antigo first—he'll be in Merica soon."[57]

Moreover, freedom festivals had demonstrated the meaning of freedom to former slaves and apprentices in the British West Indies. It was only right that this promise of freedom be extended to other enslaved people. Black speaker William Gibson explained to the gathered assembly in the Baptist church at Falmouth, on August First, 1838, "Let us pray that our brothers and sisters in other lands may be made free." While in Antigua, Thome and Kimball visited the Thibou Jarvis estate managed by James Howell. The manager took the American abolitionists to see the field gang at work. He asked them to stop and told them the visitors wanted to see how freedom was working in Antigua with the hope that it "would induce the masters in America to set their slaves free." The freed people replied: "Yes, massa, we hope dem will gib um free." In an evening meeting at a Moravian chapel, Mr. Morrish introduced the American visitors, who proceeded to explain the condition of slaves in America to the assembly. The freed people "manifested much sympathy, and promised repeatedly to pray that they might be 'free like we.'" These missionary and abolitionist reports depict the sort of universal moral reaction that the authors wanted to convey. On the other hand, it is likely that these former slaves were expressing solidarity with their enslaved brethren overseas.[58]

One final example raises the possibility of a cross-national solidarity around deprivation. Readers of the August 1847 edition of the *Missionary Record of the United Presbyterian Church* might have been struck by a small article under the subheading "Negro Gratitude and Liberality." Sometime in early May 1847, Reverend W. P. Young informed his congregation at Mount Zion

57. Brereton, "Birthday of Our Race," 73; Thome and Kimball, *West Indian Emancipation,* 23, 19.

58. Cox, *Baptist Missionary Society,* 268; Thome and Kimball, *West Indian Emancipation,* 13, 16.

in Jamaica about how "mourning, starvation, disease, and death" had "filled Ireland and the Highlands of Scotland." Two days after preaching on the famine, Rev. Young visited Cinnamon Hill village. Near the village, nailed to a tree, he came across the following letter:

> 5th May 1847
> My Dear Friend—have mercey upond the starving in England and in Scotland in Every parts of the worlds have mercy upond them for they have suffer mercy for us if it where not the good people in England and in Scotland this time we all wood have to work night and day like cattle and mule think upond this we all wood have been in Slavery this time thank be unto God for the victory he hath done come let us all try and help the starving for the Lord say he shall reward them in to the kingdom of heaven try and Give what you have got four shilling is not hard to get.

It is clear these Jamaican villagers were grateful to the English and Scottish people for their assistance in getting rid of British colonial slavery. And it is likely these freed people subscribed to notions of Christian charity toward those in need. But it is also the case that this request for subscriptions was the initiative of local villagers. Moreover, as former slaves, they could no doubt identify with the wretched conditions of those in "Every parts of the worlds." Their ad hoc whip round reflected solidarity with their oppressed fellows.[59]

It would be foolish to build too much on these cross-national connections, but it would be equally foolish to ignore them. Afro-Caribbean freed people empathized with the condition of enslaved black people in the United States because of common oppression and expectations of freedom. This solidarity could extend to other oppressed people. Meanwhile, missionaries and abolitionists simply reported Christian fellowship and Negro gratitude. This bonding also occurred among Christian missionaries in the post-emancipation British West Indies and the slave Republic. The nature of this transnational alliance and its important transformation is the subject of the following chapter.

59. *MRUPC*, August 1847, 120–21.

Chapter 2
West Indian Emancipation and the
American Antislavery Picnic

Antigua is the morning star of our nation.
Thome and Kimball, 1838

The abolition of slavery in the British West Indies in 1834–38 had a tremendous impact on people and events in the Anglo-Atlantic world. It encouraged British abolitionists to spread their antislavery wings. In late 1833, Scottish middle-class dissenters formed the Edinburgh and Glasgow Emancipation Societies. On August 1, 1834, one of the founding members of the latter society, Congregationalist Dr. Ralph Wardlaw, preached a sermon called "The Jubilee" at West George Street Chapel in Glasgow, Scotland. Dr. Wardlaw, much like Christian missionaries in the British colonies, depicted emancipation as God's work. "The day of atonement," he preached, "was a day of humble penitential confession of sins,—a day on which they [apprentices] were to 'afflict their souls,' while, at the same time, it was a day signalized by extraordinary rites of typical propriation." Over the next few decades, leading British abolitionists like Richard Davis Webb of Dublin and Liverpool-born George Thompson were drawn to America to fight against slavery as well as participate in a broader coalition of international reformers.[1]

West Indian emancipation also had an important impact on American abolitionists. It represented the first act of manumission by a major colonial power in New World slave societies. Furthermore, it served to mobilize protest against American slavery. American abolitionists used evidence from West Indian emancipation to argue for the benefits of immediate emancipation in the American South. Most important, American abolitionists began to visit the United Kingdom in search of support to oppose domestic slavery.

1. C. Duncan Rice, *The Scots Abolitionists, 1833–1861* (Baton Rouge: Louisiana State University Press, 1981), 10–11, 26, 36, 40–41, 51–52, 54, 69; Wardlaw, "Jubilee," 12; Davis, *Progress,* 119–22; *BAP,* 1:57.

During the passage of the act in 1833, William Lloyd Garrison was in Great Britain. Over the next thirty years, scores of American abolitionists would follow in his footsteps. In 1840, many attended the World's Anti-Slavery Convention in London. During the 1850s, other American abolitionists visited the United Kingdom in support of the free produce movement. Their objectives were numerous but usually included fund-raising, propagandizing abolition, and pressurizing the British government to support the termination of American slavery. According to Duncan Rice, this international role was partly a "defense mechanism against their minority position" in the United States. While abolitionists were often unpopular, this was not always true at certain times and in certain places. Most important, American abolitionists recognized the fundamental importance of the United Kingdom in the struggle against American slavery. Finally, annual commemorations and celebrations of West India emancipation would rank among the most popular and regular expressions of American antislavery politics over the next generation.[2]

British abolition had no less an important impact on American slaveholders and their supporters. It came in the aftermath of Nat Turner's bloody revolt in Virginia, the founding of the *Liberator* in Boston, and the constitutional crisis over Nullification in South Carolina. The British Empire to the south and north of the American Republic had endorsed the system of colonial emancipation. Moreover, visiting British abolitionists like George Thompson were seen by some as British-financed conspirators pushing for the overthrow of the American Republic. Finally, Southern slaveholders were to draw upon the "failures" of West Indian emancipation to oppose American emancipation. Their transnational comparisons were to become an important component of proslavery ideology over the coming decades.[3]

Before detailed exploration of these links between West Indian emancipation and American antislavery, a word must be said regarding the political economy of cotton in the Anglo-Atlantic world. Between them, slave plantations in the southern United States and proletarian factories in the northern cities of the United Kingdom dominated the global production and manufacture of cotton in the first half of the nineteenth century. Cotton production

2. Rice, *Scots Abolitionists,* 11–12, 77, 80–114, 191.

3. Ibid., 71, 74; James Brewer Stewart, *Holy Warriors: The Abolitionists and American Slavery* (New York: Hill and Wang, 1976), 71.

in the American South increased from 2 million pounds in 1791 to over a billion pounds in 1860. Cotton dominated the export trade of the United States throughout this period. From 1836 through 1840, cotton accounted for 63 percent of American exports. By 1840, the United States was producing over 60 percent of the world's cotton. Slaves grew most of this cotton. In addition, cotton built up domestic capital, attracted foreign investment, and helped fuel the industrial development of the northern states. Indeed, during the half-century prior to the Civil War, the growth of the American economy was largely fueled by the expansion of slave-grown cotton. The British industrial revolution was also fueled by cotton. Between 1846 and 1850, Britain imported four-fifths of its cotton from the United States. American cotton accounted for more than 70 percent of cotton imports to the United Kingdom. British textile factories in northern England and southern Scotland relied heavily upon southern slave cotton. What impact would the abolition of colonial slavery have on this important transatlantic economic relationship? To southern slaveholders, slavery was the only way to provide British factories with their necessary raw materials. To abolitionists, Great Britain had to be pressured because of its role in supporting American slavery through its economic reliance on slave cotton.[4]

"MORNING STAR"

The passage of British abolition encouraged American abolitionists to embrace immediate emancipation. During the 1820s, social reformers on both sides of the Atlantic opposed slavery because of its backwardness. Moreover, these reformers called for both national abolition as well as a personal commitment to the eradication of the sin of slaveholding. The result was the immediatist antislavery movement calling for direct over indirect action, the immediate rather than gradual end to slavery, and opposition to any system of apprenticeship or semi-slavery. In the words of Elizur Wright Jr., it was the duty of slaveholders to provide slaves with liberty, legal protection, and compensation.

4. Douglass C. North, *The Economic Growth of the United States, 1790 to 1860* (Englewood Cliffs, N.J.: Prentice-Hall, 1961), pt. 2; Eric Williams, *Capitalism and Slavery* (London: Andre Deutsch, 1964), 128, 162; Harold D. Woodman, "Slavery: II Economic Aspects," Houghton Mifflin, Reader's Companion to American History, http://college.hmco.com/history/readerscomp/reah/html/ah; Rice, *Scots Abolitionists*, 23.

"Also," Wright added, "it is the *duty* of all men to proclaim this doctrine, to urge upon slave-holders *immediate emancipation*, so long as there is a slave—to agitate the consciences of tyrants, so long as there is a tyrant on the globe."[5]

The institutional expression of immediate abolition came with the formation of the American Anti-Slavery Society (AASS). Six months after the British government passed colonial emancipation, sixty-two abolitionists met in Philadelphia. Their ranks included New York evangelicals led by the Tappan brothers, New England Congregationalists under Garrison, Unitarians like Samuel J. May, and Quakers like John Greenleaf Whittier. Quakers accounted for one-third of the delegates and included four women: Lucretia Mott, Lydia White, Ester Moore, and Sara Pugh. There were only three black delegates: Robert Purvis, James McCrummell, and James G. Barbadoes. Elizur Wright Jr. was elected secretary and was to serve in that capacity until 1839. Their central aim was to organize local antislavery societies to promote the principles of immediate emancipation. Garrison wrote the organization's Declaration of Sentiments demanding immediate emancipation together with condemnation of colonization, compensated abolition, legalized slavery, and racial prejudice. This platform did not ignore the limitations of British emancipation that had included a period of apprenticeship, together with a large amount of compensation to former slaveholders.[6]

Almost immediately, the AASS embarked upon a national propaganda campaign challenging American slavery. The organization sponsored a newspaper, *The Emancipator*, published in New York City, aiming for national circulation. The secretary of the AASS, Elizur Wright Jr., added his pen to those of many others churning out antislavery pamphlets. In May 1835, the AASS launched a massive postal campaign designed to flood the nation with antislavery literature. By the end of 1837, they had posted over a million pieces. Moreover, there was an important international dimension to this propaganda campaign. Having been influenced by the British campaign against slavery, together with the limitations of the implementation of colonial abolition, the

5. *BAP*, 3:8; Stewart, *Holy Warriors*, chap. 2.

6. *BAP*, 3:134, 307; Stewart, *Holy Warriors*, 51–54. Two of the black delegates saw international action. Purvis traveled to England to build solidarity against American slavery, while Barbadoes resettled his family in Jamaica in the spring of 1840 to start a silkworm business. See *BAP*, 3:81, 306. For the ideological links between immediatism and the market revolution, see Stewart, *Holy Warriors*, chap. 3.

AASS turned their attention to the propagation of West Indian emancipation as a working showcase for successful emancipation to encourage the abolition of American slavery.[7]

Between November 1836 and June 1837, James Armstrong Thome and Joseph H. Kimball toured the British West Indies. Thome was the son of a Kentucky slaveholder who increasingly opposed the institution of slavery, while Kimball emerged out of the burgeoning antislavery movement in New Hampshire. They had been "deputed" by the executive committee of the AASS. Their central objective was to break "the silence which the pro-slavery press of the United States has seemed so desirous to maintain" regarding British emancipation, with the "publication of facts and testimony collected on the spot." Their first stop was Antigua, chosen because it had abolished slavery immediately without implementing the apprenticeship system in 1834. Although they left it to readers to decide whether immediate emancipation had been "a blessing or a curse," the authors steered the evidence toward the former interpretation. For one thing, they visited St. John's and its hinterland estates rather than the more rural and isolated plantations where emancipation had been more problematic. Their focus on the Christian piety of Negroes, especially through chapel services, was obviously designed to impress American and British readers of the deserving nature of this formerly enslaved people whose cousins should also be liberated. Their conclusion was foregone: "Antigua is the morning star of our nation."[8]

Barbados was the next island they visited, chosen because of its apprenticeship system. While the system did illustrate *the good disposition of the colored people,*" both its design and practical operation pointed to the shortcomings of a gradual process of liberation. Abolition was far less effective when it was phased in rather than implemented immediately. The visitors' last stop was Jamaica, selected because of its colonial importance and comparatively greater unrest caused by abolition than elsewhere. After spending a month touring the towns and rural districts, Thome and Kimball argued that virtually all of the "causes of the ill-working of the apprenticeship in Jamaica" are "embodied in the intrinsic defects of the system itself." And the fault lay with

---

7. Stewart, *Holy Warriors*, 69–70; *BAP*, 3:134; Rice, *Scots Abolitionists*, 12.

8. StanKlos.com, "Joseph Horace Kimball," *Appleton's Cyclopedia of American Biography* (2000); Thome and Kimball, *West Indian Emancipation*, 5–52.

"the violent character of its planters," together with special justices, in whose hands apprenticeship was little better than slavery. The American abolitionists concluded their narrative with the following expectation: "Commending our narrative to the blessing of the God of truth, and the Redeemer of the oppressed, we send it forth to do its part, however humble, toward the removal of slavery from our beloved but guilty country."[9]

It is important to note the links between British abolition and American slavery exemplified by Thome and Kimball's *West Indian Emancipation*, published by the AASS in 1838. The American visitors frequently discussed the coming of emancipation and chapel watch nights with former slaves, apprentices, and missionaries. Their views were to shape American abolitionists' depiction of the advent of abolition in the British West Indies. Moreover, their tour of the British Caribbean led them to make several propositions about British abolition: the "*event* of emancipation passed *PEACEABLY*"; "*Free labor* is decidedly LESS EXPENSIVE than *slave labor*"; and emancipation "laid the corner-stone in the fabric of their [ex-slaves'] moral and intellectual improvement." This emphasis on the safety, efficiency, and progress of West India emancipation was to become central to the narrative of freedom espoused by American antislavery activists in their meetings, publications, and organizations.[10]

Moreover, abolitionists in the Caribbean bonded with their abolitionist colleagues in the United States. Reverend N. Gilbert, Anglican and proprietor in Antigua, hoped the visitors "might gather such facts during our stay in the island, as would tend effectually to remove the curse of slavery from the United States." Reverend Mathew Banks, Methodist minister of St. Bartholomews, expressed his horror of Christian slavery and its support by Methodists in the United States: "Tell our brethren of the Wesleyan connection . . . that slavery must be abolished by *Christians*, and the church ought to take her stand at once against it." The American visitors told Rev. Banks that these efforts had already started. "'That's right,' he exclaimed, 'agitate, *agitate*, AGITATE! *You must succeed:* the Lord is with you." (The Lord had surely been with Rev. Banks and his flock during the 1834 watch night in Antigua.) Rev. Horne believed the "great nation of America must now soon *toll the knell* of slavery, and this event will be hastened by the happy operation of freedom

9. Thome and Kimball, *West Indian Emancipation*, 81–84, 85, 108–14.
10. Ibid., 15, 16, 18, 21, 36, 40, 48, 55, 65. Emphasis in the original.

here." The Wesleyan missionaries at St. Johns passed several resolutions concerning the emancipation of the slaves. "That we hail with the most lively satisfaction," read one, "the progress in America of anti-slavery principles, the multiplication of anti-slavery societies, and the diffusion of correct views on this subject." These religious bonds over abolition point to the importance of intra-hemispheric connections within the Anglo-Atlantic world.[11]

FROM PULPIT TO PICNIC

In June 1842, John Anderson Collins wrote to the Boston *Liberator* with the suggestion that Garrisonian abolitionists should organize picnics to commemorate British emancipation. Mr. Collins, a rather serious-minded anticlerical from Vermont who had been educated at Andover Theological Seminary, had become general agent for the Massachusetts Anti-Slavery Society (MASS). In 1841, this thirty-one-year-old Garrisonian had embarked on a fund-raising trip to the United Kingdom "for the purpose of procuring pecuniary aid." The trip proved a financial disaster, with Collins having to borrow money from fellow MASS member and traveler Wendell Phillips to pay for his trip home. The antislavery picnic sought to propagate immediate abolition in the United States through public celebrations of the success of emancipation in the British West Indies. Collins suggested that local antislavery societies organize "an anti-slavery picnic," with a procession, banners, speeches, songs, and hymns. A few weeks later, *The Anti-Slavery Picnic* put together by Mr. Collins was printed, consisting of "original and carefully selected matter admirably adapted for recitation, declamation, singing, etc." This collection quickly became widely used at abolitionist meetings. Although its author soon moved on to utopian socialism in upstate New York and eventually various business activities and public office in California and Nevada, the antislavery picnic became an important public expression of American abolition over the next two decades. This annual commemoration represented the critical intersection of local and regional interests with the international antislavery movement.[12]

In the first decade after British abolition, public halls, meeting houses, and local churches provided the major venues for commemorations of West Indian emancipation by American abolitionists in New England. These

---

11. Ibid., 7, 21, 23, 24.

12. Studley, "August First," 567; Rice, *Scots Abolitionists*, 101–14.

annual events every August First were organized by state and local antislavery societies such as MASS, the Young Men's Anti-Slavery Society of Boston, and local auxiliaries at Pawtucket, Wrentham, and Chelsea. Congregations and friends of abolition enthusiastically gathered together for these commemorations. Around 100 to 150 people were reported in attendance at the 1838 Deerfield meeting. Full attendance was reported at celebrations in Boston and Fall River in 1838, while the 1836 Fall River event was reported to have been attended by an "immense throng [who] crowded every inch of space, cramming the vestibule, doors, etc. etc." The service usually consisted of prayers, hymns, and speeches given by local and prominent abolitionists. The hat was often passed to raise funds to fight against American slavery, sometimes with mixed results. At the 1838 meeting, $443 was obtained in cash and pledges from the audience at Marlboro Chapel in Boston. Three years later, the *Liberator* reported that "it was quite melancholy to see the celerity with which the audience departed at the mere pronunciation of the word [collection]." Resolutions praising British abolition, condemning American slavery, and calling for immediate emancipation were often passed at these commemorations. These resolutions and reports of "August First" would be sent to the *Liberator* for a wider readership.[13]

These commemorations reflected the transnational dimensions of antislavery through the participation of British abolitionist speakers together with ideological and visual connections between West Indian emancipation and American slavery. At the Philadelphia commemoration in 1836, there was a banner linking British abolition with future American emancipation. This visual connection represented one example of Anglo-American abolitionism on display at these church commemorations every August First. There were also visiting British abolitionists. George Thompson, the prominent British antislavery activist, visited the United States in 1834–35, during which time he lectured to antislavery audiences on West India Day and at other events in Boston. British abolition was often praised for providing a noble example. At their 1838 meeting, the Wrentham Anti-Slavery Society passed several resolutions, including the statement that British abolition "demonstrates the

---

13. This brief account of church commemorations is drawn from the sources listed for Table 2.1.

TABLE 2.1. Church Commemorations, 1834–1843

1834	Pawtucket, Mass.
	Lowell, Mass.
1835	Boston, Mass.
1836	Meeting House, Fall River, Mass.
	Philadelphia, Pa.
1837	Methodist Chapel, Boston, Mass.
1838	Marlboro Chapel, Boston, Mass.
	Unitarian Meeting House, Fall River, Mass.
	Methodist Meeting House, Andover, Mass.
	Salem, Mass.
	Providence, R.I.
	Pawtucket, Mass.
	Methodist Meeting House, Lynn, Mass.
	Wrentham, Mass.
	Deerfield, Mass.
1839	Chelsea, Mass.
	Concord, N.H.
1841	Marlboro Chapel, Boston, Mass.
1842	Meeting House, Scituate, Mass.
1843	Universalist Meeting House, Weymouth, Mass.

Sources: CA, August 11, 18, 1838; *HF,* August 13, 1841; *L,* August 16, 1834; August 8, 1835; August 13, 1836; August 4, 1837; August 3, 10, 24, 1838; August 16, September 6, 1839; August 20, 1841; August 12, 1842; August 11, 1843.

practicality of immediate emancipation in this country." In his 1835 address, George Thompson thought of British abolition as "maintaining order in the transition of an unparalleled revolution, without crime, without violence, without turbulence or tumult! 'Tis the death knell of American slavery." Moreover, several local auxiliaries resolved the glories of monarchical liberation versus the shame of republican slavery. Finally, the abolition of British colonial slavery was seen as a link in a chain that would eventually result in the overthrow of American slavery. This theme of the progress of abolition was reported at many of these meetings as well as in their press coverage. It was such connections that provided the framework for Anglo-American abolitionism over the next three decades.[14]

But what was the social meaning of these West Indian Emancipation Day celebrations? First, they were small, localized events. Although attended by visiting clergy, abolitionist speakers, and interested parties, August First Day represented a small-town expression of antislavery sentiment. Second, Emancipation Day was largely a thanksgiving service to God and those faithful servants (missionaries, abolitionists, etc.) who had carried, and would carry, out his work. Emancipation was God's work, as recently illustrated by British abolition. Many of these New England church services represented a day of thanksgiving similar to those arranged by Christian missionaries in their chapel services in the British West Indies. Third, British abolition illustrated that American abolition was something to be lawfully granted rather than violently seized. One of the eight resolutions passed by the Deerfield assembly in 1838 was the pursuit of "lawful means" to abolish slavery. "While we sympathize with our colored brethren," explained the antislavery society of Pawtucket at their 1834 celebration, "we most earnestly desire them to receive all injuries in patient submission, and thus by their wise and meek example, assist their friends in hastening the termination of all their wrongs." (This helps explain the pious representation of former slaves in Antigua by Thome and Kimball.)[15]

Finally, these church commemorations provided an opportunity for the small-scale mobilization of people of African descent against American slavery. African Americans were reported to have attended the 1838 Fall River meeting, the 1839 Chelsea event, and many others. Solomon Alexander, "a man of color," spoke at the 1837 Boston meeting, while a "colored choir" sang at the 1838 Marlborough Chapel meeting. Many African Americans would have learned of "August First" and its religious commemorations through the reports published in the *Liberator*.[16]

14. *L*, September 17, 1836; August 10, 1838; August 8, 1835.

15. *L*, August 16, 1834; August 24, 1838. Thome and Kimball, *Emancipation in the West Indies*, 5–52. Indeed, freed people in Antigua were so busy expressing their gratitude to God and his missionaries and attending chapel services in Thome and Kimball's account, one wonders if they ever got time to do anything else with their freedom!

16. *CA*, August 11, 1838; *L*, August 4, 1837; August 3, 1838; August 16, 1839.

These church commemorations continued into the 1850s. The Baptist Church in Fitzwilliam, New Hampshire, held a thanksgiving service in 1853.[17] But it also appears that church services became less salient and functioned differently during the 1850s. Rather than serving as congregational sites for local anniversaries, they were largely relegated to the margins, as either meeting places for the commencement of larger, outdoor public parades, or as final resting places for evening remembrances. From the early 1840s onward, scores of "August First" picnics were celebrated annually by state antislavery societies and their local auxiliaries. Large crowds of European- and African-descended peoples would assemble at a grove or small-forested area, where they would listen to antislavery speeches, collectively sing abolitionist songs and hymns, and partake of a "collation" (light repast). The abolitionist press played an important role in both advertising these events to attract participants and reporting on them afterward to spread the word. In contrast to the thanksgiving church service, the antislavery picnic was designed for public spectacle to reach as many people as possible. The skies were meant to ring with the joys of past abolition and shouts for future liberation. As we will see in chapter 6, the expansion of American slavery during the 1850s, together with increased violence and protest, rendered the church service with its small congregation, thanksgiving service, and moral suasion to overthrow American slavery, increasingly obsolete.

Several weeks after the *Liberator* first published Mr. Collins's suggestion, numerous antislavery picnics were held in the groves of Massachusetts. August First Day was reported in West Brookfield, Hubbardston, and Hingham. Five hundred people from neighboring towns attended "Freedom's Jubilee" at Temperance Grove, Dedham, southwest of Boston. The grove's tall trees, the reporter informed his readers, were reminiscent of abolition's "straight truths." The recently published *Anti-Slavery Picnic* provided celebrants with recitations, addresses, and songs. Around eight hundred people assembled for "August First" at the Grand Oak, Fall River, a small textile town in the southeast of the state. There were brass bands, along with a "juvenile" performance from the Sabbath school children. The most elaborate antislavery picnic was organized at Wood End Grove, Lynn, northeast of Boston. Between three thousand and five thousand people of mixed age, sex, and race were

17. *L*, August 19, 1853.

TABLE 2.2. The Antislavery Picnic, 1842–1860

1842	Temperance Grove, Dedham, Mass.
	Grand Oak, Fall River, Mass.
	Wood End Grove, Lynn, Mass.
	Hubbardston, Mass.
	West Brookfield, Mass.
	Willard Hall, Hingham, Mass.
	Lenox, Mass.
1843	Temperance Grove, Dedham, Mass.
	City Hall, Lowell, Mass.
	Atheneum Hall, Nantucket, Mass.
	Weymouth, Mass.
	Philadelphia, Pa.
1844	Tranquility Grove, Hingham, Mass.
	Norristown, Pa.
	Courthouse, Concord, Mass.
1845	Porter's Grove, Danvers, Mass.
	Grove, Marlboro, Ohio
	Waltham, Mass.
1846	Weare Centre, N.H.
	Island Grove, Abington, Mass.
1847	Springfield, Mass.
	Lynchburg, Ohio
	Island Grove, Abington, Mass.
1848	Wood End Grove, Lynn, Mass.
	Island Grove, Abington, Mass.
1849	Randolph, Ohio
	Hospital Grove, Worcester, Mass.
	Island Grove, Abington, Mass.
1850	Elmira, N.Y.
	City Hall, Worcester, Mass.
	Guildford, Conn.
	Island Grove, Abington, Mass.
1851	Worcester, Mass.
1852	Harmony Grove, Framingham, Mass.
	Mechanic Hall, Salem, Mass.
	Worcester, Mass.

1853	Waverley Hall, Framingham, Mass.
	St. Roman's Well, Flushing, N.Y.
	Marlborough, Pa.
1854	Grove, Hopedale, Mass.
	Island Grove, Abington, Mass.
1855	Harmony Grove, Framingham, Mass.
1856	Island Grove, Abington, Mass.
	Cummington, Mass.
	Grove, Hopedale, Mass.
1857	Island Grove, Abington, Mass.
	Grove, Hopedale, Mass.
	Longwood, Pa.
	Penningtonville, Pa.
1858	Island Grove, Abington, Mass.
	Town Hall, Marlboro, Ohio
1859	Island Grove, Abington, Mass.
	Milford, Mass.
	Florence, Mass.
	Freeman's Grove, Salem, Ohio
	Museum Hall, St. Louis, Mo.
1860	Island Grove, Abington, Mass.
	Milford, Mass.

Sources: ASB, July 25, August 15, 1845; August 13, 1847; July 28, August 11, 18, 1849; August 17, 1850; August 20, 1853; July 29, 1854; August 23, 1856; August 15, 1857; July 24, 1858; July 30, August 20, 27, 1859; *HF,* July 28, August 18, 1843; July 26, 1844; July 25, August 22, 1845; July 24, August 7, 1846; *L,* August 5, 12, 19, 1842; August 4, 11, 1843; August 3, 10, 17, 1849; August 9, 16, 1850; August 15, 1851; August 6, 13, 1852; August 12, 19, 1853; August 8, 15, 1856; July 31, August 7, 14, 21, 1857; August 6, 20, 1858; August 5, 12, 1859; August 10, 17, 1860; *NE,* August 19, 1847; *NS,* August 21, 1848; August 10, 24, 31, 1849; June 13, 1850; Federal Writers' Project, *Massachusetts;* Glick, "Thoreau and the Herald of Freedom," 200–201; Schappes, "Ernestine L. Rose," 345; Studley, "August First," 567–77.

in attendance, many hailing from the close-by towns of Danvers and Salem. There was a procession, band, bell ringing, and speeches by Wendell Phillips and Charles Remond. Also, several songs were sung, presumably from *The Anti-Slavery Picnic*. According to the reporter, this was a "true American" event, unlike July Fourth. By the end of the summer of 1842, many features of a new August First were emerging: large crowds; public processions; speeches and songs; picnicking; and widespread publication.[18]

The most spectacular antislavery picnic was held at Tranquillity Grove, Hingham, southwest of Boston, two summers later. The event had been postponed because of a thunderstorm the previous day. From dawn onward, the town's merchants, women, and the event's committee made ready, with storefront decorations, flags and bunting on the main street, and long tables and seating in the grove. Fodder for the horses and plenty of ice water were provided. The grandstand, bandstand, and seating were all checked, while flags, bunting, and mottoes were strewn between the magnificent grove oaks. Some of these read:

> True Freedom is to share
> All the chains our brothers bear.
> West India Emancipation
> 1st of August, 1834.
> True Freedom is to be
> Earnest to make others free.
> God created man free;
> Then fetter not a brother's limbs.

Most of the food was prepared by "the ladies of Hingham," and included breads, cakes, pies, tea, coffee, cream, lemons, sugar, boiled ham, fowl, fruits, raisins, and fresh vegetables. "Endless throngs" began to pour into the town by boat, carriage, and coach from Boston, as well as from surrounding Suffolk, Essex, Plymouth, and Norfolk counties. The "grand lines" began to form

18. *L*, August 5, 12, 19, 1842; Studley, "August First" 568; Federal Writers Project. *Massachusetts: A Guide to Its Places and People* (Boston: Houghton Mifflin, 1937), 231–32. According to this guide, the Fall River Historical Society was housed in a building where a "false bookcase in the parlor once concealed the entrance to a wine-cellar, a station of the Underground Railroad."

at Fountain Square under the direction of appointed marshals. White star medallions were distributed among the crowd. On one side of the medallion was a picture of a shackled, suppliant "Negro" with one knee bent, hands folded and extended, and wrists bound by chains to his ankles with the legend underneath "A voice from Great Britain to America 1834." On the medal's reverse side stood an upright "Negro" with arms outstretched, broken shackles, irons, and whip on the ground, with the outside circling legend "This is the Lord's Doing; it is marvellous in our Eyes, Psalm 118, v.23." Below center, the legend read, "Jubilee, Aug. I, 1834."[19]

The procession consisted of a crowd four-deep with "men and women, black and white, clerical and lay, rich and poor," stretching for a mile and half. According to the banners and mottoes, antislavery delegations from towns all over the state—Abington, Hanson, Hanover, Kingston, Plymouth, Lynn, Salem, Boston, Dorchester, West Roxbury, and Weymouth—were present. Many signs insisted on the instant abolition of American slavery. "Immediate emancipation" was the call from the Essex contingent. The hypocrisy of a slaveholding Christian Republic was represented on Hanson's town banner with the American Eagle trampling a prostrate slave, a bloodhound about to seize the victim, and a file of soldiers aiming muskets at his body with the motto "This is American Liberty." Another banner from a town in Essex County had the motto: "Shall a republic which could not bear the bonds of a king, cradle a bondage which a king has abolished?" This image of the slaveholding Republic was contrasted with the recent freedoms of the former colonial power. British emancipation was represented on numerous banners, one device having the hour of emancipation shown by a slave at sunrise on August First, 1834, with chains falling off his limbs, from which they were just broken, with the motto "This is the Lord's doing. Slavery abolished in the British West Indies, 1st August, 1834." The banner from the town of Dorchester paraphrased Isaiah: "Our watchword, let the oppressed go free." Emancipation was "the duty of the master and right of the slave," read one AASS banner. The procession must have been quite impressive. They "preached," according to one reporter, the "gospel to the gazers from the windows."[20]

19. *L*, July–August, 1844; *HF*, July 26, 1844; Studley, "August First," 570–77; Federal Writers' Project, *Massachusetts*, index.

20. Ibid.

Once this large crowd reached the grove, they had a counter-procession so as to witness each other. This must have been an extraordinary sight: some six thousand to eight thousand people circling one another. After nine cheers, Garrison was appointed chairman, Rev. Stearns led a prayer, while letters of endorsement were read out from John Quincy and Charles Francis Adams, who were unable to attend. At noon, the church bells rang out the "joyful jubilee." The crowd mingled around the long tables, making acquaintances, renewing friendships, and swapping news and gossip. Antislavery speeches were delivered by several speakers, including MASS lecturer John Pierpont, twenty-six-year-old fugitive and rising abolitionist star Frederick Douglass, moral reformer and abolitionist James Freeman Clarke, state legislator Seth Sprague, and William Abijah White and Oliver Johnson. After the speeches, the crowd sang songs from the antislavery hymnal. Toward evening, the crowd prepared to disperse and "the lovers of liberty turn[ed] homeward." They were accompanied by the sunset bells, which "clang[ed] out again the jubilee of August First." All declared it to be a day "long to be remembered for its social enjoyment and inspiriting association." This August First Day, wrote the reporter for the *Liberator*, echoed "the faith old in the land of the Pilgrims."[21]

Over the next decade, the antislavery picnic spread throughout the groves and public halls of Massachusetts. After 1846 and 1852, Island Grove, Abington, and Harmony Grove, Framingham, became important antislavery picnic venues chosen by MASS. (Large advertising posters for some of these celebrations continue to collect dust in the Samuel J. May Antislavery Collection in the Kroch Library at Cornell University.) Most of these public commemorations represented smaller versions of the 1844 Hingham spectacle. People would congregate in a wooded area, listen to speeches, sing songs, and raise funds to challenge American slavery. At other times, a different sort of celebration was planned. President Zachary Taylor designated August 3, 1849, as a national day of fasting due to a cholera epidemic. In response, MASS moved its celebration back two days and planned a massive celebration at Hospital

21. Studley, "August First" 576–77; *BAP*, 3:421–22, 372. This rite of liberty in Massachusetts stretched back to the 1620 emigration through August First in 1844 and on to Studley's 1944 article in the *New England Quarterly*. It is omnipresent. An earlier version of this chapter was rejected by the *NEQ* because it did not fit with this state rite of liberty.

Grove, Worcester. Their objective was to provide a counter-commemoration to highlight the contradictions of a slaveholding Christian Republic. Between three thousand and five thousand people gathered from New Hampshire, Rhode Island, Connecticut, and Massachusetts. They met to fast with the "firm resolve that Slavery shall die." Speakers Charles C. Burleigh, Reverend Theodore Parker, Adin Ballou, Phillips, Ralph Waldo Emerson, and Garrison described the "success" of West Indian emancipation, and emphasized the need for the immediate abolition of American slavery. The antislavery picnic was subsequently reported in several abolitionist papers, including the *North Star, Liberator,* and *Anti-Slavery Bugle.* The establishment of these picnics was captured in the opening remarks of one correspondent. "The Massachusetts Abolitionists have had another Mass meeting (as it is the fashion now-a-days to call them)," he or she wrote, adding, "I should perhaps say the New England Abolitionists, for numbers came to the gathering from New Hampshire, Rhode Island and Connecticut."[22]

Moreover, the antislavery picnic quickly spread to the groves and public halls of several other states, including Indiana's northern counties, parts of eastern Michigan, upstate New York, and Ohio's Western Reserve. These regions emerged as prime antislavery recruiting grounds from the 1840s onward and proved of particular interest to MASS. The Western Anti-Slavery Society (WASS), a Garrison-based group in Salem, Ohio, with its press organ the *Anti-Slavery Bugle,* organized a three-day August First near the village of Marlboro, Ohio, in 1845. A week before the event, the *Anti-Slavery Bugle* issued a call to the "Laboring man," "the Philanthropist," and "the Christian" to attend "such a gathering as will do honor to the day." "Let it be an occasion," wrote editor Benjamin S. Jones, "that shall not soon be forgotten—a day of smiles and tears, of sunshine and of shade, for we should ever rejoice with them that do rejoice, and mourn with those that mourn." Some three thousand people were reported to have attended this commemoration over the three days, some hailing from seventy miles away.[23]

The participants gathered in the grove, sang songs, and mingled around the "Fair Table," which had been prepared by the "Abolition women" of New

22. *NS,* August 10, 24, 31, 1849; *L,* August 3, 10, 1849; *ASB,* August 18, 1849.
23. Stewart, *Holy Warriors,* 78–81; *BAP,* 4:185, *ASB,* July 25, August 15, 1845.

Lisbon and Columbiana. These local antislavery women had also designed a variety of antislavery mementos, including

> toilet cushions and needle books, work bags and work boxes, dolls of both sexes and pin-cushions of various patterns, card baskets and book marks, pigs and rabbits to suit the fancy of children and shoes to fit their feet, aprons for the younger and caps for the older, dresses for the little ones, and travelling bags for those who journy [*sic*]. On the book marks, toilet cushions, and needle books there were various mottoes and verses including "THIS FOR THE SAKE OF FREE-DOM," "REMEMBER THEM IN BONDS," and "LIBERTY."

These domestic products linked the private sphere of women's work with the public sphere of women's politics. They also reflected the transnational dimensions of the antislavery picnic. This was a public commemoration of British abolition to mobilize against American slavery. Furthermore, items made by British women in the campaign against British colonial slavery were now being used in the movement against American slavery. Over the next three days, Benjamin Jones, Abigail Kelley, Stephen S. Foster, J. Elizabeth Hitchcock, and Isaac Pierce spoke to the assembly on the history of British abolition, post-emancipation conditions in the West Indies, American slavery, American abolitionists, and the politics of antislavery in the recently formed Liberty Party. "At the conclusion of our three day meeting," concluded the reporter for the *Anti-Slavery Bugle*, "we separated, many of us feeling it was good for us that we had been together."[24]

An important part of this shift from the pulpit to the grove can be seen in the development of the antislavery song. Music had always been central to antislavery expression in the Atlantic world. British congregations sang hymns in the name of universal freedom and condemnation of British colonial slavery. Watch nights and thanksgiving services in the British West Indies during the 1830s were similarly characterized by the singing of traditional hymns by former slaves led by missionaries. Antislavery supporters in New England

24. *ASB*, July 25, August 15, 1845. For the gender politics of antislavery domestic work in Great Britain and the United States, see Clare Midgley, *Women against Slavery: The British Campaigns, 1780–1870* (London: Routledge, 1992), chaps. 3, 6; Julie Roy Jeffrey, *The Great Silent Army of Abolitionism: Ordinary Women in the Antislavery Movement* (Chapel Hill: University of North Carolina Press, 1998), 108–26, 165, 246.

and elsewhere sang hymns against American slavery. This joyful chorus of Christian hymns continued into the era of the antislavery picnic. "Several beautiful original hymns were sung by a volunteer choir of gentlemen and ladies" at the Atheneum Hall commemoration on Nantucket Island in 1843. Hymns were sung at the Worcester celebrations in 1850 and 1852. An African American choir sang at the 1853 Flushing celebration. Zion's jubilee song was sung at the 1857 Hopedale commemoration.[25]

There was, however, a new development in the production, distribution, and consumption of antislavery music from the early 1840s onward. Abolitionists began to write new hymns and songs reflecting contemporary ideas, conditions, and aspirations. Instead of traditional hymns, these songs praised British abolition, condemned American slavery, and forecast emancipation. Furthermore, printers produced song sheets and antislavery works that were in demand. Antislavery societies handed out these publications at August First picnics. John Collins's *Anti-Slavery Picnic* was used at picnic celebrations in Dedham, Lynn, West Brookfield, and Hingham the same year as its publication. It was to become the "hymnal" of the antislavery picnic.[26] The exercises of the three-day commemoration in Marlboro, Ohio, in 1845, were interspersed with the singing of Whittier's "Hymn for the First of August," "Come Join the Abolitionists," and the "Disunion" song. The assembly of between seventy and a hundred people at the 1847 Emancipation Day in Lynchburg, Ohio, sang "O Pity the Slave Mother" and "Be Free, O Man, be Free." There was "excellent Anti-Slavery singing" at the Worcester event in 1849. The Rootstown Choir led the audience in Randolph, Ohio, with "God Speed the Right." Later on, they sang "Awake, ye Northern Freemen." Mrs. Abby H. Price of Hopedale wrote the "Emancipation Song" for the Worcester celebration of 1849. These crowds made the welkin, rather than the church roof, ring with the voices of the people in joyous celebration.[27]

By the 1850s, such songs had become an established part of the antislavery picnic. This can be seen clearly from the production, distribution, and usage of new song sheets. In 1850, printer R. Allen of No. 533 Lombard Street, Philadelphia, printed a song sheet titled "August 1st, 185 ." The last

<hr>

25. *L*, August 11, 1843; August 9, 1850; August 13, 1852; August 14, 1857.

26. *L*, August 5, 12, 19, 1842; August 4, 1843.

27. *ASB*, August 15, 1845; August 13, 1847; August 11, 1849; *NS*, August 10, 1849; *L*, August 10, 1849.

number of the year was deliberately omitted because, according to the song sheet itself, the song was meant to "be Sung on the 1st of August, in each and every year, at the Celebration of the British West India Emancipation." Sung to the popular tune of "Scot's Wa' Hae," it consisted of eight verses of four lines each. These verses employed the familiar antislavery rhetoric of expanding Southern slavery, Christian brotherly unification around abolition, and the need to wipe away public shame from "our" native land. The organizers of the antislavery picnic, and other such public meetings distributed these song sheets to the audience, who would then lift up their voices in a combined chorus of past celebration, present mobilization, and future liberation.[28]

Sometime during the 1850s, Prentiss and Deland of 40 Congress Street, Boston, Massachusetts, printed a song sheet called "Hymns and Songs for the Celebration of British West-India Emancipation." Its five songs explicitly linked British abolition with the struggle against American slavery. "Hymn for First of August" was written by Reverend E. Davis and sung to the tune "Scot's Wa' Hae." Its four verses praised the "glorious day" of British abolition, trumpeted those Christian "friends" who had "watched" through the night, glorified divine freedom, condemned hellish bondage, and welcomed "the shouts of freemen" to "our own fair shore." "British Emancipation," by Reverend John Pierpont, was sung to "Watchman, Tell Us of the Night." Although its four verses also praised British abolition and divine freedom, its major concern was with the juxtaposition of "ye islands disenthralled" with a "CHRISTIAN LAND" called "Freedom's Home." The third song on the sheet was the "Day of Jubilee," by A. G. Dugan, sung to "America." This short and beautiful two-verse tune anticipated the "joyful day" of God's work when "Freedom's flag unfurled, shall wave throughout the world, over every slave." The last two songs, "Right On," sung to the air of "Lenox," and "Slavery must pass away," sung to the tune "Old Hundred," repeated the themes of glorious freedom, death to despotism, and the inevitability that "slavery itself must pass away, and be a tale of yesterday." All these hymns and songs were sung by the crowd gathered for the commemoration at Island Grove, Abington, Massachusetts, in 1860.[29]

28. R. Allen, "August First Day Song Sheet, 185 ," *American Memory*, Library of Congress, reproduced online.

29. Prentiss and Deland, "West-India Emancipation Song Sheet," 1860, Pamphlets, Manuscript Room, Schomburg Center.

These antislavery songs were significant for a number of reasons. First, they represented the development of new consumption, production, and distribution patterns in the antislavery marketplace. Second, they demonstrated clear connections between British abolition and American antislavery, both in terms of the event itself, as well as through more detailed references in the song lyrics. Third, these songs pointed to the importance of feelings and emotions among supporters of the antislavery movement. Argument and reason were crucial for purposes of persuasion, but feelings were critical to their popular dissemination. As John Pierpont put it in his speech at the 1843 Dedham picnic: "That last hymn has said all. A better speech could not be made—certainly not sung . . . Is there here a heart that does not respond to every word of it? Is there a soul that does not feel that last stanza?"[30]

Although music is the food of love, orators were also featured at these antislavery picnics. Prominent white abolitionists, including Phillips, William E. Channing, Garrison, Charles C. Burleigh, Theodore Parker, Adin Ballou, and Edmund Quincy, addressed the crowds. Noted fugitives like Douglass, Samuel R. Ward, Henry H. Garnet, and Henry Box Brown, together with well-known black activists like Remond, were also regular speakers at the antislavery picnics. These famous speakers were usually invited by picnic organizers to encourage public interest and promote the event. According to the announcement for the 1844 Concord celebration, for instance, the reporter anticipated that the "fame of Mr. Emerson will no doubt attract many to the celebration." Most picnic speakers were male, but some were women. Jane Elizabeth Hitchcock addressed the 1845 Marlboro meeting. Abigail Kelly spoke at both this meeting and the 1857 Abington commemoration. Lucy Stone spoke at the 1848 Lynn picnic. Ernestine L. Rose addressed the assembly at the 1853 Flushing event.[31]

Moreover, many picnic speakers belonged to the transatlantic abolition movement. Some emigrated or visited the United States to support the cause. Russell L. Carpenter of Bristol, England, and J. B. Syme of Edinburgh, Scotland, both spoke at the 1850 Worcester meeting. John Scoble, born in England and a British West Indies traveler, spoke at the 1851 Plymouth meeting, and later addressed the church congregation of Henry Ward Beecher. The

30. *HF*, August 18, 1843.
31. See sources listed in Table 2.3.

following year, he took over the reform colony of Dawn, Canada West. Rev. Oughton, an English Baptist missionary to Jamaica since 1835, toured the United States in the fall of 1851. Reverend Henry Bleby, a missionary from Barbados, spoke at the 1858 Abington meeting. On the other hand, American abolitionists went to Europe and Canada to spread the word. Douglass toured the United Kingdom twice, while Parker Pillsbury visited once in 1854.[32]

Table 2.3 provides a breakdown of these orators and their orations at antislavery picnics. It includes invited speakers and those who addressed the crowd. There were probably other speakers who went unreported. Many August First orations were not reproduced because of the cost of printing or lack of print space. The major exception was the Garrison press. Both the *Liberator* and the *Anti-Slavery Bugle* reprinted a number of these speeches. The orators' words would be written down by a reporter using an early form of phonetic shorthand. The speeches at the 1849 Worcester picnic, for example, were captured "by Mr. Parkhurst, the skilful phonographic reporter," and reproduced in the next issue of the *Liberator*[33] (see those orators marked with daggers in Table 2.3). Several abolitionist speakers had their addresses reprinted as separate pamphlets. Such publications served to raise funds as well as to spread the antislavery message beyond the ken of those who heard it in the grove (see those orators marked with an asterisk in Table 2.3).

Although there has been some scholarly interest in these orations, it remains largely confined to a debate on the moral progress of emancipation. According to David Davis, Ralph Emerson's 1844 Concord address at Concord demonstrated that "British emancipation was both proof of moral progress in history and the harbinger of a new era when the masses would awaken and apply an absolute moral standard to every public question." More recently, John Stauffer has examined some of Frederick Douglass's Emancipation Day speeches critiquing the notion of moral progress.[34] This is all interesting stuff, but an examination of picnic orations reprinted in newspapers and published as separate pamphlets suggests a much richer and muscular

---

32. Ibid.

33. *L*, August 10, 1849.

34. David B. Davis, *The Problem of Slavery in Western Culture* (Ithaca: Cornell University Press, 1970), 25–26; John Stauffer, "American Responses to British Emancipation: The Problem of Progress," *Sisterhood and Slavery: An International Conference*, October 25–28, 2001, Gilder Lehrman Center, Yale University.

TABLE 2.3. Picnic Orators and Orations, 1842–1859

1842	Wendell Phillips, Charles L. Remond, Lynn, Mass.
	William E. Channing,* Lenox, Mass.
	Samuel J. May, E. D. Hudson, John P. Jewett, West Brookfield, Mass.
1843	John H. Pierpont, Dedham, Mass.
	C. Pierce, Nantucket, Mass.
	William L. Garrison, Phillips, May, Lowell, Mass.
	Charles C. Burleigh, Philadelphia, Pa.
1844	Ralph W. Emerson,* Pierpont, Frederick Douglass, William A. White, Concord, N.H.
	Garrison, Phillips, Pierpont, Douglass, James F. Clarke, White, Seth Sprague, Oliver Johnson, Hingham, Mass.
1845	Benjamin S. Jones, Abigail Kelly, Stephen S. Foster, Jane E. Hitchcock, I. Pierce, Marlboro, Ohio
	Emerson,† Waltham, Mass.
1847	William B. Calhoun, R. B. Hubbard, Dr. Lyman, Henry B. Stanton, Springfield, Mass.
	J. McMillan, J. Hambleton, Lynchburg, Ohio
1848	Edmund Quincy, Phillips, T. T. Stone, Rev. Shackford, W. G. Allen, Lucy Stone, Lynn, Mass.
1849	Burleigh,† Theodore Parker,† Adin Ballou,† Phillips,† Garrison, Worcester, Mass.
	Johnson, J. Heaton, Randolph, Ohio
1850	Samuel R. Ward, Henry H. Garnet, James W. Loguen, Remond, Elmira, N.Y.
	Garrison,† May, Burleigh, Russell L. Carpenter, Remond, Quincy, Phillips, Foster, J. B. Syme, Worcester, Mass.
	G. W. Perkins,* Guildford, Conn.
	Ward, Garnet, Auburn, N.Y.
1851	Phillips,† Worcester, Mass.
1853	Douglass, Burleigh, Phillips, Parker, Framingham, Mass.
	Ernestine L. Rose,† Garrison, V. W. Wilkins, T. Van Renssalaer, Flushing, N.Y.
1854	Garrison,* Abington, Mass.

(continued)

TABLE 2.3. continued

1856	Thomas W. Higginson, Phillips,[†] Abington, Mass.
	Burleigh, Cummington, Mass.
	Ballou, Hopedale, Mass.
1857	Kelly-Foster,[†] John S. Rock,[†] Miss Gardner, Clarke, Remond, Abington, Mass.
	W. S. Haywood, Hopedale, Mass.
1858	A. B. Way, Reverend R. Morrow, Reverend R. T. Taylor, B. S. Jones, Marlboro, Ohio
	Reverend Henry Bleby,[*†] Abington, Mass.
1859	Quincy,[†] Abington, Mass.
	Parker Pillsbury,[†] Milford, Mass.
	Philip P. Carpenter, St. Louis, Mo.

Sources: ASB, August 15, 1845; August 13, 1847; August 11, 18, 1849; August 17, 1850; August 23, 1856; August 15, 1857; July 24, August 7, 1858; August 13, 20, 27, 1859; *FDP*, February 23, 1855; *HF*, July 28, August 18, 1843; July 26, August 16, 22, 1844; *L*, August 12, 19, 1842; August 11, 1843; August 9, 16, 1850; August 15, 1851; August 12, 1853; August 8, 15, 1856; August 7, 21, 1857; *NE*, August 19, 1847; *NS*, August 21, 1848; August 10, 31, 1849; June 13, 1850; *BAP*, 1:81, 359, 404, 3:335, 372, 392, 465–66; 4:192, 252, 302; Davis, *Slavery in Western Culture*, 25–26; Glick, "Thoreau and the Herald of Freedom," 196; Lader, *Bold Brahmins*, 103, 106; Schappes, "Ernestine L. Rose," 345; Studley, "August First," 576.

*Published in pamphlet.

[†]Published in newspaper.

body of Anglo-American abolitionist thought. In search of this wider dimension, we conclude this chapter with an analysis of three prominent picnic orators and their orations: Wendell Phillips at Worcester in 1849; Ernestine L. Rose at Flushing in 1853; and Reverend Henry Bleby at Abington in 1858. These three speakers represent a cross-section of abolitionist voices: the antislavery stalwart; the universal reformer; and the Anglo-Caribbean traveler.

Furthermore, their three speeches over a ten-year range register some of the changes in antislavery thought during a critical period of antislavery agitation. Also, attention to the parenthetical descriptions of crowd responses to various points by the speakers—applause, laughter, cheers—allows us to hear the crowd rather than simply assume that speakers like Emerson and Douglass spoke for the assembled. Finally, all three speakers and their orations point to the transnational dimensions of West Indian emancipation and the struggle against American slavery.

Wendell Phillips was born of patrician roots in Massachusetts and Harvard-educated. According to his most recent biographer, the Boston Brahmin identified with an Anglo-American tradition of republican liberties and patriot-heroes. After the murder of abolitionist editor Elijah P. Lovejoy in 1837, Phillips devoted his life and not inconsiderable fortune to the abolition of American slavery, endorsing the cause of moral persuasion espoused by his friend Garrison.[35] Throughout the 1840s, Phillips was a regular speaker at antislavery picnics. As a member of MASS, Phillips helped arrange the massive picnic commemoration at Worcester in 1849. The major theme of his 1849 address was to contrast the success of British abolition with the challenges of overthrowing American slavery. He did this in four ways.

The first was to trumpet the glories of British abolition. This anniversary, he said, "represents for us the greatest day in the sweep of time; when nearly a million of fetters were stricken from human limbs." In other words, this was a historic occasion deserving of serious commemoration. Second, he compared the "anti-slavery enterprise" of England with that of America. He differed with a previous speaker, Theodore Parker, who claimed it had been an easier task in England. Although American slavery was indigenous (here) rather than colonial (over there), Phillips argued, visiting former slaves like William and Ellen Craft and Frederick Douglass provided an "irresistible appeal" to the stoking of antislavery agitation in the United Kingdom. Also, although the British Parliament had sovereign power to abolish colonial slavery compared to an American Congress inhabited by powerful slave interests, extralegal means like "Hearts, Thoughts, Dollars, Truth," especially in the Northern states, "will find a way." Perhaps the only difference between the

---

35. James B. Stewart, *Wendell Phillips: Liberty's Hero* (Baton Rouge: Louisiana State University Press, 1986), xi, 12, 29, 31, 59, 63, 69, 104, 112, 115, 135, 161, 189, 205.

two places, said Phillips, was that "social prejudice against color" was absent in England, making it easier to abolish slavery.[36]

The third point Phillips made echoed that of Thome and Kimball published eleven years earlier. West India emancipation had been safe: "To the honor of the colored race, to the hope of humanity, to the joy and gratitude of every believer in a just Ruler of the Universe, we are able to look back upon that eventful scene in the history of the race, and recollect that it was not sullied by one single act of vengeance; by one single expression of unkindness; by one single drop of bloodshed." This was essentially propaganda for the immediate abolition of American slavery. (As chapter 1 has demonstrated, while British abolition did not bring the anticipated racial blood-bath, neither was it altogether quiet, orderly, and controlled.) Also, Phillips thought much of the debate about the "success" of West India emancipation was simply wrongheaded. While abolition's opponents pointed to the drop in sugar production as evidence of emancipation's failures, supporters pointed out that the "slave worked on the second day of August." Phillips thought both were off because it was as "if there were nothing but sugar in God's world!" Finally, Liberty's hero proposed a means for ending American slavery. He called for rebellion: "I want an organized rebellion. I want a legal rebellion. I want a recognized rebellion. I want a State rebellion. I want a legislative rebellion. I have no regard for what is called constitutional law." He advised his audience to "Go home, make anti-slavery to be everything, a reality and I will find you the men."[37]

It is unclear whether the crowd of three thousand to five thousand followed the speaker's advice. More evident was their response to some of Phillips's points. The phonographer reported two occasions of "(Applause)" and one time of "(Laughter)." After advising the crowd to go home and mobilize, Phillips joked "and you shall have Robert Winthrop for an anti-slavery lecturer." The audience no doubt appreciated the sarcastic reference to a conservative state politician who sought good relations with Southern states by not discussing American slavery. Earlier on in the speech, the audience applauded

36. *BAP*, 3:373; Lawrence Lader, *The Bold Brahmins: New England's War against Slavery, 1831–1863* (New York: E. P. Dutton, 1961), 83–85; *L*, August 3, 1849. Phillips's 1849 Worcester speech was reprinted in the *NS*, August 31, 1849, and the *L*, August 17, 1849. It was also summarized in the *ASB*, August 18, 1849. Racial prejudice in Britain and its encounter by visiting black abolitionists is examined in chap. 7.

37. *NS*, August 31, 1849.

Phillips's praise of William Wilberforce's part in British abolition "as evidence of a life well spent." The audience also cheered the speaker's concluding remark that collective antislavery activism would result in a "First of August when we may speak well of ourselves instead of the English, and we shall have feasts instead of fasts, one end of the country to the other." It is likely that the Worcester audience both approved of Anglo-American abolitionists like Wilberforce and Phillips, as well as the positive link between British and American emancipation. Phillips was to go on to speak at the next two "August Firsts" at Worcester and over the next several years at various state antislavery picnics.[38]

The same year Wendell Phillips spoke at Framingham, several hundred black and white people gathered at the grove of St. Roman's Well, Flushing, New York, to celebrate the anniversary of West India emancipation. The meeting had been organized by the recently revived New York Anti-Slavery Society (NYASS). After a prayer led by black minister Rev. Campbell and songs sung by a black choir, the main address was delivered by Garrison. His oration was followed by that of Ernestine L. Rose, the daughter of a Polish rabbi who had emigrated in 1827 and later joined up with the Utopian Socialist movement of Robert Owen in England. In 1836, she migrated to the United States with William E. Rose, husband and fellow Owenite, and became involved in various reform movements. In 1850, she served on the business committee, alongside Douglass and Garrison, at the first National Women's Rights Convention in Worcester. Upon being introduced, Rose stepped forward to much applause from the assembly. Her address was primarily concerned with juxtaposing British abolition with American slavery and natural rights with all forms of human bondage. What a contrast, Rose noted, between July Fourth, a commemoration of "the utterance of a great truth," and August First, "a practical application of it." Despite the adoption of the Declaration of Independence, "the United States of America are guilty of outrage and recreancy to their own principles in retaining slavery." Despite "oppression and tyranny in her midst," however, Great Britain "has shown a noble example to the world in emancipating all her chattel slaves." Furthermore, Rose went on to challenge the arguments of opponents of emancipation,

38. Ibid.; *BAP,* 4:390; *ASB,* August 17, 1850; August 23, 1856; *L,* August 9, 1850; August 15, 1851; August 12, 1853.

especially the threat by Southerners to secede from the Union. The slave South, she pointed out, depended upon the North for its teachers, professors, craftsmen, laborers, and food growers. Most important, Rose pointed to the contradiction between natural and inhuman rights. "Slavery is," she said, "not to belong to yourself—to be robbed of yourself." She went on to draw a parallel between enslavement and patriarchy by arguing that, like slaves, women were denied the natural right of human liberty. All women, she asserted, were "excluded from the enjoyment of that liberty which your Declaration of Independence asserts to be the inalienable right of all." And in succinct language, she concluded: "Emancipation from every kind of bondage is my principle."[39]

Along with her persuasive universal message, Rose also appears to have been an excellent and witty public speaker. The crowd who listened to her address at Flushing laughed at her comments on over a dozen occasions. Most of their humor derived from the speaker's satirical attacks on the slave South and her stabs at its slaveholders. The South, for instance, lagged way behind the North: "Indeed, so greatly impoverished is the land in the South that it is a positive fact, that I once saw a cow held up while she was fed." Rose's satirical jab at American Southerners' threats of dissolution—"I should be very sorry to leave you"—met with several bursts of laughter. This was especially poignant since Garrison, with his well-known advocacy of dissolution from the slaveholding Christian Republic, had preceded her on the speaker's platform. Certainly the funniest gag was Rose's jibe at Southern laziness and anti-abolition by offering a Southern gentleman with whom she was conversing "something to do, were it to give me a coat of tar and feathers." This was met with "Great laughter and applause." Given her apparent success at Flushing, it seems odd that this appears to have been Rose's only August First address. This might be because she was destined to become, in the words of one recent scholar, the "chief orator and linguist of the international women's movement."[40]

39. *L*, August 19, 1853; Morris U. Schappes, "Ernestine L. Rose: Her Address on the Anniversary of West Indian Emancipation," *Journal of Negro History* 34, no. 3 (July 1949): 346–47; Anderson, *Joyous Greetings*, 47–52; Rose's 1853 Flushing speech was reprinted in the *NASS*, August 13, 1853; *L*, August 19, 1853; *NYDT*, August 5, 1853. For an early commentary on women abolitionist leaders in Massachusetts, see Lader, *Bold Brahmins*, chap. 4.

40. Schappes, "Rose," 347–55; Anderson, *Joyous Greetings*, 47.

Five summers later, Reverend Henry Bleby, a visiting Methodist missionary from the British colony of Barbados, was invited by MASS to deliver the keynote address at the antislavery picnic organized at Abington. The intervening years had witnessed growing violence, as exemplified in Bloody Kansas, physical attacks in the U.S. Senate, and armed showdowns over fugitive slaves. The minister had been an eyewitness to the Jamaican slave revolt of 1831 and had written an account, *The Death Struggles of Slavery*, published in 1853. The West Indian visitor began his speech by informing the assembly that he had been an "eyewitness" during that "insurrection" that "hastened on the crisis of the movement for West India emancipation." The resolve of some 50,000 Jamaican slaves "to strike a blow for freedom" informed the "public mind" in Great Britain that among the slaves there was a "determination to be free." Rather than abolition being only God's work, the listeners were informed, it was the slaves themselves who began the process of emancipation. The speaker went on to depict this Jamaican slave revolt as a rite of liberty over death. Rev. Bleby recalled his interview with Sam Sharpe, the leader of the revolt. He asked the condemned man why he led a revolt. "'Sir,' said he, 'in reading my bible, I found the white man had no more right to make a slave of me than I had to make a slave of the white man—(applause); and I would rather go out and die on that gallow, than live a slave.' (Loud applause)." The crowd clearly approved of Sharpe's "manly courage." It is perhaps not surprising that the slave rebel leader's invocation of Patrick Henry should have met with the enthusiastic approbation of the descendants of an American revolutionary tradition.[41]

This was a rather unusual account of West Indian emancipation. Rev. Bleby, however, soon returned to the more familiar representation of emancipation as part of the Christian jubilee. He had been present at abolition, where he "saw the monster [slavery] die." Thanksgiving services were held at midnight in a large church attended by thousands of enslaved people. He read Leviticus 25:10. Both the kneeling and silent prayers were broken only by irrepressible "sobs of emotion." The clock struck "the knell of slavery."

41. Craton, *Testing the Chains*, 299–300, 313, 319; Henry Bleby, *Speech of Rev. Henry Bleby, Missionary From Barbados, on the Results of Emancipation in the British West Indies Colonies, delivered at the Celebration of the Massachusetts Anti-Slavery Society held at Island Grove, July 31st, 1858* (Boston: R. F. Wallcut, 1858), 10, in *Slavery Pamphlets*, vol. 65, no. 11, Beinecke Library, Yale University. Bleby's 1858 speech is also reproduced online at *American Memory*, item 99.

"A burst of joy rolled over that mass of people." They "literally shouted" the jubilee hymn. These accounts of the destruction of the monster slavery and watch nights were common in both the British West Indies as well as the United States. Rev. Bleby's conclusion—that "emancipation in the British West Indies is no failure"—was also a part of this Anglo-American narrative and met with enthusiastic applause from his Island Grove audience.[42]

While care should be taken not to exaggerate the significance of Rev. Bleby's 1858 speech at Abington, it did reflect some important changes in the relationship between West India emancipation and American antislavery. Both the watch night and the success of abolition were familiar features of the Anglo-American abolitionist narrative. But a decade of violence during the 1850s and the urgency of the times promoted new themes. Slaves in revolt, not simply hard-working Christian abolitionists, had helped begin the process of British abolition. Rev. Bleby made slave rebels the heroes of West Indian emancipation, in both his book and his anniversary speech. Presumably, it would take a similar form of violent protest to terminate American slavery. Emancipation was and must be the consequence of revolutionary violence, not a boon of the state. Moreover, liberty was a universal theme that beat in the breast of every human being. Jamaican slave rebels were engaged in a national liberation struggle. "I could not but drop a tear," recalled Bleby in witnessing Sharpe being led to the gallows, "to see a man like that put to death, whose only crime was that he made an effort to recover that liberty which is the right of every human being." Presumably the same was true of his American cousins. Bleby's remarks on emancipation in the British West Indies were important because of what they suggest about slave resistance, links between British abolition and American slavery, and the success of emancipation in the British West Indies. The speech was to subsequently reach a wider audience when publisher R. F. Walcutt of Boston distributed it as a separate antislavery pamphlet.[43]

What was the historical significance of the antislavery picnic? In the first place, it resembled the thanksgiving service with the emphasis on temperance,

---

42. Bleby, *Speech of Rev. Henry Bleby,* 14–35.

43. Ibid. There are some interesting parallels between Bleby's interview with the jailed Sharpe and Thomas Grey's jail interview with Nat Turner. See Kenneth S. Greenburg, *The Confessions of Nat Turner and Related Documents* (Boston: Bedford Books, 1996), 38–58.

respectability, and emancipation as God's work. Moreover, religious rites continued to influence the antislavery picnic. Participants often sat down to what the press usually described as a "collation," or a religious light meal. "Quaker matrons" prepared the food at the 1845 Marlboro event. Prayers were usually given and hymns sung. And the hat was passed to raise funds to challenge American slavery. The press often reported the antislavery picnic as a "Christian jubilee."[44]

Despite these similarities, however, the antislavery picnic was different from the thanksgiving church service in several ways. In the first place, it was designed to be a much larger public visual event. These were popular open celebrations rather than small closed commemorations. This was exemplified in the shift from the collation to the picnic.[45] Furthermore, the August First picnic was a political event. Sometimes issues were debated. At the 1845 Marlboro meeting, there was a discussion over the proslavery and antislavery nature of the recently formed Liberty Party. There was a discussion of several antislavery resolutions at the Randolph meeting in 1849. Other times, the antislavery picnic represented a political coming-out. Emerson used the 1844 commemoration to announce his allegiance to abolition. The 1853 Flushing event advertised the reformed New York Anti-Slavery Society; it was also the place where Rose made her statement about the universality of human liberation. And these picnics were genuine democratic assemblies. As one reporter observed about the 1846 Weare picnic, not only were these meetings called "to break the chain of the bondman," but they also represented "free gatherings of the people, back among the hills of the country." Such meetings were "where all feel an interest—and [were] of a character that will draw out the people."[46]

In addition, the explanation for the timing and transformation of the antislavery picnic must be understood within specific historical conditions. New struggles, generational shifts, and increasing tension over the expansion

44. *ASB*, August 15, 1845; August 15, 1857; July 24, 1858; *L*, August 13, 1852; August 15, 1856; Schappes, "Rose," 345.

45. Along with publicizing New England abolitionism, it is likely that the antislavery picnic was meant to attract other abolitionists after the division of the movement in 1840. For concise narratives of the "Great Schism" in the United States and in the United Kingdom, see Stewart, *Holy Warriors*, 88–96; Rice, *Scots Abolitionists*, chap. 4.

46. *HF*, August 6–7, 1846; *ASB*, August 15, 1845; August 11, 1849; Schappes, "Rose," 344, 354.

of American slavery, together with the nature and direction of the antislavery movement, explain the advent and take-off of the antislavery picnic during the early 1840s. The emphasis on the right to resist, acknowledged in the opening of Rev. Bleby's oration, was the culmination of a decade of violence, protest, and a different August First organized by people of African descent in North America.[47]

Finally, the significance of the antislavery picnic can be gleaned from the opposition it elicited. In preparation for the 1850 event, MASS was branded as being composed of "fanatics, madmen, incendiaries, disorganizers, traitors, comeouters, infidels," according to supporters of Southern slaveholders. The celebrations of 1857 worried some Southerners and defenders of slavery. The *Newberry Rising Sun* of South Carolina castigated "nigger papers" that promoted emancipation, since nowhere had a colony of "Negroes" left alone prospered because their "[racial] habits are [the] same." The *Boston Courier* condemned August First Day at Abington because it was moving the country toward "disunion and political anarchy." According to the *St. Louis Republican*, the commemoration of West Indian emancipation constituted a faithfully observed anniversary "where Abolitionism is most rampant and wears its most aggressive respect." The keynote speaker of the 1859 celebration in St. Louis, Missouri, received the following note: "St. Louis, July 31, 1859. Mr. P. Carpenter:—A Committee of fifty staunch men of which I have been elected Foreman, has been appointed for the purpose of tarring and feathering and riding you on a rail should you dare to attempt the lecture tomorrow night as advertised." The note was addressed to "Phil. P. Carpenter, Abolition, nigger-thieving Lecturer," and signed by "Zachariah Browning, foreman." Carpenter went ahead with his speech, but the "fifty staunch men" failed to show up.[48]

One of the most important consequences of the antislavery picnic was the expansion of antislavery activism and protest. This was particularly evident in the participation of people of African descent at these public meetings, whether as attendees, speakers, or fugitives. The consolidation of American slavery and the increasingly violent nature of the era, however, led to the

47. See chap. 6.
48. *NS*, August 24, 1849; *L*, August 7, 21, 1857; *ASB*, August 20, 1859.

emergence of a different August First and the remaking of the antislavery picnic in the image of African American liberation. Abolitionists and activists of African provenance throughout the Atlantic world were soon to shape the event in their own ways for contesting American slavery, challenging white racism, and constructing an international politics of racial solidarity. It is that process, and the most important commemorative festival among people of African descent in the ante-emancipation United States, to which we now turn.

Chapter 3
August First in Afro-America

We had met [in San Francisco] to dig the grave of Slavery.
Thomas H. Ward, August 1, 1854

Around 10:00 A.M. on August 1, 1842, a street procession of black men and boys with banners commemorating temperance and West Indian emancipation wound its way through the Moyamensing section of Philadelphia. Local white residents attacked the parade, the marchers retaliated, and a street battle ensued. The police and mayor were called in, but mob violence and street fires continued into the evening. One consequence was the destruction of black-owned property. Robert Purvis, wealthy local citizen and prominent black abolitionist, despaired: "I am convinced of our utter and complete nothingness in public estimation." The "cause" of the altercation, it was later revealed, was due to a mistaken interpretation of a public banner. The marchers had carried a banner called "Liberty or Death" supposedly depicting the menacing figure of a "Negro" and a town in Haiti during a massacre of whites by slaves. In actuality, the banner had the figure of an emancipated slave pointing with one hand to broken chains at his feet, and the other to the word *liberty* in gold letters over his head. The burned town was really a rising sun with a sinking ship representing the dawn of freedom. Mayor Scott expressed his surprise at such misrepresentation, but noted "public tumults" usually occurred from similar "perversion[s] of truth." On the banner's reverse side was the sign, Young Man's Vigilant Association of Philadelphia.[1]

This street parade is instructive for several reasons. First, it points to the international dimensions of abolition and slavery during the nineteenth century. Americans either celebrated, or condemned, West Indian emancipation. Furthermore, it suggests new public forms of celebration and mobilization

---

1. *L*, August 10, 19, 1842; Howard H. Bell, "National Negro Conventions of the Middle 1840s: Moral Suasion vs. Political Action," *Journal of Negro History* 42, no. 4 (October 1957): 247–48; *BAP*, 3:389–92; *HF*, September 2, 1842.

against American slavery. People were marching in the streets to display and trumpet their commemoration. It also highlighted the dangers of public space for African Americans. Indeed, these dangers were serious enough for the National Convention of Colored People—due to meet in Philadelphia—to cancel their summer meeting. Most important, this commemorative march occurred at a time when the struggle against American slavery was undergoing a basic strategic shift from moral reform to more militant and demonstrative expressions.

One of the major weaknesses of the historical scholarship on Emancipation Day celebrations has been its skirting of the temporal, spatial, and political dimensions of freedom festivals. Thus, August First is treated as an unchanging event, either as a nation-building exercise or as a forum for elite control, when in actuality its social forms, participants, and political significance underwent significant transformation from the 1830s through the 1850s. This chapter examines the changing nature of August First through the analysis of two major social forms—church rites and public rites—and why these took on special significance at particular moments. These events took place and were designed to respond to a larger political context.

Moreover, simply counting and describing Emancipation Day celebrations in enthusiastic pursuit of either an American or African American political tradition tells us little about how and why August First took on special meaning in various places. The popularity of the anniversary in Ohio, for instance, is better explained in relation to the expansion of slavery, fugitive slave paths, and the emergence of a new generation of antislavery activists and organizations. If the national *lieu de memoire* downplays the local, it also overlooks the international aspects of West Indian emancipation celebrations. This chapter pursues the diasporic dimensions of August First in terms of participants, ideas, the nature of the event itself, and its connections. The primary objective is to show the importance of the event's place in ante-emancipation cultural and political life.

Finally, the focus on commemorative celebrations primarily as memory-work and the construction of a usable past detracts from the role of such celebrations in popular mobilization against the oppressive weight of American slavery. Of course memory-work was important, but what were its politics and in what ways *specifically* did these challenge American slavery and racism? August First was an important site for political mobilization whose primary objective in linking emancipation with enslavement was both the celebration of the former together with the overthrow of the latter. In contribution to debates over seasonal rituals of social inversion, the argument here is that August First functioned as an annual public expression of opposition to slavery.

CHURCH RITES

The antislavery press reported over thirty annual August Firsts in northern states between 1834 and 1842. Occasionally these gatherings were held in a colored schoolhouse, debating hall, or white church, but the vast majority took place in established black churches. These meetings were often addressed by local antislavery leaders prominent in their communities: David Ruggles in New York; Samuel R. Ward, and Henry Highland Garnet in New York and New Jersey; and William C. Nell and William L. Garrison in Boston. Most August Firsts were held in 1838 and the following year, presumably in celebration of the early termination of the system of apprenticeship in the British West Indies and the complete end of chattel slavery. These commemorations were held in the key seaboard centers of Philadelphia, New York City, and Boston with the largest number of black inhabitants, although there were numerous gatherings in smaller towns and villages. The commemorations were

TABLE 3.I. August First in Church, 1834–1842

1834	Belknap Street Church, Boston, Mass.
	Philomathean Hall, New York City, N.Y.
1835	?
1836	African Episcopal Church, Philadelphia, Pa.
	Baptist Church, Catskill, N.Y.
1837	?
1838	Colored Methodist Church, Newark, N.J.
	Colored Presbyterian Church, Newark, N.J.
	Zion's Church, New York City, N.Y.
	Bethel Church, New York City, N.Y.
	Zion's Baptist Church, New York City, N.Y.
	Asbury Methodist Church, New York City, N.Y.
	First Colored Presbyterian Church, New York City, N.Y.
	Baptist Church, Albany, N.Y.
	School House, Madison, N.Y.

TABLE 3.1. continued

	Second Presbyterian, Watertown, N.Y.
	Methodist Chapel (white), Utica, N.Y.
	Bethel Church, Cincinnati, Ohio
	Belknap Street Church, Boston, Mass.
	Philadelphia, Pa.
1839	Philips Sunday School, New York City, N.Y.
	First Colored Presbyterian Church, New York City, N.Y.
	Colored Methodist Church, Newark, N.J.
	Colored Presbyterian Church, Newark, N.J.
	Belknap Street Church, Boston, Mass.
	Bethel Free Church, Troy, N.Y.
	Colored Methodist Episcopal Zion Church, Newburgh, N.Y.
	Second Baptist Church, Detroit, Mich.
1840	First Colored Presbyterian Church, New York City, N.Y.
	Zion's Baptist Church, New York City, N.Y.
	Belknap Street Church, Boston, Mass.
	Colored School, Wilmington, Del.
1841	Concord, N.H.
1842	Belknap Street Church, Boston, Mass.

Sources: *CA*, July 21, 28, August 11, 18, 25, 1838; July 20, 27, August 17, September 28, August 31, 1839; August 1, 15, 1840; *E*, August 11, 1836; *HF*, August 20, 1841; *L*, August 9, 30, 1834; September 17, 1836; August 3, 10, 1838; August 9, 16, 31, 1839; August 14, 19, 1840; *BAP*, 3:17, 132–35, 188, 305, 447; Rhodes, *Shadd Cary*, 19.

mostly reported by the Boston *Liberator* and the New York *Colored American*, usually under the subheading "First of August." Their primary objective was to encourage the celebration of an important antislavery anniversary and garner support for American abolition. The press coverage also sought to challenge the Gag Rule that had tabled all discussions of antislavery petitions by the U.S. Congress in 1836.[2]

2. "The country newspapers are beginning to speak out: who shall gag them?" *CA*, August 18, 1838.

Although there were some minor differences, the social organization of August First was fairly similar. The upcoming meeting would be advertised in the antislavery press in the weeks preceding the event. This responsibility, together with the arrangements of the day—program, speakers, printed materials—would be left to an organizing committee made up of prominent local citizens. S. R. Alexander, D. D. Rue, Eli Leason, W. Prescott, and Thomas Dalton, for instance, arranged the Belknap Street Church celebration in Boston in 1839.[3] The usual program for the day would be the election of officials, praying, readings from either the Bible or the British Act of Emancipation, a commemorative address or oration, and the singing of hymns. Sometimes there would be a collection. Often antislavery resolutions were passed, including agreement to publish the proceedings in the abolitionist press. On occasion, the event concluded with a temperance dinner.[4]

The institutionalization of the black church was crucial to August First and the antislavery movement. One of the first independent institutions, the church represented an important shared space for congregating, praying, and organizing by African Americans. The roots of some of the major black church denominations lay in racial exclusion and independent formation during the late eighteenth and early nineteenth centuries. The most prominent included St. Thomas Episcopal Church of Philadelphia, founded by Absalom Jones in 1794; the First African Baptist Church of Boston, founded by Thomas Paul in 1805; the African Union Methodist Episcopal Church of Wilmington, formed in 1813; and the First Colored Presbyterian Church of New York City founded in 1822 by Samuel E. Cornish. Much of the expansion of these denominations and others, however, occurred with the emergence of the American antislavery movement. Between 1830 and 1844, it has been estimated the African Baptist Church grew from 10 to 34 congregations. The African Methodist Episcopal Church, with congregations in New England, Ohio, Indiana, and Canada West, increased from 86 to 296 between 1836 and 1846. Dozens of other congregations were also founded during this period. These black churches played an important role in the antislavery movement. This sacred space served several secular purposes, including meeting place, schoolhouse, and sanctuary for fugitive slaves. Black clergymen used

3. *CA*, August 31, 1839. For other organizing committees, see *CA*, August 17, 1839; August 15, 1840; *L*, August 14, 1840.

4. This outline of church August Firsts draws from the sources cited in Table 3.1.

the church to castigate American slavery. This was especially true with regard to fugitive slave clergymen like James W. C. Pennington, Samuel R. Ward, Jermain W. Loguen, and Henry Highland Garnet.[5]

Many black clergymen and local leaders were attracted to an agenda of moral reform. This doctrine maintained that social ills could be eradicated through individual moral improvement, and entailed self-help, education, the work ethic, and sobriety. The positive result would be the uplift of the individual, the striking down of prejudice, and the abolition of American slavery. This agenda was institutionalized through the founding of the American Moral Reform Society (AMRS) during a National Convention meeting at the Wesley African Methodist Church in Philadelphia in 1835. Its members endorsed "Education, Temperance, Economy, and Universal Liberty." Auxiliary societies were organized in Pittsburgh, Baltimore, Providence, Troy, and New Jersey, while temperance groups, education associations, and religious societies were encouraged to affiliate with the AMRS. Although mandated to become a national and racially integrated organization, it remained dominated by the African American elite in Philadelphia. Afro-Philadelphia businessman William Whipper outlined the key components of this moral reform agenda in his address at the 1835 meeting:

> We shall endeavour to promote education, with sound morality, not that we shall become "learned and mighty," but "great and good." We shall advocate temperance in all things, and total abstinence from all alcoholic liquors. We shall advocate a system of *economy*, not only because luxury is injurious to individuals, but because its practice exercises an influence on society, which in its very nature is sinful. We shall advocate universal liberty, as the inalienable right of every individual born in the world, and a right which cannot be taken away by government itself, without an unjust exercise of power.

The social values of temperance, education, and universal liberty were prominently displayed on August First in black churches throughout the 1830s and early 1840s.[6]

5. James O. Horton and Lois E. Horton, *In Hope of Liberty: Culture, Community and Protest among Northern Blacks, 1700–1860* (New York: Oxford University Press, 1997), 138; *BAP*, 3:35–36, 188, 447.

6. *BAP*, 3:8–14, 129–30, 146, 149, 152–53.

Temperance was especially important to the moral reform movement because of its indispensable link with colored people's uplift and economic independence. The organization of abstinence among Afro-Americans began in local temperance societies in New Haven and New York City in 1829. By the mid-1830s, it has been estimated that nearly every black community in the free states had at least one local, regional, or national temperance society in its midst. Literary, benevolent, and political societies advocated abstention from the consumption of alcohol. Black clergymen established local abstinence societies, temperance grocery stores, and boardinghouses.[7] The advent of August First brought with it an opportunity for the further propagation of temperance principles. The colored female citizens of the Literary Association who met at St. Thomas Episcopal Church in Philadelphia to commemorate British emancipation in 1836 read chapters, listened to addresses, and dined on bread and water. About eighty colored people "partook of an excellent dinner, served up in fine style, and on strict temperance principles," at the Marlboro Hotel during the anniversary of West India emancipation in 1839. A year later, a similar group at the same venue "proclaimed liberty to their masticating machinery" in "industrious spirit." The celebrants at Wilmington's August First in 1840 "partook of a sumptuous repast which Mr. Hubert had prepared for the occasion, on strictly temperance principles." At Marlboro Chapel's August First in Boston, William C. Nell proposed a temperance toast: "May it prove the cornerstone on which the colored American shall safely erect the temple of his own independence."[8] These temperance dinners reflected the moral reform agenda of the black elite. Later on, however, communal eating and drinking at antislavery picnics and parades was to assume less didactic and more independent forms.

August First in the black church also provided opportunities for the social politicization of a younger generation. Young people were critical to the moral reform movement. They needed to be conditioned into better ways of moral improvement, social uplift, and community leadership. Beginning in

---

7. *BAP*, 3:17–18, 194–95.

8. *L*, September 17, 1836; August 9, 16, 1839; August 14, 1840; *CA*, August 31, 1839; August 15, 1840. Temperance was not part of the missionaries' August First in the British West Indies. Meanwhile, apprentices and freed people regularly consumed alcohol during their celebrations and anniversaries of freedom.

the late 1830s, juvenile antislavery societies were formed throughout the free states to prepare a later generation of antislavery leaders. August First became an important public venue for both socializing the young as well as displaying their fitness for future citizenship. At the 1839 Troy celebration, it was reported that the "exercises of these dear children" of the Yates Juvenile Antislavery Society "were conducted with great decorum, and we enjoyed great delight in listening to the melodious sonnets which flowed from their lips in praise of Freedom's God." The following year, a procession of singing children bearing flowers filed into the galleries two-by-two in Belknap Street Church. Songs from the juvenile choir accompanied the Emancipation Day service at Chardon Street Chapel in Boston three years later. On July 30, 1840, black entrepreneur and abolitionist Abraham Shadd lectured the gathering at a black schoolhouse in Wilmington: "It is our imperative duty as well as interest, to use every exertion to elevate the character of the free colored population." This social politicization of a younger generation on August First was an important part of the moral reform agenda of black elites in the United States as well as Christian missionaries in the British West Indies.[9]

Although August First reflected the importance of the black church, together with the opportunities for elite stewardship in moral reform, they were important transnational events. This was evident in several ways. Thome and Kimball's *West India Emancipation* became an important source to African Americans for learning about British abolition. The *Colored American* regularly included extracts from this book, as well as testimonials to its authenticity during the late 1830s. In 1838, the commemoration of the end of apprenticeship was marked by watch nights in black churches in the northern states. "Pursuant to previous notice," reported the *Colored American*, "a very large and respectable assemblage of colored citizens, convened at Bethel church [Cincinnati, Ohio], on Tuesday evening, July 31st, at half past 11 o'clock." During the fifteen minutes before midnight, a "breathless silence prevailed throughout the assembly." At 12:00, the choir and congregation "struck up the jubilee

9. *CA*, September 28, 1839; *L*, August 14, 1840; August 11, 1843. For the social politicization of children on Emancipation Day in the British Caribbean, see Cox, *History of the English Missionary Society*, 253, 266–71; Phillippo, *Jamaica*, 71. For similar processes in Canada West, see *L*, August 20, 1852, *VF*, August 13, 1851. For its counterpart in the United Kingdom, see Linda Colley, *Britons: Forging the Nation* (New Haven: Yale University Press, 1992), 226–27.

hymn." The following year, at the Twentieth Street Presbyterian Church in Troy, New York, D. A. Payne addressed the congregation on the abolition struggle in Great Britain and the advent of West India emancipation. Then "he read from Thome and Kimball's Journal, that inimitable description of the glorious scene which was witnessed in the Temples of the living God, when the midnight clock tolled the death knell of Slavery." [10]

Moreover, West Indian visitors sometimes participated at August Firsts in the United States. Rev. Clark, a Baptist missionary from Jamaica, addressed the August First audience at Madison in 1838. The meeting was held in a schoolhouse because *"the use of the meeting house was denied."* "Think of that!" fulminated the editors of the *Colored American,* "meeting houses in central New York closed against a West India minister, who wished to tell the benefits of emancipation." [11]

These transnational connections were most evident from resolutions passed at August First meetings during the first decade after British abolition. There were several aspects to these resolutions. First, there was the ritualization of gratitude. Christian missionaries insisted that apprentices and former slaves in the British West Indies be thankful for being granted the boon of freedom in the Caribbean. The expression of thanksgiving for God's work in the past and prayer for the future also characterized black church commemorations in the United States. The *Colored American* called for widespread thanksgiving services in 1838: "Let those of us who may be permitted to see the memorable first of August, with our *enfranchised* brethren across the waters, appear before God at early dawn in his sanctuary, there to praise him for the conquests of holy principles, and to plead with him to break the oppressors rod, that the oppressed of our own land may go free."

Moreover, some meetings used the occasion to express publicly their identification with slaves in the American South, as well as former slaves in the British colonies. In 1836, the Catskill assembly resolved to "stand by our friends and brethren in the south" since "Anti-Slavery effort has emancipated 800,000 slaves in the British Colonies." The organizing committee for Emancipation Day in Newark "deem[ed] it to be our duty to celebrate the first day of August, 1838, the day which brings entire freedom to all our brethren in

10. *CA*, March 25, 1837; June 9, July 28, August 25, 1838; September 28, 1839.

11. *CA*, July 28, August 18, 25, 1838; September 28, 1839; August 1, 1840. Italics in the original.

the British West India Islands, in a manner alike expressive of our joy produced by that happy event, and our deep and increasing commiseration for the bound and bleeding slave at home." At the Bethel Church commemoration in Cincinnati, the congregation approved of the sentiment that the event "inspire the people of color throughout the continent of America, with the warmest feelings of gratitude to him who has promised that 'Ethiopia shall stretch forth her hand,' and become a people, for in the commencement of this glorious work we may mark the budding of its fulfillment." At the 1839 meeting in Detroit, it was resolved that "free people of color throughout the United States, ought to celebrate the first of August as a day dear to us which gave liberty to our brethren in the West Indies."[12]

Most important was the commemoration of West Indian emancipation for the purposes of mobilization against American slavery. David Ruggles, a twenty-six-year-old former businessman, abolitionist, and leader of the New York Committee of Vigilance, addressed the assembly at the Baptist church in Catskill in 1836. Its primary purpose, he said, was to declare war on all forms of legal and illegal slavery together with helping fugitives escape the clutches of slaveholders and city officials. He spoke in support of a resolution that the antislavery effort "clearly indicates the spirit of determined opposition," with the "prediction that slavery is doomed finally to perish." After expressing their joy over the success and righteousness of British abolition, the colored citizens of Utica in 1838 resolved to "press forward courageously in their noble enterprise." They also expressed their regard for veteran British abolitionist George Thompson, hoping to enlist his support in the struggle for "our poor enslaved brethren," and planned to publish the proceedings in the colored press. The following year, the celebrants at the Newburgh event unanimously adopted six resolutions. These included giving thanks for British abolition, praise for Garrison's actions, and the condemnation of slavery for its "violation of the rights of man." The final two resolutions condemned racial prejudice, concluding that "good moral character and a proficiency in learning or literature" was the universal test of superiority. Meanwhile, the New England Freedom Association, a newly formed black vigilance committee, proclaimed universal liberty through their banner, "Liberty inherent the birthright of all," at the 1843 anniversary.[13]

12. *CA*, July 21, 28, August 25, 1838; August 17, 1839; *E*, August 11, 1836.
13. *E*, August 11, 1836; *CA*, August 25, 1838; August 17, 1839; *L*, August 11, 1843.

PUBLIC RITES

August First Day commemorations in black churches continued into the 1850s, but they declined in number, and began to play a less important role. Rather than serving as congregational sites for the event, they were largely relegated to the margins, serving as either initial meeting places or for an evening remembrance.[14] My research has uncovered 117 references to annual August Firsts between 1837 and 1861 in antislavery and local press reports. This is a minimum estimate for two reasons. Even the most careful and detailed search might overlook some mention of these celebrations. Also, some newspaper references to August First defy numerical count. In the summer of 1855, for instance, the *Frederick Douglass' Paper* noted the "day was appropriately celebrated in various other places, in this, and other States." The *Poughkeepsie Eagle* reported in 1860: "Spirited celebrations were held in New York, Boston, and other large cities."[15] Occasionally these gatherings were held in a black church or local hall, but the vast majority consisted of public parades and park picnics. Some of these picnic spots, like Parker's Grove in New Bedford, Arthur's Grove in Pittsburgh, and Judge Bennet's Grove in Buffalo, were temporarily loaned out by propertied whites opposed to American slavery. Other meeting places were fair grounds and public lands.

The temporal and spatial dimensions of the public August First were especially important. From the early 1840s onward, African Americans organized, attended, and celebrated scores of West India Emancipation celebrations annually in the villages, towns, streets, and cities of northern and western states. Although some black communities like New Bedford's began their annual commemoration in 1844, most communities turned to the public August First during the 1850s. This was largely due to the emergence of key issues around American slavery, antislavery, and racial politics: the passage of the Fugitive Slave Act and federal-state tensions over its implementation, together with the Kansas-Nebraska controversy and the expansion of American slavery. "Notices of FIRST OF AUGUST celebrations, gather thick and fast about us," reported the *Frederick Douglass' Paper* in late

14. For later church commemorations, see *NYDT*, August 2, 1855; *WAA*, August 10, 31, 1861; *L* August 9, 1861. For the church as meeting place and concluding service, see *PT*, August 9, 1859.

15. *FDP*, August 10, 1855; *PE*, August 4, 1860.

July 1855. "The day will be more generally celebrated, than at any other period." [16]

Moreover, these commemorations expanded across the nation. Much like the thanksgiving service in church, the public August First was held in the key Atlantic seaboard cities, as well as at smaller places inland. What is most striking is the geographical spread of August First into small urban areas in western Pennsylvania and Midwestern states like Ohio, Indiana, Illinois, and Minnesota during the 1850s. These areas saw an increase in the numbers of people of African descent due to a combination of the Underground Rail-road, relatively safer remove from Southern slavery, and access to southwest-ern provinces of British Canada. After the admittance of California into the Union in 1850, African Americans immigrated westward, and, from 1854 onward, celebrated August First in San Francisco, Sacramento, and Placer-ville. With the expansion of American slavery and the take-off of the fugitive slave movement, the Midwest became an important regional hub of August First meetings. In 1856, for instance, it was reported from Ohio that the "FIRST OF AUGUST was much more celebrated this year than usual." [17]

The annual celebration was reported by white antislavery newspapers (*Liberator, Antislavery Bugle*), the black abolitionist press (*Colored American, Frederick Douglass' Paper, North Star, Anglo-African*), and the local print media (*Poughkeepsie Eagle*). These newspapers supported the celebration and gave it extended cover-age under the subheading "First of August" or "Anniversary of British Eman-cipation." Some of the local press used the same subheadings but were much more opposed to antislavery. They often reported the event in less flattering terms and used it as an opportunity to spread racist caricatures. According to the *Brooklyn Daily Times*, the 1859 celebration at Morris Grove, Long Island, "was a burlesque as marked as an opera of the Christy's Minstrels." The same tabloid ended its account of the following year's celebration with a description of a fight between "two stout ladies" called "Clarissa" and "Sarah," watched by "colored gentlemen, with the love of fun which is characteristic of their race, looking on without interfering." The "Spy" began its report of the Au-gust First in Harlem in 1861: "Reader were you ever at a picnic where the gentlemen were far less numerous than roosters in a barnyard?" [18]

16. *FDP*, July 27, 1855. For the 1850s events, see chap. 6.
17. *ASB*, August 23, 1856.
18. *BDE*, August 3, 1859; August 2, 1860; *AA*, August 17, 1861.

The public August First usually consisted of "picnics, parades, public meetings and abundant speeches." Committees of arrangement with prominent black citizens usually organized the event. This involved letter writing, printing handbills, securing halls and groves, preparing refreshments, booking musical accompaniment, sending out invitations, fund-raising, and event advertising. Readers of the July 31, 1851, edition of the *Frederick Douglass' Paper* would have come across the following notice: "FIRST OF AUGUST CELEBRATION. The Colored Citizens of Lockport and Geneva, intend to celebrate the 1st of August in their respective towns. Addresses are to be delivered in Geneva by Messrs. Ward, Remond, and Johnson; in Lockport by the Rev. Amos Beman, and by Frederick Douglass, if his health will permit." People would usually assemble in the early to late morning at a railway terminus, city hall, or local church. Celebrants were often "arrayed in their best attire." Led by a grand marshal and marching to the tempo of one or several brass bands, they "paraded the principal streets of the city." The procession was often quite spectacular, with various "colored societies" dressed in their order's regalia bearing banners, flags, and slogans. In the parade would be carriages bearing well-dressed black youngsters. Independent colored militias consisting of young black men bearing arms would provide an escort, especially during the 1850s. Having reached their destination—usually a wooded grove, local park, or fairground—the assembled crowd sang songs and listened to antislavery speeches. Afterward, they would sometimes engage in "sports upon the grass" and games like "blind man's bluff" and "old man and woman." They would dine and dance, the "festivities" continuing "until a late hour." [19]

Both Benjamin Quarles and Mitch Kachun have provided useful and detailed descriptions of these Emancipation Day celebrations.[20] They downplay, however, the relationship between public celebrations and the larger system of racial politics. The following section explores this dialectic in three ways. First, we focus on the unique significance of black public parades together with the cultural aspects of the antislavery picnic. Second, we explore the transnational connections between West Indian emancipation and American antislavery in the Atlantic world. Most important, we examine the role of August First in political mobilization for the overthrow of American slavery.

19. This account draws upon the sources listed for Table 3.2.
20. Quarles, *Black Abolitionists,* 116–42; Kachun, *Festivals of Freedom,* 54–96.

TABLE 3.2. August First in Public, 1837–1861

1837	Broadway Hall, New York City, N.Y.
	Geneva, N.Y.
1838	Broadway Tabernacle, New York City, N.Y.
1839	Philomathean Hall, New York City, N.Y.
1840	Rochester, N.Y.
1841	Williamsburgh, New York City, N.Y.
	Wilmington, Del.
1842	Moyamensing, Philadelphia, Pa.
	Lowell, Mass.
1843	?
1844	Grove, Columbus, Ohio
	Parker's Grove, New Bedford, Mass.
1845	Providence, R.I.
	Parker's Grove, New Bedford, Mass.
1846	Parker's Grove, New Bedford, Mass.
1847	Academy Grove, Canandaigua, N.Y.
	Parker's Grove, New Bedford, Mass.
1848	Washington Square, Rochester, N.Y.
	Auburn, N.Y.
	Parker's Grove, New Bedford, Mass.
1849	Cincinnati, Ohio
	Grove, Flushing, Ohio
	Grove, Laceyville, Pa.
	Parker's Grove, New Bedford, Mass.
	Judge Bennett Park, Buffalo, N.Y.
1850	Wesleyan Church, Cleveland, Ohio
	Grove, Harrisville, Ohio
	Salem, Ohio
	Parker's Grove, New Bedford, Mass.
1851	Parker's Grove, New Bedford, Mass.
	Arthur's Grove, Pittsburgh, Pa.
	St. Clairsville, Ohio
	Worcester, Mass.
	Lockport, N.Y.
	Geneva, N.Y.

(continued)

1857 Parker's Grove, New Bedford, Mass.
      Mark Rock, R.I.
      Canandaigua, N.Y.
      Grove, Springfield, Ohio
      Fair Grounds, Canandaigua, N.Y.
      Galesburg, Ill.
      Livingston's Woods, Poughkeepsie, N.Y.
1858 Parker's Grove, New Bedford, Mass.
      College Hill, Poughkeepsie, N.Y.
      Morris Grove, Long Island, N.Y.
      Myrtle Avenue Park, Williamsburgh, N.Y.
      Grove, Springfield, Ohio
      Christiana, Pa.
      Haddington Grove, Philadelphia, Pa.
      Grove, Nicollet Island, Minn.
1859 Parker's Grove, New Bedford, Mass.
      Morris Grove, Long Island, N.Y.
      Sacramento, Calif.
      Grove, Harrisville, Ohio
      Fox's Grove, Poughkeepsie, N.Y.
      Fair Grounds, Richmond, Ind.
      Grove, Geneva, N.Y.
      Grove, Harrisburg, Pa.
1860 Parker's Grove, New Bedford, Mass.
      Myrtle Avenue Park, Williamsburgh, N.Y.
      Park, Geneva, N.Y.
      Hudson, N.Y.
      Hayce's Grove, Alliance, Ohio
      Fair Ground, Yonkers, N.Y.
1861 Fair Ground, Yonkers, N.Y.
      Forest Hill Grove, Utica, N.Y.
      Harlem, New York City, N.Y.
      Bellvue Garden, New York City, N.Y.
      Myrtle Avenue Park, Brooklyn, N.Y.
      Red Bank, N.J.
      New Brunswick, N.J.

(continued)

Fackler's Grove, Leavenworth, Kans.
Belle Isle, Detroit, Mich.
Smith's Hill Grove, Providence, R.I.
Grove, Harrisburg, Pa.
Iron City Park, Pittsburgh, Pa.
McFarland's Grove, Pittsburgh, Pa.
Breed's Grove, Pittsburgh, Pa.
Desplains, Chicago, Ill.
Watkins, N.Y.
Ward's Wood, Springfield, Ohio
Grove, Groton, Conn.
Parker's Grove, New Bedford, Mass.

Sources: AA, August 6, 1859; July 27, August 10, 17, September 14, 1861; *ASB*, August 18, 1849; July 20, August 10, 17, 24, 1850; August 9, 16, 1851; August 14, 1852; August 6, 27, 1853; August 4, 11, 1855; July 19, August 9, 23, 1856; August 27, 1859; August 11, 1860; *BDE*, August 2, 3, 1858; August 3, 27, 1859; August 2, 1860; *CA*, July 15, 29, August 5, October 28, 1837; July 21, 28, September 22, 1838; August 17, 1839; September 5, 1840; August 14, 1841; *E*, August 24, 1837; *FDP*, July 24, September 4, 1851; August 12, 26, 1853; June 23, August 18, 25, September 22, October 20, 1854; July 27, August 10, 17, 24, September 28, 1855; *HF*, September 2, 1842; *L*, August 19, 1842; August 15, 1851; August 19, 1853; August 15, 1856; August 14, 1857; August 6, 13, 20, 1858; August 5, 26, September 2, 1859; *NASS*, August 12, 19, 26, 1847; *NE*, August 14, 1851; August 5, September 16, 1852; August 18, 1853; August 17, 1854; August 9, 1855; *NYDT*, August 2, 1855; *NS*, May 26, July 14, August 4, 11, October 13, 1848; April 20, May 11, June 29, July 27, August 10, 17, 31, 1849; *Palladium of Liberty*, August 14, 1844; *PE*, August 8, 1857; August 7, 1858; August 6, 1859; August 4, 1860; *PT*, August 4, 11, 1857; August 9, 1859; *BAP*, 3:177, 179, 389–92; Bell, "Negroes in California," 154; *Frederick Douglass Papers*, 3:183–84, 214– 15, 366–67; Brown, *Life of William J. Brown*, 131; Grover, *Fugitive's Gibraltar*, 230, 261; Jackson, "Anglo-African," 345–46; Muelder, *Fighters for Freedom*, 219; Pease, *Diary of Samuel Rodman*, 261–62, 293, 330; Phillips, *Freedom's Port*, 174; Quarles, *Black Abolitionists*, 116–17; Sterling, *Making of an Afro-American*, 83, 107–8, 138; White, "Civil Rights Agitation," 18.

During the antebellum decades, public politics emerged at local and national levels. As cities grew and the suffrage expanded, so did a public politics characterized by mass-based parties, public meetings, and a popular press. This new urban culture was further reflected in the growth of public amusements, sporting events, popular lectures, and public ceremonies. As Mary Ryan has observed, by 1850 "Americans had found their ceremonial métier in the cultural performance of the parade." "Filing through the streets with banners and a band," she continues, "was an everyday occurrence in the ante-bellum years, a mode of celebration enjoyed by hundreds of militia units, trade associations, fire companies, political parties, reform associations, ethnic brotherhoods, and simple revelers." Commemorative celebrations organized by African Americans were also influenced by the advent of mass politics. The spread of this popular political culture even affected slaves in the Upper and Lower South.[21]

It is important not to forget, however, that American public space was potentially dangerous for people of African descent. A scheduling conflict over the usage of the Chatham Street Chapel between the New York Sacred Music Society and celebrants of New York State's 1827 emancipation law led to major attacks on black people and their property between July 9 and 12, 1834. The following summer, anti-abolition rallies attracted huge crowds. The same day a meeting of the New York State Antislavery society at Utica saw the mobbing of Garrison in Boston. During the mid-1830s, the *Liberator, Philanthropist,* and *Emancipator* reported 157 anti-abolitionist mob actions throughout the northern states. Between the early 1830s and the early 1840s, there were riots in Philadelphia, Boston, Dayton, and Cincinnati in which blacks were attacked by whites. Such regular occurrences encouraged some to avoid public events altogether because they were considered to be too dangerous. The response of many others, however, was that since property was being burned and black people were being singled out for physical attack, it made sense to organize more collectively in the name of self-defense.[22]

21. Mary P. Ryan, *Women in Public: Between Banners and Ballots, 1825–1880* (Baltimore: Johns Hopkins University Press, 1990), 13–14, 22; Davis, *Parades and Power*; Steven Hahn, *A Nation under Our Feet: Black Political Struggles in the Rural South from Slavery to the Great Migration* (Cambridge, Mass.: Harvard University Press, 2003), 55.

22. Jeffrey, *Silent Majority*, 49; Paul L. Gilje, *The Road to Mobocracy: Popular Disorder in New York City, 1763–1834* (Chapel Hill: University of North Carolina Press, 1987), 162–70; Richards, *The Slave Power*, 130; *L*, August 12, 19, 1842; Davis, *Parades and Power*, 46; Horton and Horton, *Hope of Liberty*, 243–44.

From the early 1840s onward, African Americans paraded through the "principal streets" of dozens of villages, towns, and cities in commemoration of West Indian emancipation. The 1848 commemoration at Rochester consisted of a "large procession" of local benevolent societies, clergy, orators, schoolchildren, organizers, citizens, and strangers who "proceeded through the city to Washington Square." At Buffalo the following year, a procession was formed "with carriages from which were displayed beautiful and appropriate Banners, presenting a grand and imposing spectacle." The procession at Richmond, Indiana, in 1859 "marched through diverse streets, with music and banners, making a grand display." The local white citizens of New Bedford must have become accustomed to the annual colored public holiday. The 1844 commemoration was marked by "a very respectable procession preceded by a band of colored musicians, mounted marshal, and cavalcade with a large number on foot with banners indicating different associations of women for mutual aid and improvement." The annual parade five years later was attended by "many from abroad and they made a striking appearance with their band and procession and showy costumes." At the 1851 celebration, the "various Masonic and other lodges, the school children, and a large number of the colored population, formed a procession, and escorted by bands of music, paraded the principal streets to John A. Parker's Grove, where dinner was had." By moving through the principal streets, African Americans were temporarily seizing public space often denied them by a hostile racial climate.[23]

Music provided by brass bands played an important part in these West Indian Day parades. The New York Brass and Howard Clary's Band from Boston provided the marching music at New Bedford in 1851, while the uniformed Flockton's Brass Band regularly struck up at the Poughkeepsie celebrations in the late 1850s. The Philadelphia Brass Band played at the 1859 Harrisburg event, while the Salem Brass Band and the Alliance Brass Band played at August First in Ohio in 1856 and 1860 respectively. The New Bedford parade in 1858 was accompanied by the North Bridgewater Brass Band consisting of eighteen pieces led by George E. Kingsly, along with the Malden Brass Band led by Thomas H. Perkins and the Rhode Island Brass Band from

23. *NS,* July 14, August 4, 1848; August 10, 1849; *ASB,* August 27, 1859; Zephaniah W. Pease, ed., *The Diary of Samuel Rodman, 1829–1859* (New Bedford, Mass.: Reynolds Printing Co., 1927), 261, 293; *NE,* August 14, 1851.

Providence. The Providence band had played the previous year at the Mark Rock commemoration.[24]

Not all brass bands contracted to play by organizing committees fulfilled their obligations. The Wallace Band had been engaged to play at the Morris Grove celebration in 1855, "but when its members saw how very black some of the picnic-ing [*sic*] faces were, they backed out of their engagement and went home with dumb bugles and reversed bassoons. Play their sweet music in the ears of niggers? Not they! WALLACE'S is a high-toned band. Their instruments of brass and their stringed instruments create symphonies that are fit to delight the ears of only white folks." It is interesting to note that, given the racial climate, any white bands were willing to participate at black celebrations in the first place. At any rate, the newspaper reporter went on to recommend that colored people needed to provide their own music.[25]

African Americans, however, had been providing their own music for quite a while. Numerous black men who fought during the colonial wars were military musicians. Francis "Frank" Johnson led one of the finest professional colored bands, which performed in England for Queen Victoria. Other noted black bands included Matt Black's All Negro Marching Band and Hazzard's Band from Philadelphia; Peter Guess's Band from Boston; Samuel Dixon's Brass Band from Newburgh; and the Scioto Valley Brass Band, the Roberts Band, and the Union Valley Brass Band from Ohio. Many of these bands played on August First. A band of "colored young men" played martial music for the Groton celebration in 1861, while the "Social Band" played the Pittsburgh event in full regalia. Three bands played at Urbana in 1856, including one "colored" band. Harry Cragg's "celebrated colored band" played the Red Bank celebration. Three bands accompanied the procession at Dayton, while Wolf's Brass Band headed the Columbus commemoration, both in 1854. "The noble 'Brass Band' from Stoughton," played at New Bedford in 1853 and 1856. These "privileged characters, generally—marched and played orderly as well as excellently. They assumed no 'airs,' white or black, but what were pleasing to the people and . . . with the character of the day and the event. They gave the utmost satisfaction; and they will, doubtless, be called

24. *FDP*, August 10, 1855; *L*, August 15, 1851; August 14, 1856; August 6, 1858; *PE*, August 7, 1858; *PT*, August 9, 1859; *WAA*, August 6, 1859; *ASB*, July 19, 1856; August 11, 1860.
25. *NYDT*, August 2, 1855.

again when music is wanted to celebrate the victories of freedom. They were not only good musicians, but well behaved gentlemen."[26]

According to one scholar, brass bands merely "added a martial atmosphere to the parade."[27] The evidence suggests otherwise. These bands provided work for musicians as well as a forum for social interaction. Such bands were often made up of budding musicians who sought an outlet for their interests and conviviality. Furthermore, these brass bands provided musical uplift as well as order for the participants. The band at Cincinnati "discoursed most excellent and spirit stirring music." At Pittsburgh, "M'Cargos band discoursed sweet music," while an anonymous band led the Smyrna commemoration with a "correct and tasteful execution of their music." Harry Cragg's famous band played waltzes and "the Star-Spangled Banner." They provided martial order and rhythm to these parades. Also, these songs and tunes united celebrants, providing a collective identity to diverse groups of people who had gathered from afar. Finally, their musical sounds publicly announced this annual celebration throughout the streets, squares, and parks. This was the colored folk's annual celebration and, much like former slaves in the British West Indies during Jonkonnu, crop-over, and Carnival, they would be heard![28]

Behind the brass bands marched colored societies, usually dressed in their full regalia. Some represented older expressions of moral reform such as the temperance movement. The United Benevolent Temperance Society marched at the 1858 Poughkeepsie event, while the Daughters of Temperance marched in Harrisburg the following year. Other organizations had emerged out of the need for social provision, mutual protection, and communal obligation among African Americans living and working in Northern towns and cities. The Order of United Colored Americans marched in Cincinnati in 1852 and Dayton in 1854. The Sons of Liberty also marched in Dayton. Lodges of the Odd Fellows and the Good Samaritans marched in the Harrisburg and New

26. Clifford E. Watkins, "Marching Bands," *EAACH*, 3:1687–92; *WAA*, August 10, 17, 1861; *ASB*, August 23, 1856; *FDP*, August 12, 1853; August 17, 1854; *L*, August 19, 1853; August 15, 1856; *NE*, August 17, 1854.

27. Gravely, "Dialectic of Double-Consciousness," 304.

28. *ASB*, August 14, 1852; August 27, 1853; *FDP*, August 26, 1853; *NE*, September 16, 1852; *WAA*, September 14, 1861. My thanks to Sam Floyd for discussions on the importance of this black musical tradition.

Bedford parades. The Young Men's Morning Star marched at New Bedford and Providence. Members of the Carlisle Club and Toussaint L'Ouverture Club marched at the Harrisburg celebration. Members of the Union Club marched at New Bedford.[29]

Numerous other colored societies marched at these annual commemorations. No less than thirty-two societies were expected to march in the Long Island procession in 1855. The First Colored Independent Philanthropic Grand Lodge of Free and Accepted Masons of the State of New York intended to march at Newark in 1852. The Sons of Protection marched in their order's regalia in Salem, Ohio, in 1855. From Cincinnati, it was reported that "other organizations of our colored friends" marched in Dayton's 1854 processional.[30]

The participation of these reform and benevolent societies highlights the communal importance of West India Day in African American life and culture. Prominent organizations and institutions turned out to march in public. These local societies recognized the importance of this event. Furthermore, the parades advertised the extent of social organization among African Americans not always apparent to those from outlying areas. Moreover, their marches must have been visually stunning. Various "colored societies, in full regalia, with broad sashes, and scarves of red, blue and yellow, and with banners, badges and mottos, dazzling in the sunlight, and floating in the breeze," lit up the 1855 New Bedford parade. One young participant could still vividly recall these parades thirty years later.[31]

These "colored" societies marched with banners, flags, and mottoes proclaiming their political beliefs. Banners marked "Liberty the birthright of all" and "Equal Rights to all" announced adherence to the philosophy of natural rights. The desire for a free republic was displayed in such mot-

29. *NE*, September 16, 1852; August 17, 1854; *PE*, August 7, 1858; *WAA*, August 6, 1859; *L*, August 15, 1851; August 19, 1853; August 15, 1856; Brown, *Life of Brown*, 131; Monroe N. Work, "Secret Societies as Factors in the Social and Economical Life of the Negro," in *Democracy in Earnest*, ed. James E. McCulloch (Washington, D.C.: Southern Sociological Congress, 1918), 342–50; Moses Dickson, *Manual of the International Order of Twelve Knights and Daughters of Tabor, containing general laws, regulations, ceremonies, drill, and a Taborian lexicon* (St. Louis, Mo.: A. R. Fleming, 1891).

30. *ASB*, July 19, 1855; *FDP*, July 27, 1855; *NE*, August 5, 1852; August 17, 1854.

31. *FDP*, August 10, 1855; Brown, *Life of Brown*, 131.

toes as "no union with slaveholders," and "america! [*sic*] with all her faults we love her still." Popular abolitionist images of "Am I not a Man?" and "Am I not a Brother?" conveyed sentiments of the universal brotherhood of man. British abolition as the triumph of God's will was evoked on the reverse of these images with "broken fetters, riven chains, and the disenthralled bondman, with outstretched arms, and heaven-erected face." The commemorative importance of emancipation was suggested by the inscriptions "the day we commemorate," "in commemoration of West Indian Emancipation, Aug. 1, 1834," "would that we were free," "Liberty to the British West Indies," and "This Day the Manacles fell from 800,000 human beings, Aug. 1, 1834."[32] These visual aids depicted the dominant ideas and beliefs of those on parade. They further provided other participants, as well as casual onlookers, with easy-to-read signs and symbols of the social meaning of this event. William Nell reported that flag displays at the 1848 Rochester celebration functioned so that "the uninitiated learned the *why* and *wherefore* of this gathering of freemen."[33]

Young people also marched on August First. Children paraded annually at the New Bedford celebration. Five carriages of 125 children belonging to Freedom's Juvenile Singing School plus carriages with Sabbath school children marched in 1856. This commemoration also saw a phalanx of a hundred boys bearing the banner "Let the Oppressed go free." Moreover, youthful participants spoke at Emancipation Day celebrations. Children addressed the crowd at the Lefferts Park commemoration in 1861. Children from the Sabbath schools "of the several colored churches, together with scholars of the colored primary school" in San Francisco "recited some fine selections of prose and poetry." The *Christian Recorder* recommended an August First in Washington, D.C., partly to "afford the little folks an opportunity of giving expression to their thoughts and feelings on the subject."[34]

32. *L*, August 19, 1853; August 15, 1856; Grover, *Fugitive's Gibraltar*, 262; *WAA*, August 17, 1861; *FDP*, August 10, 1855; *ASB*, July 19, 1856.

33. *L*, September 1, 1848, quoted in Rael, *Black Identity*, 61; Figes and Kolonitski, *Interpreting the Russian Revolution*, chap. 2. I was reminded of the visual power of signs and symbols during mass antiwar demonstrations in Toronto and New York City during the spring of 2003. Perhaps the best, though, was at the September 24, 2005, antiwar rally in Washington, D.C. Coming just after Hurricane Katrina, it refined the iconic 1960s slogan: "Make Levees not War."

34. *L*, August 15, 1851; August 19, 1853; August 15, 1856; *WAA*, August 10, 1861; *FDP*, October 20, 1854; *CR*, June 28, 1862.

Much of the focus on the education of African American children in the antebellum North has been on formal schooling and institutions of learning. Participation of young people on August First, however, suggests an important public expression of social politicization. Event organizers arranged for local churches and schools to turn out their young members on these occasions. There were two main reasons. Such events taught the younger generation the social mores of community such as discipline, manners, and temperance. J. H. Perkins explained to the Cincinnati crowd that "we must educate them [our children] morally, practically, and intellectually, make them mechanics, and tillers of the soil, producers as well as consumers." A party of youngsters "took the liberty of going in bathing" at Groton, but were quickly stampeded "on seeing a gentleman approaching carrying a long stick." Moreover, these parades of smart and well-behaved youth were designed to impress local onlookers with a spectacle of respectability. One reporter for the *Liberator* commented approvingly on the acknowledgment by their fellow classmates of an open carriage with schoolchildren decorated with evergreen and flowers. Not only were these youngsters on the path toward self-improvement, but their respectability offered a challenge to racial subordination and the denial of the rights of equal citizenship.[35]

After the parade, the celebrants ended up at a local park or wooded grove for a picnic. Sometimes these were low-key affairs. The local newspaper reported that the Poughkeepsie commemoration in 1859 "did not appear to be quite as large as last year." But one of the most remarkable features of these public August Firsts was their sheer magnitude. Around 1,000 people attended the annual picnics at Flushing in 1849 and Canandaigua in 1857. There were 2,000 people at Harrisville in 1850 and Christiana in 1858. Between 3,000 and 4,000 folks celebrated August First at Cincinnati in 1852, New Bedford in 1853, and Poughkeepsie in 1858. The largest crowds appear to have turned out for West India Day during the mid-1850s, with 5,000 reported at Clifton Park and Urbana and 7,000 at New Bedford.[36]

35. *WAA*, August 17, 1861; *NS*, September 7, 1849; *L*, August 15, 1851.

36. *PE*, August 6, 1859; *ASB*, August 18, 1849; August 10, 1850; August 23, 1856; Frederick Douglass, *The Frederick Douglass Papers*, Series I, Speeches, Debates, and Interviews, vol. 3, ed. John W. Blassingame (New Haven: Yale University Press, 1985), 183, 214; *L*, August 20, 1858; *NE*, September 16, 1852; *FDP*, August 12, 1853; August 10, 1855; *NYDT*, August 2, 1855.

Many Americans of European descent attended August First parades and picnics. Hundreds were at Pittsburgh's annual celebrations. Of the 1,000 people gathered at Morris Grove, Brooklyn, "perhaps one fourth were white folks." Of the 3,000 to 4,000 people at Poughkeepsie in 1858, probably "one third, and perhaps more [were] white." At least 2,000 whites attended the Urbana meeting in 1856. Women made up much of the crowd. There were "equal" males and females in attendance at the 1858 commemoration at Poughkeepsie. On the way home to his mother's house in New Bedford, Quaker whaling merchant Samuel Rodman encountered "a gratified audience of about a thousand people, a majority of whom were white and more than half women," at an August First celebration.[37]

There are several explanations for this participation by Euro-Americans. Some came for the sport. The reporter on the 1855 Brooklyn event believed that a "knot of rustics left their fields and came up in the afternoon, doubtless for a little fun." Some crowds can be understood within the context of an emerging public leisure culture associated with antebellum modernization, although this would not explain their motivation. It is not unlikely, however, that many white participants supported and sympathized with an increasingly important date in the antislavery calendar primarily because they opposed slavery. The reporter of the 1856 Urbana commemoration noted that the celebrations "were got up by the colored people," while "the whites gave them the encouragement of their presence." Many women who annually attended August First at New Bedford were supporters of abolition, much like those ordinary black people who protected fugitives, supported runaways, and pursued other antislavery activities without belonging to abolitionist organizations or institutions.[38]

The abolitionist press remained almost silent on the gender and racial makeup of these crowds. This was partly because of their belief that abolition

---

37. *NYDT,* August 2, 1855; *PE,* August 7, 1858; *FDP,* August 10, 1855; *L,* August 19, 1853; *ASB,* August 18, 1849; August 15, 1856; Pease, *Diary of Samuel Rodman,* 330; Jeffrey, *Great Silent Army.*

38. *FDP,* August 10, 17, 24, 1855; *ASB,* August 23, 1856; Jeffrey, *Great Silent Army;* James O. Horton and Lois E. Horton, *Black Bostonians: Family Life and Community Struggle in the Antebellum North* (New York: Holmes & Meier Publishers, 1979), 99, 110–13. One of the drawbacks with national and elite-based approaches toward August First is its silencing of important acts of racial solidarity.

was a universal cause beyond any given social group. Furthermore, advertising racially mixed groups, especially with colored men and white women, would only aid detractors of antislavery in their charges of racial amalgamation and equality. Even so, a careful reading of the abolitionist and local press reveals large black crowds assembling for parades and picnics on August First. At 4:00 P.M., on August I, 1855, there were 750 "people of color" at Morris Grove, Long Island. John J. Moore reported "some sixteen hundred colored people in San Francisco," although late arrangements meant that "only the children with their parents and friends" attended the city celebration in 1854. Crowds of around three thousand "colored" people attended the Cincinnati celebration in 1852, the Urbana meeting in 1856, and the Poughkeepsie event in 1858. Frederick Douglass reported that from "three to four thousand person [*sic*], young and old, male and female," participated in the New Bedford celebration in 1853. The reporter estimated that there "could not have been less than five thousand colored people on the ground" at Clifton Park on Staten Island in 1855. At the Christiana commemoration in 1858, "W.W.B." reported the "largest meeting of colored persons that I ever met at one time." These were large crowds at a time when such assemblies were rare in the Northern states and prohibited in the slave South. Indeed, they were probably among the largest independent gatherings by people of African descent in nineteenth-century America. Not until the post–World War I parades organized by Marcus Garvey's United Negro Improvement Association (UNIA) would there be similarly sized urban gatherings by people of African descent.[39]

These August First picnics were often very social and convivial occasions. One well-documented example was the August First picnic held at Clifton Park, Staten Island, in 1855. Before 10:00 A.M., the streets were alive to the sound of drums. (Recall the role of drum playing in Emancipation Day parades in the urban West Indies during the 1830s.) By early afternoon, "there could not have been less than 5,000 colored people on the ground." Local fashions were evident. "Colored ladies are so fond of gaudy hues," sneered one reporter, "that we fancied a great many rainbows had been cut into small

---

39. *L*, August 20, 1858; *NYDT*, August 2, 1855; *Frederick Douglass Papers*, 3:183; *ASB*, August 10, 1850; *L*, August 15, 1856; *FDP*, September 4, 1851; August 12, 1853; October 20, 1854; *NE*, September 16, 1852.

pieces to adorn the persons of these 'images of God, cut in ebony.'" "Colored vendors" provided the crowd with fruits, vegetables, meats, and assorted "condiments." There were also sports upon the grass, "rollings and rumblings to and fro." The day ended with a ball in the evening, followed by "firing pistols and crackers in the streets until a late hour." As the reporter put it, this event represented "a good time without the white folks around."[40]

Music, dancing, and balls were especially popular at the conclusion of August First commemorations. "Merry" dances were held at New Bedford (1853), San Francisco (1855), and Springfield (1857). Emancipation balls were enjoyed at Dayton (1854), Harrisburg (1859), Geneva (1860, 1861), Chicago (1861), and Groton (1861). Celebrants "trip[ped] the fantastic toe" at Miller's Hall, Poughkeepsie, and Springfield, Ohio." At the San Francisco celebration of 1855, it was reported that "dancing, although not in the program, was evidently more enjoyed than anything else." "With a majority of the colored people in this city," it added, "dancing is the acme of human happiness."[41]

Numerous reports commented on "belles" at these dances and events. Some of the "girls" at Springfield were described as "dazzlingly beautiful." "Colored ladies" were dressed in "gaudy hues" at Staten Island. "One Venus," noted the reporter, "especially struck us, with bare shoulders and arms, and a Bloomer hat upon her woolly head," while others were of a "rich mahogany color" with "several very fine specimens." The ladies all looked "fine" at Groton, "but in the eyes of many fortune seemed to favor Miss P. S-n, of Norwich, Connecticut." At Harlem's ball, there were "neatly" dressed ladies, all anxiously pursued by "roosters in a barn."[42] Despite their derogatory tone, such accounts hint at important social aspects of August First Day celebrations. Many people attended these events in their best clothes as part of a respectable agenda. The sartorial choices of some women, however, were clearly the result of fashion consciousness. Unlike today's mass media marketing, these fashions reflected an individual sense of identity, self-expression, and style. Moreover, dances, balls, and festive occasions must have provided the

40. *NYDT,* August 2, 1855.

41. *L,* August 19, 1853; August 4, 1857; *FDP,* September 28, 1855; *NE,* August 17, 1854; *AA,* August 6, 1859; *WAA,* August 17, 1861.

42. *L,* August 14, 1857; *WAA,* August 10, 17, 1861; *NYDT,* August 2, 1855.

means for social intercourse and sexual encounters among African Americans that might otherwise have been hard to realize in small villages and towns. More salacious detail, while hinted at in the hostile white press, remained mute in the black and white "respectable" antislavery press.

Indeed, most reports of August First came from abolitionist and local newspapers primarily concerned with representing Emancipation Day celebrations as spectacles of respectability. Innumerable reports, for instance, ended with favorable descriptions of the participants' behavior. August First at St. Clairsville, Ohio, was celebrated by "colored people" with "decorum and social enjoyment." "At their second of August celebration," in Cincinnati reported "P," there was "not one drunken man on the ground, and the behaviour for so large an assemblage was quite as unexceptional as any similar one among whites would have been." Frederick Douglass was no less impressed with New Bedford's celebration, which "was well conducted, well begun, [and] well ended." "No visitors," concluded the *Poughkeepsie Eagle* of the 1859 celebration, "that ever honor us with their presence conducted themselves with more propriety than marked the movements of all who assembled to honor the day so dear to their affections." It is not unlikely that such descriptions of good conduct express the implicit tension between representing antislavery sentiment as being popular and social concern over the collective behavior of such large gatherings of colored people.[43]

Much like reports of quiet and sober abolition in the British colonies by officials and missionaries, however, we should be wary of the assignment of polite corporate behavior to Afro-American crowds. The evidence is scant, but suggestive. Pittsburgh's commemoration had been enjoyed for years, but 1861 was celebrated "with more than ordinary zest." "From the appearance of some of them on their return in the evening," reported the *Poughkeepsie Eagle*, "it was evident that they had enjoyed it in [a] manner peculiar to such public occasions." In the *Evening News* of Springfield, Ohio, the "colored brethren" "put up at the Willis, patronized the saloons, visited dry-goods palaces, and made themselves generally prevalent." "Dancing, although not in the pro-

43. *ASB*, August 9, 16, 1851; *NE*, September 16, 1852; *FDP*, August 12, 1853; *PE*, August 6, 1859; Rael, *Black Identity*, 65–68. For a comparative study of "polite" crowds in industrializing English cities, see Mark Harrison, *Crowds and History: Mass Phenomena in English Towns, 1790–1835* (Cambridge: Cambridge University Press, 1988), chap. 7.

gram, was evidently more enjoyed than anything else," wrote the rather exasperated "Nubia," of the San Francisco celebration in 1851. Moreover, racist local newspapers like the *Brooklyn Daily Times, Brooklyn Daily Eagle,* and the *New York Daily Times* caricatured the event. At the 1855 Brooklyn celebration, it was reported that "one yellow girl indignantly repudiated the charge of black skin. She had never been so insulted before. Black she was not and black she would never be." At the 1858 Morris Grove celebration, it was reported that "casks of lager and demi-johns of liquids, which from the exhilarating effect produced on those who appeared to test their contents bore a suspicious resemblance to *eau de vie.*" At the same event two years later, it was reported that "two stout ladies got into a dispute on the respective merits of their spouses. 'Clarisa' had the best of the argument but the worst of the fight, for on round 1st Sarah struck her twice on the nose, and knocked her partly out of time."[44]

Despite meticulous organization and careful preparation, August First did not always go to according to plan. One drunken Irishman insisted at the Columbus celebration that "he could whip 'anny Nagur on the ground,'" while other white men drank from their pocket flasks, yelled out, and retired to adjacent woods from whence they commenced "hooting and shouting." At the 1855 Staten Island event, a "colored lady got into a quarrel with an Irish laborer, who had laughed . . . at the procession." "'They lifted the American flag,' she said, 'and that's what you and your people can't dare to do without a lie.'" The daytime picnic at Desplains, Chicago, was followed by an evening oration and ball at Witkowsky Hall, which went very smoothly until "broken up by a party of drunken soldiers, who were at first driven off, but subsequently returned with reinforcements, and demolished chairs, benches, and etc." The Yonkers celebration had to be cut short because of the failure of "Mr. Griffin and the white man who keeps the bar to fulfill their promises with regard to their quota of the expenses of the celebration." The same thing had happened the year before. During the speeches at Poughkeepsie, the platform for speakers collapsed: "crack, crack, crash, crash, went the unstable frame, and down came the boards, timbers, orators, officers, reporters, black and white, Quaker and elders, in one conglomerate mass of pine, hemlock

44. *NYDT,* August 2, 1855; *WAA,* August 10, 1861; *PE,* August 4, 1860; *FDP,* September 28, 1855; *BDE,* August 3, 1858; August 2, 1860.

and humanity!" One journalist "saw a good sized board strike Mr. Douglass upon the head." There were no major injuries, a wagon was substituted, and the orators resumed their speaking.[45]

It is clear that August First played a significant part in black cultural and political life. These occasions drew together large groups of people from various regions on a regular basis for the purposes of commemoration as well as conviviality. It also served as an opportunity for the black elite to propagate their agendas both at the event itself as well as in its subsequent reporting. It is important, however, not to ignore the international dimensions of these annual celebrations. These local celebrations were invariably connected to broader events and places.

While local speakers predominated, sometimes speakers attended from farther afield. James A. Thome, fresh from his recent visit to the British West Indies, spoke for nearly an hour at the Broadway Tabernacle meeting in New York City in 1837, refuting "all the arguments leveled against IMMEDIATE EMANCIPATION" and praising former slaves for "the cultivation of virtuous habits" and "intellectual improvement." A certain "colored speaker" called Mr. Walker, who served as presiding officer at the 1853 celebration in Mount Pleasant, Ohio, had spent two years in Liberia, West Africa. Palmer, who had recently visited the West Indies, addressed the same gathering in Ohio. The well-traveled John Butler attended the New Bedford event the same year. A fugitive from Virginia, he had "tilled the soil of Canada; trimmed the ships and delighted [*sic*] the lamps of New Bedford; traversed more than half the globe, and hunted gold in California." Along with speakers, many people attended from afar. A "considerable number from abroad, and among them a few from Canada," were reported at the 1848 Rochester event. Port towns like New Bedford with their maritime commerce, whaling industry, and transient seamen often provided an international crossroads.[46]

45. *FDP,* August 18, 1854; September 28, 1855; *NYDT,* August 2, 1855; *WAA,* August 10, 1861; *Frederick Douglass Papers,* 3:214–15.

46. *CA,* July 29, August 5, 1837; *ASB,* August 27, 1853; *FDP,* August 12, 1853; *NS,* August 11, 1848; Grover, *Fugitive's Gibraltar,* 6–8, 10, 56. New Bedford during the early 1850s was also the starting place for Herman Melville's brilliant novel *Moby Dick,* whose international seafaring proletariat on the *Pequod* proved incapable of resisting the charismatic individualism of Captain Ahab.

Moreover, these August First commemorations belonged to a world of Atlantic abolition. In 1848, France sneezed and Europe caught cold. The result was a series of European revolutions and the abolition of slavery in the French and Danish Caribbean colonies. Elaborate arrangements were made for the Rochester celebration, including the reading out of both the British and French Acts of Abolition. The following year's celebration in Buffalo was an international event. Crowds bought antislavery goods made in England. The British Act of Abolition was read out aloud. There were numerous toasts, including one made to liberty, equality, and fraternity. In 1850, Brazil finally agreed to the abolition of its slave trade. Three years later, an August First in Philadelphia called for the death of Brazilian slavery. At some August First anniversaries, the American Declaration of Independence was read, while others were somewhat ambivalent. At the 1837 August First in New York City, it was pointed out that had the colonies remained British, there would have been no slaves in the existing United States after 1834.[47]

Along with public parades, convivial picnics, and their international dimensions, annual commemorations of West Indian emancipation played an important role in organizing political mobilization against American slavery. This was evident on several fronts. On the most basic level, annual commemorations served as an important opportunity for black organizations and antislavery newspapers to fund-raise for the cause. A box was placed near the entrance of Broadway Hall to collect funds for the committee at the 1837 meeting. The colored people of Geneva resolved to celebrate August First and "raise some funds for the *Colored American*." The following year, celebrants at the August First in New York City were invited to dine at the Temperance Eating House on the corner of William and Ann streets for $6.14 admission "for the benefit of the A. S. Society."[48]

More directly, West Indian Emancipation celebrations served as a nexus for both the self-defense of fugitive slaves as well as physical resistance against the institution of American slavery. The New York Committee of Vigilance and the New England Freedom Association, black vigilance committees in

47. The international nature of August First orations is examined in more detail in chap. 7.

48. *CA*, July 29, 1837; July 28, 1838.

New York and Boston respectively, played prominent roles in August First meetings in 1837 and 1843. The Sons of Protection organized and carried out the August First in Salem, Ohio, in 1856. Moreover, defenders of fugitives used August First as a means to bring attention to the plight of runaway slaves as well as to celebrate successful defenses. The Shadrach case was discussed at the 1851 and 1853 New Bedford August First, while the 1858 August First in Christiana celebrated its earlier success. Finally, fugitives were prominent at these events. They included famous antislavery speakers like Douglass, Ward, and Garnet, but also ordinary fugitives, who participated in Emancipation Day celebrations at Deer Creek, Salem, and Springfield, Ohio, throughout the 1850s. August First provided channels of fugitive communication where information was gathered and politics disseminated. We will see the extent to which fugitives played a central role in this fight against American slavery during the 1850s in chapter 6.[49]

Most important, annual celebrations of West Indian emancipation contributed to popular mobilization for the overthrow of American slavery. This can be seen in the transformation of the National Black Convention (NBC) movement. The first phase of NBC was largely unaffected by West Indian emancipation. National conventions of colored citizens convened every year between 1830 and 1835 in Philadelphia. These meetings were dominated by an older generation of wealthy free blacks, church elders, and white philanthropists. They condemned slavery but were mainly concerned with propagating moral reform. These conventions proved largely unsuccessful in establishing local conventions, while annual conventions were not held for the next several years.[50]

This began to change, however, with the emergence of a new set of challenges together with a generation of black leaders hailing from local organizations. In 1837–38, the Pennsylvania legislature restricted the vote to white males. Over the next few years, black opposition to this racist disfranchisement culminated in a state convention of colored freemen in Pittsburgh in August 1841. The planned convention in Philadelphia for 1842 was canceled

---

49. *CA*, July 29, 1837; *L*, August 11, 1843; August 15, 1856; *ASB*, July 19, 1856.

50. Stewart, *Holy Warriors*, 95–98, 135–36; Bell, "Negro Conventions," 247–50; *BAP*, 3:413–14; Blackett, "Freedom," 119.

because of popular violence earlier that summer. On August 15, 1843, however, over fifty black delegates from at least twelve states assembled in Buffalo, New York. They were concerned with self-improvement through temperance, moral reform, and antislavery. They also debated the need for a national colored press and the development of a frontier agricultural community. This traditional platform was balanced by the convention's endorsement of the recently created Liberty Party. Formed in 1839, this new party sought the end of American slavery through the political mobilization of voters. This embrace of the politics of slavery represented a fundamental divergence from Garrisonian abolition and its refusal to participate in the politics of a slaveholding Republic.[51]

The Buffalo convention is, of course, familiar to scholars for the debate over physical violence to overthrow American slavery. The hour-long "Address to the Slaves" by Henry Garnet had his audience both laughing and crying, but was firm in its concluding call for armed struggle against slaveholders: "If you must bleed, let it all come at once—rather *die freemen than live to be slaves.*" The address was turned over to a revising committee consisting of Garnet, Douglass, A. M. Sumer, S. H. Davis, and R. Banks. The convention rejected the revised message by one vote.[52] It seems rather ironic that an address to the slaves has largely been examined as a debate among free black leaders. Far less attention has been paid to possible links between slave revolt and black abolitionists. On the most obvious level, Garnet's address should be seen in relation to the emerging militancy gaining ground around the self-defense of fugitive slaves and mobilization against American slavery. More specifically, it is possible that Garnet's address was itself a *response* to slave actions. On August 13, 1841, the *Herald of Freedom* published an article under the subtitle "Attempted Insurrection." The editors of this prominent antislavery newspaper anticipated the opponents of armed struggle at the Buffalo convention in their endorsement of peaceful abolition. "While we deeply deplore any attempt on the part of the blacks to resort to violence to regain their rights or avenge their wrongs," wrote the editor, "we cannot help regarding it as the natu-

51. Ibid.

52. Bell, "Negro Conventions," 250–52 (italics in the original); William S. McFeeley, *Frederick Douglass* (New York: Norton, 1991), 105–6; *BAP,* 3:491.

ral consequence of the oppressions to which these miserable beings are subjected." This familiar abolitionist rejection of revolutionary violence to overthrow American slavery was followed by a summary from the New Orleans papers of late July containing "an account of the discovery of an intended revolt of slaves in Louisiana and Mississippi, which has produced a great sensation." "There was a systematized plan, it is stated, in which the negroes from Bayou Sara to Natchez were combined to rise and murder the whites." An overseer accidentally discovered the plot, and the following morning slaves were examined and confessions were extracted. "The alarm was immediately spread abroad, arrests were made to various plantations, and it was found by the confessions that they were all agreed in the main facts, that there was to be a general rise, and that the first of August was the day agreed upon."[53]

The NBC has been interpreted in various ways. Howard Bell argues for a shift from moral persuasion to political action during the mid-1840s. James Stewart writes that the convention movement provided a forum for leaders to debate, identify on racial grounds, and organize against oppression. Numerous other scholars have traced the demise of the NBC due to ideological struggles over black emigration during the 1850s.[54] Less comment has been made concerning the diasporic dimensions of the NBC, especially with regard to West Indian emancipation. There were several important aspects to this relationship. August First Day provided preparation and consolidation for political organization. On Monday, August 2, 1852, the colored citizens of Cincinnati held their anniversary of West India emancipation. A few evenings later, they held a meeting "for the purpose of appointing delegates to the approaching Cleveland convention." The Colored Men's Republican Club bivouacked in Myrtle Avenue Park in preparation for the August First celebration in 1860. Furthermore, the NBC had an obvious impact on Emancipation Day. During his speech at the 1853 New Bedford commemoration, William J. Watkins referred to the recent colored convention held at Rochester, saying, "we intend

53. *HF,* August 13, 1841.
54. Bell, "Negro Conventions"; Stewart, *Holy Warriors,* 136. Numerous new works on antebellum black life inexplicably pay little attention to the NBC. See Horton and Horton, *Hope of Liberty;* Milton C. Sernett, *North Star Country: Upstate New York and the Crusade for African American Freedom* (Syracuse: Syracuse University Press, 2002); Kachun, *Festivals of Freedom.*

to agitate, agitate, agitate." The language of convention was increasingly used to report August First Day. The writer "Spectator" described the 1850 Harrisville event as a "Convention" of "near two thousand people" assembled in a grove at the Methodist Protestant church. Thomas Jefferson, chairman of the organizing committee for the August First celebration, respectfully informed the citizens of the United States "that they will hold a Grand Convention of the Anniversary of the West India Islands on the 1st day of august, 1854, in the city of Dayton!"[55]

Moreover, August First celebrations also served to promote the abolition of American slavery. A large meeting of the "Colored Visitors and others" held at Bannaker House, Cape Island, in 1855 hailed the anniversary of emancipation and lamented "that the United States, although boasting of her liberty and republicanism, still hold in slavery 3 1/2 millions of our brethren." This meeting further resolved "that it is the indispensable duty of our people to use every effort for the overthrow of slavery, and for the acquisition of our rights in this the land of our nativity." Having described the wonderful August First celebration in Richmond, Indiana, in 1859, J. Greenly Ampey went on to compare: "But we have a greater work to do than our West India Brothers. They only had eight hundred thousand galling yokes to break; we have four millions of these to destroy and grind to powder before our glorious work is done." The chairman of the organizing committee for the fifteenth anniversary of West India emancipation in Cleveland wrote to the *Anti-Slavery Bugle* with the following information: "we have thought it proper to call a Mass Convention Celebration, to meet in the city of Cleveland, on Thursday, August First, 1850, whose object shall be to adopt some plan best calculated to promote the cause of Freedom, and arrest the onward march of American Slavery."[56]

In this chapter, we have explored two important social forms of August First in Afro-America and how these changed over time. Moreover, we have challenged the national characterization of this event with a focus on its transnational dimensions. One of the most important objectives has been to ar-

55. *NE*, September 16, 1852; *BDE*, August 2, 1860; *L*, August 19, 1853; *ASB*, August 10, 1850; *FDP*, June 23, 1854.
56. *FDP*, August 24, 1855; *ASB*, July 20, 1850; August 27, 1859.

gue for West Indian Emancipation Day celebrations as an important site for black popular politics, especially political mobilization against American slavery. Both aspects—transnationalism and antislavery mobilization—were to become especially prominent in the British colony of Canada West during the 1850s. Their nature, explanation, and significance for subsequent events is the focus of the following two chapters.

Chapter 4
Black Loyalists in Canada West

*WE, the coloured inhabitants of Canada, most respectfully, most gratefully and
most loyally approach your Gracious Majesty, on this, the anniversary
of our death to Slavery, and our birth to Freedom.*
Citizens of Toronto, August 1854

On August 1, 1854, hundreds of Canadians of African descent from southern Lake Ontario descended upon Toronto "to celebrate the emancipation of the negroes in the West Indian Islands." They marched, prayed, cheered, and gave thanks to Great Britain for its benevolent act of abolition passed over two decades earlier. Who were these Afro-Canadians? How did their August First celebration compare to those organized by American antislavery societies, as well as those by African Americans? Most important, what do such events tell us about the social politics of black people in Canada during this period?[1]

For years, Canadian historians ignored the black experience altogether. One major exception was University of Western Ontario Professor Fred Landon and his pioneering work on slavery, antislavery, and border politics published in the *Journal of Negro History* during the 1920s.[2] The first serious professional study of the historical experience of black people in Canada was researched and written during the social upheavals of the 1960s, and eventually published in 1971. Robin Winks's *The Blacks in Canada: A History* represented a meticulously researched survey with four key aims. It sought to examine prejudice in Canada; to provide a contrast with American views on immigration and identity; to view the "Negro" historically; and to examine English blacks as a neglected aspect of Canadian-American cultural relations. Despite

1. *PF*, July 29, August 5, 12, 1854. An earlier version of this chapter and the following one was presented at the Society for Historians of the Early American Republic conference at the University of Montreal, July 2006.

2. See the entries listed in the bibliography. It might be noted that the *Journal of Negro History* was diasporic in its coverage of black history during its first few decades of publication after 1915–16.

its impressive research—Winks used only half of the materials collected for the book, and deposited the rest at the Schomburg Center—the work reflected an older view of blacks as victims and subjects of the historical process. Much like two other influential books published around this time—Winthrop Jordan's *Black over White* and David Brion Davis's *Problem of Slavery*—Winks's *Blacks in Canada* largely represented "what the Negro had visited upon him." [3]

During the 1970s, and spurred by the bicentennial of the American Revolution, scholars began the first serious examination of African American fugitive slaves during and after the revolutionary decades. The result has been a rich debate on the nature and ideology of black loyalists throughout the Anglo-Atlantic world. More recently, scholars have focused on antislavery in Canada, especially its major organizations, prominent individuals, and competing ideologies. [4]

Unlike scholars of Afro-America, however, historians of the black experience in Canada have paid little attention to Emancipation Day celebrations. Most scholars note that it was an important event symbolizing unity and racial identity among people of African descent, but provide little further comment. Robin Winks, Jason Silverman, and the editors of the second volume of *The Black Abolitionist Papers* dealing with Canada all note that blacks in Canada celebrated abolition in the British West Indies, and that it was culturally important, but make only scattered references to the event. Daniel Hill describes several Emancipation Day parades between the mid-1830s and the 1850s, but is mute on their social meaning. The most thoroughly researched account by Silverman and John McKivigan offers a brief cross-border examination of Emancipation Day celebrations in upstate New York and Canada West

3. Robin W. Winks, *The Blacks in Canada: A History* (New Haven: Yale University Press, 1971); Robin W. Winks Collection, Schomburg Center. The Winks Collection contains numerous copies of obscure journal articles, letters, and documents.

4. Jason H. Silverman, *Unwelcome Guests: Canada West's Response to American Fugitive Slaves, 1800–1865* (Greenwood, Conn.: Associated Faculty Press, 1985); James W. St. G. Walker, *The Black Loyalists: The Search for a Promised Land in Nova Scotia and Sierra Leone, 1783–1870* (New York: Dalhousie University Press, 1976); John W. Pulis, ed., *Moving On: Black Loyalists in the Afro-Atlantic World* (New York; Garland, 1999); Barry Cahill, "The Black Loyalist Myth in Atlantic Canada," *Acadiensis* 29, no. 1 (Autumn 1999): 76–87; *BAP*, 2:xxiii–xxviii, 31; Jane Rhodes, *Mary Ann Shadd Cary: The Black Press and Protest in the Nineteenth Century* (Bloomington: Indiana University Press, 1998).

during the 1850s. It concludes that the event was a ritual of celebration in which free blacks defined themselves variously as Americans, Canadians, and "conflicted" Afro-Americans. This account ignores important celebrations prior to the 1850s; defines ritual as an unchanging entity; and focuses on one aspect of Emancipation Day speeches—the abolitionists' contrast of monarchical republicanism with republican slavery—at the expense of the event's changing context and rich social meaning.[5]

This chapter and the one that follows support the work of those scholars who argue for the importance of black history, the role of black historical agency in the making of Canada's past, and the significance of August First celebrations. But they go further in a number of important ways. Drawing upon research in black, abolitionist, and local newspapers published in the United States and Canada West from the late 1830s through the early 1860s, they provide the first systematic analysis of these annual commemorations and their changing social meaning. These contemporary reports suggest that West Indian Day anniversaries were among the most important public celebrations by black people in Canada during the nineteenth century. Moreover, these annual events are analyzed within a transnational framework. While scholars usually see these gatherings in local or national terms, we examine them within a diasporic context of imperial abolition, American slavery, and international diplomacy, together with the shifting movement of fugitives, free blacks, and ideas of emancipation. Finally, these celebrations are examined for more complicated notions of black identity beyond the familiar paradigms of integration versus separation, double-consciousness, and Christian universalism. It is evident that public commemorations of emancipation in the 1830s were different from those of the 1850s, and that these served as important public displays of changing political identities among Canadians of African descent.

This chapter makes two arguments. An older generation of black settlers born in Canada and located in eastern Ontario pursued a politics of patriotism and loyalty to the British Crown through military service, political

5. Winks, *Blacks in Canada*, 111–12, 146, 214; Silverman, *Unwelcome Guests*, 86, 120, 153; *BAP*, 2:80, 175; Daniel G. Hill, *The Freedom-Seekers: Blacks in Early Canada* (Agincourt: Book Society of Canada, 1981); John R. McKivigan and Jason H. Silverman, "Monarchical Liberty and Republican Slavery: West Indian Emancipation Celebrations in Upstate New York and Canada West," *Afro-Americans in New York Life and History* 10 (January 1986): 14–15.

support for Tory candidates, and patriotic demonstrations. Moreover, annual celebrations every August First served as important public displays of an Anglo-Canadian political identity. This patriotism was symbolized in the social forms of the commemoration: enthusiastic cheering for the British monarchy; the consumption of tea; and attendance at Anglican Church services.

This chapter (and the following) has three major objectives. The first is to examine an important black institution in Canadian history that has been relatively ignored compared to a scholarly preoccupation with race relations. The second goal is to demonstrate the historical specificity of these freedom festivals by showing how the "rite" changed over time and its consequences. It is clear that the public celebration of British abolition reflected some of the burgeoning tensions between an older generation of loyalists and a younger generation of fugitives, especially during the 1850s. These changes and tensions are examined in chapter 5. The third purpose is to provide an international approach to emancipation and slavery challenging national frameworks that have largely shaped previous historical investigations of these questions. It is only through this broader focus that we can begin to unearth the range and extent of black agency around questions of slavery, abolition, and post-emancipation in the modern world. We begin though with a brief account of the making of imperial slavery and its unmaking through colonial emancipation.

UNMAKING IMPERIAL SLAVERY

The early decades of the eighteenth century saw the takeoff of French colonial slavery in the Caribbean colony of St. Domingue and the mainland colonies of Louisiana and New France.[6] The Bourbon state pursued mercantilist policies legally regulating the transoceanic slave trade, plantation production, and the management of enslaved Africans. By mid-century, Louisiana and St. Domingue had become slave societies in contrast to New France, a society with slaves. In 1759, there were 3,604 slaves in New France, of which

---

6. From colonial settlement to 1763, much of eastern Canada was known as New France. Between 1763 and 1841, the British divided the region into Upper Canada (present-day Ontario) and Lower Canada (present-day Quebec). From 1841 until 1867, these were known as Canada West and Canada East respectively. Our focus in this chapter and the next is upon Canada West (Ontario). See *BAP,* 2:xxviii; Rhodes, *Shadd Cary,* 233n15.

1,132 were Africans and the others "Panis." These others hailed from one of the First Nations, the Pawnee Indians. About three-fourths of all slaves were engaged in domestic work, with the rest in agricultural production. Although slavery in New France was less harsh than that practiced in the Caribbean and Louisiana, it was not benevolent enough to deter fugitive escapees. Both Joseph Odel and Peter Lawrence ran away from Nova Scotian slavery in 1792 according to an advertisement seeking their recapture in *The Royal Gazette*. These escapees were ancestral cousins to later generations of fugitives from North American slavery.[7]

As a result of the British defeat of the French in the global Seven Years' War, the Bourbon state ceded its mainland colonies east of the Mississippi to Great Britain. The British colonial slave system in the Caribbean and on the mainland consolidated the system of slavery in Canada. Legal guarantees protecting property rights in slaves were extended to slave owners at least three times between 1763 and 1790. Especially prominent was a 1790 Imperial Act designed to encourage immigration to British North America, providing for free importation of "Negroes, household furniture, utensils of husbandry or clothing." This act, together with migration to the Maritime Provinces as a result of the American War of Independence, resulted in an increase in the black population in British Canada. Some 30,000 "Empire Loyalists" eventually settled in Nova Scotia. Over 3,000 of these were freeborn blacks who chose to settle voluntarily. This was not the case with 1,232 enslaved Africans, who were forced to emigrate with their loyalist owners. Moreover, as Barry Cahill has recently argued, fugitive slaves were *not* black loyalists, since those "who defected to the British [during the Revolutionary War] were seeking refuge from slavery, not from rebellion." Several months after a major slave rebellion had broken out in northern French St. Domingue in August 1791, relocated Africans in Nova Scotia set out for the newly founded British colony of Sierra Leone on the West African coast in search of free lives removed from New World slavery. It is important to emphasize these broader

---

7. Robin Blackburn, *The Making of New World Slavery: From the Baroque to the Modern, 1492–1800* (London: Verso, 1997), chap. 7; Winks, *Blacks in Canada*, chap. 1; *The Royal Gazette and the Nova Scotia Advertiser*, July 3, 1792, reproduced in Hill, *Freedom-Seekers*, 9. For a clear distinction between societies with slaves and slave societies, see Ira Berlin, *Many Thousands Gone: The First Two Centuries of Slavery in North America* (Cambridge, Mass.: Harvard University Press, 1998).

colonial dimensions of the slave and free experience in the late eighteenth-century Atlantic world.[8]

Although British colonialism strengthened slavery in Canada, it remained a colony with slaves rather than a colonial slave society. The absence of natural factors for plantation production (i.e., soil, climate), harsh frontier conditions, the preponderance of domestic slaves, and the lack of a major slaveholding class prevented the development and consolidation of African slavery in Canada. In 1793, the newly appointed lieutenant governor of Upper Canada, Colonel John Graves Simcoe, introduced a bill outlawing the importation of slaves into the colony. One article—"No Negro or other person [Pawnee] who shall come or be brought into this province [Upper Canada] . . . shall be subject to the condition of a slave"—repealed the 1790 law. Although opposed by farmers who worked slaves in the fields and slave traders who profited from slave sales, the legislation passed the Canadian House of Assembly. All those enslaved were unaffected, but those slaves imported would be freed, while all children born after the bill passed were to be liberated when they reached the age of twenty-five years. While this imperial law represented a compromise over slavery and only affected one province, it began the process of gradual abolition. William Osgoode, the chief justice of Lower Canada, drafted the 1793 bill. Ten years later, Osgoode ruled that slavery was inconsistent with British law. His ruling drew upon the Somersett Case of 1772, in which Lord Mansfield had decided that fugitive James Somersett could not be re-enslaved after living in England because English law did not approve of slavery. Although the 1803 decision did not abolish slavery, it freed three hundred enslaved Africans in Lower Canada. This mixture of legislative and judicial action, together with prominent colonial legislation like the legal abolition of the British slave trade (1807) and the Amelioration of Slavery Acts (1823), effectively ended slavery in the British North American provinces. When the Abolition of Slavery Bill was implemented in 1834, its impact was negligible in British Canada, liberating the remaining fifty slaves.[9]

8. Winks, *Blacks in Canada*, chaps. 2 and 3; Walker, *Black Loyalists*, 12, 40, 57; Pulis, *Moving On*, chap. 1; Cahill, "Black Loyalist Myth," 79; Carolyn E. Fick, *The Making of Haiti: The Saint Domingue Revolution from Below* (Knoxville: University of Tennessee Press, 1990).

9. Winks, *Blacks in Canada*, chap. 4; Silverman, *Unwelcome Guests*, chap. 1; William R. Ridell, "The Slave in Upper Canada," *Journal of Negro History* 4 (October 1919): 372–95; *BAP*, 2:4; Hill, *Freedom-Seekers*, chap. 2.

This gradual transition toward abolition in British Canada stood in marked contrast to the expansion of American slavery in the aftermath of the successful struggle for colonial independence. During the 1790s, slavery was expanding in the American South but contracting in the northern United States and British Canada. One could see this pattern clearly in 1793. As part of a nation-building compromise over slavery, the U.S. Congress passed a Fugitive Slave Act that year providing federal support to slaveholders for returning runaway slaves. At the same time, several northern states were sentencing chattel slavery to a slow death: by 1793, for instance, slavery had been legally abolished in Vermont, Massachusetts, Pennsylvania, Rhode Island, and Connecticut. (It should not be forgotten that New York State did not finally terminate slavery until 1827; four hundred slaves were recorded in the 1830 Pennsylvania Census; and some Africans remained enslaved in Connecticut until the 1840s.) Meanwhile, across the border, Governor Simcoe implemented his slave trade bill the same year. These regional differences in the 1790s had become more entrenched by the 1830s. Plantation slavery in the Upper South increasingly gave way to the expansion of cotton and slavery in new southwestern states through the development of a booming internal slave trade. When British abolition was passed in 1833, therefore, slavery was doomed in the British Empire but spreading as part of the new transcontinental American Empire. The two imperial powers clashed over the question of fugitive slaves.[10]

After the passage of British abolition, fugitives from American slavery increasingly sought refuge in the colony of Canada. By 1840, Robin Winks estimates there were 12,000 fugitive slaves living in British Canada. Their status prompted American slaveholder requests for extradition. Recognizing the irrelevance of American fugitive laws in British Canada, U.S. slaveholders tried to use an 1833 British-Canadian extradition act for returning escaped criminals as a means of repatriating fugitive slaves. Three cases involving fugitive escapees from Kentucky, and American requests for their extradition between 1833 and 1837, tested Anglo-American relations. Thorton and Rutha Blackburn were arrested in Detroit, Michigan, under the 1793 Fugitive Slave Act, but were rescued by their supporters and crossed to Canada.

10. *BAP*, 3:26–27, 179; William L. Freehling, *The Road to DisUnion: Secessionists at Bay, 1776–1854* (New York: Oxford University Press, 1990), 502–4; Franklin and Schweninger, *Runaway Slaves*, 160.

Solomon Mosely stole himself and his master's horse, was arrested, and was ordered returned, but a group of antislavery supporters helped him to escape to British Canada. Jesse Happy also stole himself and a horse to aid his escape. These fugitives' thefts were considered instrumental to personal escape by the colonial authorities. As Sir Francis Bond Head, lieutenant governor of Upper Canada, put it in a letter to Lord Glenelg, the colonial secretary in London: "it may be argued that a slave escaping from bondage on his master's horse is a vicious struggle between two parties of which the slave owner is not only the aggressor, but the blackest criminal of the two—it is the case of the dealer in human flesh versus the stealer of horse flesh."

This pattern of fugitive escapes, extradition requests, and colonial denials continued until the Nelson Hackett case in 1842. Hackett, a self-emancipated slave from Arkansas, stole a horse, coat, saddle, and gold watch, as well as himself. Since some of these items were not considered indispensable to his escape, the governor-general ordered Hackett's return for criminal intent according to the 1833 treaty. This was the first time a fugitive had been returned from Canada West. The combination of abolitionist furor and the legal ambiguities of the Hackett case resulted in the passage of the 1842 Webster-Ashburton treaty of extradition. Although some abolitionists feared the new law would create new slave catchers, it appears that no fugitive was extradited from British Canada under the 1842 treaty.[11]

These fugitive cases between 1833 and 1842 highlight three important points concerning the relationship between imperial abolition and American slavery. First, American fugitives deemed British soil safer after the legal abolition of colonial slavery in 1833. Although they were to subsequently encounter racism and exclusion in Canada from European settlers, fugitives were *originally* motivated by their belief in greater liberties under the British flag. As William and Jane Pease pointed out over forty years ago: "If the tales of a Canadian paradise were in part misleading, perhaps it was just as well, for they guided the Negro to a land where the law both promised and gave what in the United States was denied him."[12] Second, British denials

---

11. Winks, *Blacks in Canada*, 168–77; Silverman, *Unwelcome Guests*, 36–44; *BAP*, 2:4–6.

12. Jane H. Pease and William H. Pease, *Black Utopia: Negro Communal Experiments in America* (Madison: State Historical Society of Wisconsin, 1963), 46; Silverman, *Unwelcome Guests*, provides the most persuasive case for racism toward fugitives in Canada.

of American extradition can best be understood within the broader context of an imperial commitment toward abolition and paternal governance. Sir Francis Head's words connote the clearest moral reasoning over the question of slavery. The position of American fugitives in British Canada had already been determined by the *Somersett v. Stewart* case of 1772, together with imperial abolition policies in 1807 and 1833. Slavery was illegal throughout the British Empire; any former slave was instantly free on British soil; and the British Empire was de facto a benevolent organization. (This had been the didactic purpose of official celebrations and watch nights in the British West Indies during the 1830s.) Third, black and white mobs of antislavery activists often proved more important in the freeing of fugitives than either British legal decisions or Anglo-American diplomacy. The Blackburn family and Solomon Mosely were all freed through armed struggle. This collective stance represented a continental means of self-defense and liberation with spatial extensions into the northern United States and Canada West.[13]

This continental expansion also characterized August First commemorations. One of the key questions chapters 4 and 5 seek to answer is: How was it that a law freeing a mere handful of slaves in British Canada provided the basis for one of the largest public commemorations among blacks in Canada from the late 1830s onward? Before tackling this question, however, it is important to sketch out some spatial, temporal, and demographic dimensions of black life in mid-nineteenth-century British Canada. This will provide a useful basis for understanding the origins, nature, and social meaning of August First.

Between 1840 and 1860, the black population in Canada increased fourfold, from 12,000 to around 50,000. This increase largely occurred during the 1850s. The Fugitive Slave Act drove fugitive slaves as well as free blacks into British Canada. According to the Canadian Census of 1861, there were 17,149 black residents in the province of Canada West. This figure might have represented a severe under-count, since recently arrived black inhabitants had reason to be suspicious of officialdom. Many inhabited small towns and villages throughout the province. There were, however, two distinct regional hubs. An older community of black people lived in the lakeshore cities and towns of Toronto, Hamilton, Brantford, St. Catherines, Niagara,

13. Silverman, *Unwelcome Guests,* 37; Winks, *Blacks in Canada,* 169–70. Crowd historians inexplicably continue to ignore these abolitionist "mobs." See Gilje, *Road to Mobocracy.*

and Ancaster on the southern fringes of Lake Ontario. These black folks began serious celebrations of Emancipation Day from the late 1830s onward and are the focus of this chapter. In the aftermath of the Fugitive Slave Act, increasing numbers of fugitives relocated to small settlements and towns in the two counties of Kent and Essex in the western district of Canada West between Detroit and Lake Erie. These towns—Chatham, Raleigh, Harwich, Camden, Amherstburgh, Colchester, Sandwich, and Windsor—contained large percentages of black residents.[14] We examine their August First celebrations during the 1850s and how these differed from those organized in the more easterly district in the following chapter. The central concern of both chapters is the ways in which these commemorations provided public displays of political identities among Canadians of African descent, how these changed, and what they reveal about ideological and political differences among black people in Canada.

LOYALIST RITES

As a result of the American Revolution, between 200,000 and 500,000 Euro-Americans, Native Americans, and African Americans left colonial America and relocated to Canada, England, Africa, Germany, and the Caribbean in one of the largest migrations in the modern Atlantic world. While there has been a great deal of scholarly attention on white loyalists, it was not until the mid-1970s that historians began to examine black loyalists. James W. St. G. Walker argued that fugitive slaves were American loyalists to whom the American Revolution represented a war of independence. Those slaves who flocked to the Union Jack in pursuit of freedom demonstrated their loyalty to the Crown during the American Revolutionary War as well as during the War of 1812. Others have challenged what they describe as the pernicious myth of "Black Loyalists" because of its implicit assumption that slaves were "would-be Tories." According to Barry Cahill, "Slaves chose liberty from slavery, not loyalism, and were only able to do that because the imperial authorities were

---

14. Winks, *Blacks in Canada*, 169, 176, 240; *BAP*, 2:16–19; Alan R. Douglass, *Uppermost Canada: The Western District and the Detroit Frontier, 1800–1850* (Detroit: Wayne State University Press, 2001), 7–8; Barry Noonan, ed., *Blacks in Canada, 1861: Censuses of Ontario, Quebec, and New Brunswick* (Madison: University of Wisconsin Press, 2000), 531, 532, 536, 537, 545.

offering it under the emergency powers provided for in the declaration of martial law."[15]

In contrast to these debates over the revolutionary era, there has been less attention to later generations of black loyalists in Canada. Although some scholars have pointed to an Anglo-Canadian identity among blacks, there is little historical explanation of how and why such an identity emerged.[16] Moreover, there has been no detailed examination of the various ways in which Canadian blacks expressed their identity with British interests. Most important, scholars have ignored the social meaning of patriotism among Canadian-born blacks. The conceptualization of black loyalists offered here is twofold: a tradition of imperial emancipation with roots in the 1770s Anglo-Atlantic world; and immigration to British Canada because of greater prospects and hopes than a society with American slavery. Black loyalists expressed their Anglo-Canadian identity through military service, political participation, and patriotic demonstrations. Their patriotism was paraded annually through well-organized, well-documented, and lucid public expressions of loyalty toward the British Crown. The most important public expression of this identification with British interests occurred every August First through commemorations of British abolition.

Afro-Canadians expressed their loyalty through military service to the British colonial state. There was a long record of this military service at local, regional, and national levels for the British Empire. During the American War of Independence, black men served in several regiments, including the Ethiopian Regiment and the Black Pioneers, as well as the civil branches of the British army. Between the mid-1790s and 1815, Roger Buckley estimates over 30,000 black men served in twelve West India Regiments, with probably twice as many working in an auxiliary capacity. After the creation of the British colony of Sierra Leone in West Africa during the early 1790s, blacks along with whites regularly served in the local militia. Largely created for imperial projects and colonial defense, military service offered financial bounties to free blacks, freedom to slaves, and the promise of land to veterans. According to Crown Land Papers for Upper Canada in 1826 and 1828,

---

15. Pulis, *Moving On*, xiii; Walker, *Black Loyalists*, 1–17, 389; Rhodes, *Shadd Cary*, 29; Cahill, "Black Loyalist Myth," 83, 86–87.

16. *BAP*, 2:345; Silverman, *Unwelcome Guests*, 35–36.

"tickets of location to men of color for lots on Wilberforce Street (Township of Medonte)" were issued to fifteen black ex-servicemen.[17]

Black soldiers played an especially important role in defending British Canada. In December 1837, Upper Canada political leader William Lyon Mackenzie led an independence movement against British colonial rule. Within a month, nearly a thousand black men had volunteered to serve the Crown. Governor Head wrote: "They hastened as volunteers in wagon-loads to the Niagara frontier to beg from me permission that in the intended attack upon Navy Island they might be permitted to form the forlorn hope." Black men in Chatham formed their own militia from 1837 through 1843. Eventually, five black companies were authorized, although none reached full strength. After the independence revolt was suppressed in 1838, these black units remained in uniform. Captain Alexander MacDonald's company from Chatham worked on the Cayuga road from Niagara Falls to Simcoe. Disputes broke out between the troops and white civilians in Chatham, Chippewa, Hamilton, and St. Catherines. According to the local press, the whites rejoiced at the removal of the troops, to whom they ascribed "a great deal of mischief, [and] rioting." It is not unlikely that white civilians, after the insurrection had been quelled and they felt safe, quickly became intolerant of local black military power. Over the course of 1842–43, these troops were removed from the area to the Welland Canal to keep the peace between feuding immigrant Catholic and Protestant Irish workers. After the canal was opened in June 1850, the militias were officially disbanded, but soldiers stayed around. The editor of the *Provincial Freeman* reported "we frequently meet colored men who are pensioners." Also, veterans often settled throughout the Niagara region, where they participated in the self-defense and rescue of fugitive slaves from the United States.[18]

Black soldiers publicly displayed their patriotism at August First anniversaries. At the West India Day meeting in Toronto in 1839, Philadelphia

17. Pulis, *Moving On*, chap. I; Roger Norman Buckley, *The British Army in the West Indies: Society and the Military in the Revolutionary Age* (Gainesville: University Press of Florida, 1998); Craton, *Testing the Chains*, 169–70; Walker, *Black Loyalists*, 192, 288, 388, 339; Hill, *Freedom-Seekers*, 74–75.

18. Silverman, *Unwelcome Guests*, 35, 50; Winks, *Blacks of Canada*, 151–52; *Hamilton Argus*, August 29, 1842, and the *Chatham Journal*, January 22, April 23, 1842, in Robin W. Winks Collection, Reel 4; Hill, *Freedom-Seekers*, 118–25.

Lutheran clergyman Jehu Jones observed "a regiment composed entirely of colored men," led by white officers. "Great confidence is reposed in this regiment," the visiting minister added, "and they have the most important post, in consequence of their acknowledged loyalty to the British Crown." Although unnamed, this regiment was probably one of the five black regiments mobilized to quell McKenzie's revolt. Two years later, the regiment made the decision to march during the Toronto parade. Wilson R. Abbott, a prominent black citizen who helped to organize the event, had also served in the militia during the 1837 rebellion.[19]

The Emancipation Day celebration held at the militia parade ground at Chatham, on August 4, 1842, also afforded a public expression of patriotism through military service. Residents were awakened at dawn by a twenty-one-gun salute. A company of a hundred black soldiers marched through the town. They attended a dinner "beneath an arbor of boughs sixty feet long," followed by speeches. Josiah Jones gave the keynote address. Born in Tennessee in 1816, Jones had moved to Chatham, becoming a farmer, member of a Baptist church, and militiaman. He began by expressing his gratitude at the large assembly gathered to celebrate this "glorious day of liberty." He then reminded his audience that the British government had "emptied their Coffers of Twenty millions of Pounds" to free "our foreign friends." Such an act was unforgettable and "our gratitude shall be manifested on every suitable occasion." We are known "to be true British subjects and all of the most loyal kind." The enslaved of the South, "the tigers," only need to hear the roar of John Bull and they "would burst in sunder their prison house, and sweep with the bosom of destruction, the enemies of liberty and of humanity." The celebration concluded with an evening dance at the military barracks.[20]

This enthusiasm by black men in Canada West for military service continued into the 1850s. The Crimean War of 1854–56 saw colonial Britain allied with colonial France to support the ramshackle Ottoman Empire as a bulwark against Russian imperial designs. On June 23, 1855, the black

19. *BAP,* 2:76–83, 304; Hill, *Freedom-Seekers,* 183.

20. *Chatham Journal,* August 6, 1842, in *BAP,* 2:95–96; Hill, *Freedom-Seekers,* 182–83. This type of link between Southern slaves ("tigers") and British imperial might ("John Bull") suggests that Southern slaveholders were not totally paranoid about the destabilizing impact of British emancipation on their own interests.

community in Chatham, led by Isaac D. Shadd, Delaware freeborn and subscription agent for the *Provincial Freeman*, and Harvey C. Jackson, former coach driver and antislavery activist, held a "Mass Meeting" at the First Baptist Church. They passed four resolutions expressing their loyalty to the British Crown and readiness to fight on its behalf. The first served to "make known our willingness and determination to assist in arresting the usurpations of Russia or any other power." Having the "privilege of a home on British Territory," they further resolved to "aid in any and every case" that would be "serviceable." Furthermore, the assembly expressed their deep sympathies "in the loss of those brave and gallant troops" who had fought Russian oppression. The final resolution reminded each member of the audience of "his duty to stand in defense of the Government that shields him from oppression."[21]

One good example of this military service was the formation of the Queen Victoria's Rifle Guards, a volunteer black militia company. Philadelphia-born Robert Jones considered immigrating to Liberia during the mid-1850s, but ended up settling in Hamilton, Canada West. He worked as a barber and assisted recently escaped slaves. In order to elevate "the condition of the colored people in Canada," Jones organized a military company. With the support of regular army officers Major J. T. Gilepon and Sir Allan McNab, Jones helped write a petition to the Governor General Sir Edmund Walker Head. His request was granted and the company was organized. Mr. Howard was elected captain. The positions of first lieutenant and ensign were passed to John Henry Hill and his uncle Hezekiah Hill. Both were fugitive slaves from Petersburg, Virginia. Robert Jones was made first sergeant.[22]

The organization of this company highlights several important issues. Much like black militias formed in the United States during the 1850s, it represented independent organization. Unlike such black militias, however, this company had the official sanction of the colonial state. Moreover, the personnel were fugitives who had self-emancipated themselves and decided upon armed self-defense. Indeed, this was made easier by the juxtaposition of imperial emancipation with American slavery.[23]

21. Judd, *Empire*, 94; *PF*, June 30, 1855, in *BAP*, 2:321.

22. Robert Jones to William Still, August 9, 1856, in *BAP*, 2:345–48.

23. The role and function of black militias in the Atlantic world is explored in chap. 6.

Along with military service, blacks in Canada demonstrated their Anglo-American identity through local participation in Canadian politics. From the 1830s through the 1850s, black voters consistently supported Tories and Conservatives in local and provincial elections. In August 1833, English emigrant John Prince arrived in Sandwich with his family and servants. In the general election of 1836, he was returned as politician for Essex County. During the outbreak of Mackenzie's Rebellion the following year, he was appointed colonel and became quite notorious after the battle of Windsor for executing prisoners, some of whom had killed a black Canadian. Over the next two decades, black voters in Kent and Essex counties regularly supported Col. Prince in local elections. They also held their annual celebration of West Indian Day emancipation on his Sandwich estate. By the mid-1850s, however, the political relationship had soured. Col. Prince's endorsement of racist Conservative politics in reaction to the influx of fugitive slaves into the region served to alienate many black voters.[24]

Black support for Conservative politics was especially prominent in the eastern lakeshore district. The colored citizens of Hamilton applied to the local Board of Police to protest their exclusion from public schools even though they paid taxes. Since no redress was forthcoming, they wrote a petition to the governor dated October 15, 1843. They argued that this type of discrimination was not even practiced in the United States: "for the children of color go to the Public Schools together with the white children, more especially in Philadelphia, and I thought there was not a man to be known by his colour under the British flag, and we left the United States because we were in hopes that prejudice was not in this land, and came to live under your Government."[25] Conservative support was especially prominent in Toronto, where the mayor relied on the black vote. During the early 1840s, the mayor and city council received several petitions signed by scores of prominent black citizens requesting that traveling players and circus actors from the United States be prevented from singing "Jim Crow" songs and racist portrayals of "other Negro characters." In the past, such performances had ridiculed the "African character," resulting in "many broils and suits between the white and

24. Winks, *Blacks in Canada*, 214–15; Robin W. Winks Collection, Reel 10; *BAP*, 2:322, 382.

25. "Petition of the Coloured People of Hamilton, Oct. 15, 1843," in Robin W. Winks Collection, Reel 5. See also "Petition from the Negroes in the Town of Simcoe, December 12, 1851."

colored inhabitants of this city." Apparently the show went on but without the negative songs in order to "to save the feelings of the gentlemen of color" who supported the city administration. One of those colored gentlemen was Virginia-born businessman and former militia member Wilson Ruffin Abbott. In late 1847, Abbott and forty-five other prominent black citizens from Toronto sent a letter to the attorney general of Canada East expressing thanks for support from American abolitionists. They introduced themselves as "loyal and dutiful subjects of her Majesty's just and powerful government." Four years later, Abbot was to be one of the founding committee members of Canada's major abolition society.[26]

It is worth noting that black Canadians were acting politically on a regular basis at the same time that civil rights and the ballot were being withdrawn from African Americans in the Northern U.S. states. By 1840, some 93 percent of the black populace lived in states that had legally or practically excluded them from the suffrage. In New Jersey, Pennsylvania, and Connecticut, they were disenfranchised after having once had the right to vote. By 1860, only Maine, New Hampshire, Vermont, and Massachusetts allowed black men the suffrage; New York, Ohio, and Michigan also allowed the black vote, but with restrictions. These limited political rights at the state level were confirmed through the Supreme Court ruling on the Dred Scott case in 1857 denying Americans of African descent civil rights under the U.S. Constitution.[27]

Along with military service and political participation, black Canadians regularly demonstrated their Anglo-American identity through public displays of patriotism. August First was to become the most vivid public demonstration of this loyalist patriotism toward Great Britain. It started off in a fairly moderate fashion with several small commemorations being held in Montreal, St. Catherines, and London in 1834 and 1835.[28] The complete termination of the apprenticeship system together with the defeat of McKenzie's Rebellion in 1838, however, appears to have encouraged more elaborate celebrations. Philadelphia clergyman Jones, on a visit to Toronto during the summer of 1839, provided a detailed account of that city's Emancipation Day. The event was organized by some of Toronto's black elite, including Method-

26. Robin W. Winks Collection, Reel 4; Winks, *Blacks in Canada*, 149–50; *BAP*, 2:303–4; *VF*, March 12, 1851.

27. Litwack, *North of Slavery*, 75; Horton and Horton, *Hope of Liberty*, 169, 258–59.

28. According to the *L*, September 20, 1834, an Emancipation Day festival was observed in Montreal by "the few sons of Africa" there.

ist minister William H. Edwards and other members of the city's Abolition Society, which had been formed in 1833. Although Rev. Edwards was the only one mentioned by name, it is fair to assume that many of those who had gathered several months earlier, in January 1838, to protest American slavery, thank Britain for abolition, and promote Canada as Canaan, either helped to organize or participated in the 1839 celebration. These included barber and Baptist minister Stephen Dutton; dyer and antislavery activist William Augustus; bootmaker and church trustee Mathew B. Truss; veteran, barber, and abolitionist William Hickman; baker and local leader Richard Burke; and businessman and abolitionist George Brown. The latter was to become quite prominent in leading protests against racist theater productions in Toronto during the early 1840s.[29]

The day began at 11:00 A.M. with a sermon in Westly Chapel, Hospital Street, delivered by Reverend William Miller of Philadelphia, a prominent Methodist, Freemason, and abolitionist. According to Rev. Jones, "his subject was sublime, full of thrilling interest, not only to the loyal subjects of Toronto, but to Britons everywhere." After the prayer, there was a procession to the recently constructed city hall at Front and Jarvis streets. At 2:00 P.M., Reverend Henry James Grasett, the curate of the St. James Anglican Church in Toronto, "delivered an eloquent discourse on British West Indian Emancipation." (The summer before, Grasett's fellow Anglican clergyman, Rev. Brathwaite, had delivered a similar uplifting thanksgiving address to former apprentices at Barrouallie, St. Vincent, in the British Caribbean.) The parade reassembled and marched to the Commercial Hotel, also on Front Street, "where the rooms were handsomely decorated, with evergreens and the British flag, beautifully unfurled, in token of protection to the oppressed." Under this spectacular canopy of loyalist images and symbols, the celebrants partook of "a superb dinner," after which the "Queen and Royal Family's health" was drunk to and cheered. The event ended "without the slightest accident or disorder" to mar Rev. Jones's "first impressions under the British Crown."[30]

Although the day was officially over, Rev. Jones was invited to a tea party organized by the ladies of Toronto "in honor of the day." Originating as a courtly ritual in the late seventeenth century, the drinking of tea had become

29. *CA*, September 14, 1839, in *BAP*, 2:76–83; Hill, *Freedom-Seekers*, 79.

30. Ibid. Compare this Toronto Emancipation Day banquet with those held on planter estates in the British West Indies.

a symbol of British imperial power and popular consumption a century later. By the time of the 1839 celebration, the drinking of tea had become firmly entrenched as a British "cultural habit." After this social engagement, Jones returned to his lodgings "to contemplate on the magnanimity of the British nation, who under God, had given liberty to all her slaves."[31]

We, too, might reflect on this 1839 commemoration and its social meaning. Toronto's black elite organized a major Emancipation Day celebration to demonstrate their fidelity to the British Crown. Moreover, the urban procession, the places visited, and the visual aids publicly expressed this loyal identity. Indeed, even though Rev. Jones's account reveals his desire to portray Canada in the best possible light to encourage black emigration, it is clear that this was not the point of the actual commemoration itself. Rather, the constant evocation of monarch, nation, flag, and Church points to the public expression of an Anglo-American identity by blacks in Canada at precisely the moment when British abolition, an anti-colonial revolt, and expanding American slavery were most pronounced.[32]

Although these patriotic demonstrations by black loyalists continued into the 1850s, they were also transformed by events in the United States and the continental expansion of antislavery mobilization. Six months after the passage of the Fugitive Slave Act, the first major antislavery organization was formed in British Canada. In February 1851, the Anti-Slavery Society of Canada (ASSC) was formed at City Hall, Toronto. According to one newspaper report, the "meeting was called to enable the citizens of Toronto to enter their protest against the manifold and unspeakable iniquities of Slavery, and a very interesting and effective demonstration it certainly was."

These local citizens included Protestant clergy, businessmen, and professionals, and prominent black abolitionists such as Abbott and Brown. Several

31. James Walvin, *Fruits of Empire: Exotic Produce and British Taste, 1660–1800* (New York: New York University Press, 1997), chap. 2. My grandmother personified this cultural habit with her insistence that tackling a problem is best begun with drinking a cup of tea. She remained oblivious of tea's bitter colonial roots.

32. This veneration for the *scepter'd isle* recalls John of Gaunt's famous lines in William Shakespeare, *Richard II*, II;I;50: "This blessed plot, this earth, this realm, this England." Compare, for example, black abolitionist William P. Powell's words at an August First in 1861: "What has made that speck of earth, that sea-girt isle and secured for her to the end of time, the fear, wonder and admiration of the whole world, great, glorious and free?" *AA*, August 10, 1861.

resolutions were passed demanding slavery's immediate extinction, condemning the Fugitive Slave Act, and praising American abolitionists. The purpose of the meeting was expressed in the fourth resolution: "That a society be formed called 'the Anti-Slavery Society of Canada,' the object of which shall be to aid in the extinction of Slavery, *all over the world,* by means exclusively lawful and peaceable, moral and religious." Its auxiliary, the Toronto Ladies' Association for the Relief of Destitute Colored Fugitives, was formed in April 1851. By year's end, the two groups had raised $1,108 for fugitive relief efforts, while the Ladies' Association had assisted over a hundred black families. Over the next two years, the ASSC became a national organization with auxiliary branches in Kingston, Hamilton, London, and St. Catherines around southern Lake Ontario.[33]

One of the most successful agents of the new organization was Samuel R. Ward. Slave-born on October 17, 1817, the Wards fled north, where the son attended school and became a teacher. On August 1, 1838, young Samuel addressed a prayer meeting at the Colored Methodist Church in Newark, New Jersey, in commemoration of emancipation in the British West Indies colonies. After marriage to Emily Reynolds of New York and gaining license to preach in the Congregational Church, Ward spent the 1840s preaching, engaging in antislavery activities, and writing. As a member of the Syracuse Vigilance Committee, Ward helped rescue fugitive slave William "Jerry" McHenry from federal officers in October 1851. To escape possible arrest and imprisonment for resisting the 1850 Fugitive Slave Act, Ward and his family relocated to the relative safety of Toronto, British Canada. In Toronto, Ward continued his antislavery activities, joining the executive committee of the ASSC in late 1851. The following year, on behalf of the ASSC, Ward was sent on a speaking tour throughout Canada West. "While in this service," Ward later wrote in his autobiography,

> it was my duty to travel all over the country, giving facts touching American slavery, seeking to awaken an interest against slavery in Canada, asking aid and kindness towards such fugitives as needed help, forming auxiliary societies, seeking to show the influence correct sentiment might have upon the adjoining States, and doing all

---

33. *VF,* March 12, 1851; *BAP,* 2:165, 222–23; Winks, *Blacks in Canada,* 253–57. The italics are mine.

TABLE 4.1. Loyalist August First, 1839–1861

1838	Toronto
	London
	Windsor
	Prince Estate, Sandwich
1839	Toronto
	London
	Windsor
	Prince Estate, Sandwich
1841	Toronto
	London
	Windsor
	Prince Estate, Sandwich
1842	Toronto
	London
	Windsor
	Prince Estate, Sandwich
	Militia Parade Grounds, Chatham
1843	Toronto
	London
	Windsor
	Prince Estate, Sandwich
1844	Toronto
	London
	Windsor
	Prince Estate, Sandwich
	Drummond Hill, Niagara
1845–50	Toronto
	London
	Windsor
	Prince Estate, Sandwich
1851	Toronto
	London
	Prince Estate, Sandwich
	Chatham
1852	Toronto

(continued)

	London
	Windsor
	Prince Estate, Sandwich
	Hamilton
1853	Toronto
	London
	Windsor
	Prince Estate, Sandwich
1854	Toronto
	London
	Windsor
	Prince Estate, Sandwich
	Chatham
1855	London
	Chatham
	Hamilton
	Toronto
	Windsor
	Prince Estate, Sandwich
1856	Toronto
	Chatham
	London
	Windsor
	Prince Estate, Sandwich
1857	Hamilton
	London
	Windsor
	Chatham
1858	Hamilton
	Toronto
	Windsor
	London
1859	Toronto
	Clairmont Park, Hamilton
	London
	Kingston

TABLE 4.1. continued

1860	Chatham
	Toronto
1861	Hamilton

Sources: CA, September 14, 1839; *Chatham Journal*, August 6, 1842; *FDP*, August 11, 1854; *DG*, August 3, 1854; August 2, 1856; August 3, 1858; August 2, 1859; August 2, 1860; *HS*, August 6, 1852; August 4, 1854; August 4, 1856; August 3, 1857; August 2, 1858; August 2, 1861; *L*, September 20, 1834; August 20, 1852; August 26, 1859; August 31, 1860; August 23, 1861; *NE*, August 7, 1851; July 29, 1852; *PF*, June 24, July 1, 29, August 5, 12, 19, 26, 1854; June 23, 1855; July 12, 19, 1856; July 25, August 15, 22, 1857; *BAP*, 2:76–83, 95–96, 295–96, 382–85; Kachun, *Festivals of Freedom*, 61–62; McKivigan and Silverman, "Monarchical Liberty," 9; Riddell, "Interesting Notes," 195–98; Silverman, *Unwelcome Guests*, 86; Walton, "Blacks in Buxton and Chatham," 73; Winks, *Blacks in Canada*, 111–12, 214; Robin W. Winks Collection, Reels 4, 10.

that could be done, by advice, encouragement, and any other means, to promote the development, the progress, all the best moral and material interests, of the coloured people.

It was this work that led to the organization of several ASSC branches in Hamilton, Windsor, and Kingston.[34]

Moreover, this period saw the emergence of an antislavery press for the first time in British Canada. Although many Canadian newspapers refused to endorse abolitionism, this was not the case with the *Toronto Globe*, edited by Scottish emigrant George Brown. Established in 1844, the *Toronto Globe* was soon to become the most influential newspaper in British Canada. It also increasingly attacked American slavery with editorials on the evils of slavery

34. Samuel Ringgold Ward, *Autobiography of a Fugitive Negro: His Anti-Slavery Labours in the United States, Canada and England* (London: John Snow, 1855); Ronald K. Burke, *Samuel Ringgold Ward, Christian Abolitionist* (New York: Garland, 1995); *BAP*, 2:292. The quote comes from p. 162 in the electronic version of Ward's *Autobiography*.

and the problems of fugitives in Canada West. As Brown reminded his readers in reporting an August First in Toronto:

> Most other civilized nations have followed the example thus nobly set them, and have issued the decree that the "slave shall go free." To the disgrace of the United States, they now stand almost alone in seeking to continue and perpetuate this horrid, inhuman, God-delaying system. Light will, however, doubtless, break in also upon this yet benighted Land, and the day cannot be far distant, when, either by physical or moral force, the American slave shall stand up, possessed of all those inalienable rights with which he has been endowed by his Creator, even life, liberty, and the pursuit of happiness.[35]

In March 1854, the *Provincial Freeman* began regular weekly publication from Toronto under the nominal editorship of Samuel Ward. With Ward in the United Kingdom from 1853 through 1855, the day-to-day running of the *Provincial Freeman* fell to Mary Ann Shadd. Free-born in Wilmington, she became a teacher in black schools in the mid-Atlantic region. In 1851, Shadd moved to Windsor, where she opened a school for black children. The following year she published *A Plea for Emigration or, Notes of Canada West* which, in the words of Shadd's foremost biographer, "was an unabashed propaganda tract that exaggerated the benefits of the Canadian haven while ignoring many endemic problems." From its founding, the *Provincial Freeman* was dedicated to antislavery, temperance, and educational reform. Many readers addressed their letters to the editor, "Dear Madam." In 1855, the newspaper relocated to Chatham in western Ontario.[36]

It was through the pages of the *Provincial Freeman* that readers first encountered advertisements for the August First celebration of 1854. On June 13, a large meeting of black residents was held in the First Baptist Chapel on Queen Street in Toronto. The strikingly named Charles Freeman served as secretary, while Providence-born activist and ASSC office agent Reverend J. B. Smith chaired the meeting. They passed several resolutions. One was to "celebrate that glorious event . . . when the British nation did honour itself and justice

35. *PF*, August 12, 1854; *DG*, August 3, 1854.
36. *BAP*, 2:192, 216, 237; Rhodes, *Shadd Cary*, 35, 43–44.

to 800,000 of her Colored Subjects." They also resolved to convene on August 1 at 5:00 A.M. for a thanksgiving service at the Second Wesleyan Chapel on Richmond Street. They agreed to meet at 9:00 A.M. at Government House on King Street, and meet up with visiting friends from Hamilton. The service was to be held at St. James Cathedral, after which there would be a procession through the principal streets to government grounds for a dinner and addresses. A soiree and fireworks would end the day. The management committee included several prominent black citizens of the city: Chairman J. Harper; saw factory owner Thomas W. F. Smallwood; and billsticker and provisions provider William H. Harris. It is important to note the extent of these preparations. They reflected an established black elite who recognized the public significance of this event. This event, they agreed, would be "more imposing than has ever been done heretofore." The stated objective was to attract a "large gathering of the friends from all parts of the country and the States." The undeclared one was to trumpet their own leadership.[37]

The celebration passed off much as it had been advertised in the press. The inhabitants of Hamilton took a short trip across Lake Ontario on the sailing ship the *Arabian*. They were welcomed to Toronto by President Smallwood. In his brief address, he castigated the "disloyal sentiments" of those who thought "because we did not achieve it ourselves, it is disgraceful for us to celebrate this day." After the sermon by Rev. Grasett, the celebrants "paraded through the principal streets" and three hundred men, women, and children sat down to a "sumptuous dinner." Three cheers were given to the queen, after which local white attorney G. Dupont Wells was requested to read an address to the queen. The monarch was thanked for the "boon" of freedom on behalf of all the "colored inhabitants of Canada." Furthermore, these subjects were "at your service." Moreover, only loyalty was possible from "such a people" in "your mighty dominions" for whom "his chains fall from him." If her colored subjects had any faults, these were due to the "brutalizing cup of slavery," which the "invigorating food of education" would remove. The address concluded with the desire that God "bless your majesty as a Queen, bless you as a wife, bless you as a mother." After the speech, several toasts were made to the queen, the British military, the provincial governor, the *Provincial Freeman*, and the two brass bands. In the evening, a soiree was

37. *PF,* June 24, July 29, 1854; *BAP,* 2:158, 160, 235, 513; Hill, *Freedom-Seekers,* 87.

held at the newly organized Society of Odd-Fellows. After the drinking of tea, there was a grand display of fireworks.[38]

What was the social meaning of this 1854 emancipation celebration in Toronto and how did it compare to past celebrations? There were similar public expressions of patriotic loyalty through thanksgiving, cheers for monarchy, and Anglican services. Indeed, the *Provincial Freeman* reported that "Canadians, red-men, and colored men have within the last three months addressed the Throne, with expressions of loyal attachment to the Queen and Constitution of Great Britain." The emphasis on patriotism and public expression of Anglo-American identity linked the 1854 celebration with earlier ones held at Chatham, Toronto, and elsewhere.

Annual commemorations of British abolition remained an important part of Afro-Canadian life. Members of Toronto's and Hamilton's black communities continued to sail up and down the southern shores of Lake Ontario every August First to celebrate emancipation. The order of the day continued as before, with public processions through the major streets, antislavery speeches, dinner, and a soiree. Many of the same people were involved in the day's proceedings: Smallwood helped with the organization; brass bands and social orders like the Freemasons and the Sons of Temperance marched on a regular basis; and Rev. Grasett continued to bless this divine moment. Moreover, the rites of loyalty were unmistakable through the waving of the Union Jack, the drinking of tea, and cheering the British monarchy. Blacks in Canada continued to assemble every year to celebrate the passage of abolition and to express their gratitude to the British government for this boon of freedom. Although few of them had actually been emancipated, this anniversary became the most important collective public expression of their political identification as Anglo-Americans.[39]

But it must not be forgotten that events of the early 1850s transformed August First celebrations in a number of important ways. The passage of the Fugitive Slave Act in the United States had forced fugitive slaves and free blacks to relocate to British Canada. One significant consequence was the

38. *PF,* August 5, 1854; *Toronto Colonist,* reprinted in *HS,* August 4, 1854; *BAP,* 2:295–96.
39. *PF,* June 23, 1855; May, 17, 1856; August 22, 1857; *HS,* August 4, 1856; August 3, 1857; August 2, 1858; *DG,* August 2, 1856; August 3, 1858; August 2, 1859.

continental expansion of fugitive movement, together with antislavery mobilization through new organizations, new institutions, and participation by
the print media. In addition, the celebration of emancipation was now linked
to the overthrow of American slavery. What had previously been a public
commemoration of patriotism was transformed into a mobilization against a
continental and global problem. Moreover, a Toronto-based elite assumed the
leadership of all black people in Canada, delivering the "Address to Queen
Victoria" on behalf of all the "colored inhabitants of Canada." They con-
gratulated themselves that "everything passed off quietly, and, we trust, satis-
factorily to all concerned."[40] This was class leadership through the familiar
politics of respectability. This elaborate celebration was a vindication of black
middle-class leadership. It was also very similar to the actions of black elites in
the United States and in parts of the British Caribbean, who sought to carve
August First celebrations in their own image. Most important, this Afro-
Canadian loyalist elite found it necessary to be proud, and even loud, because
it faced a challenge to its leadership emanating from a new generation of fugitive slaves. It is to these fugitives, their remarkable antislavery mobilization,
and their different August First in southwestern Ontario, that we now turn.

40. *PF,* August 5, 12, 1854.

Chapter 5
Fugitive Slaves in Canada West

While we shall rejoice at the noble act of the British Government in letting "the oppressed" of our
race go free and with thousands of self-emancipated ones *[my emphasis] now protected*
in the enjoyment of liberty on the Queen's soil—let us not forget to sympathize with and
labor for the emancipation of the three millions and a half of our enslaved countrymen
who are tyrannically held to labor by the American despots.
Voice of the Fugitive, *July 30, 1851*

As a result of the passage of the Fugitive Slave Act in 1850 in the United States, many fugitive slaves and free blacks left the Northern states for the comparative safety of British Canada. It has been estimated that about three thousand fugitives relocated in the months immediately following ratification of the law. Fugitive slaves like Anthony Hollingsworth, Daniel Lockhart, Fred Wilkins, and Jerry McHenry, all of whom had been rescued from American slave catchers, also relocated to Canada. Those who aided and abetted their escape, like Samuel Ward and John Lisle, also moved to Canada to avoid federal prosecution. Furthermore, numerous fugitives worked their way via the Underground Railroad through the Midwestern states of Ohio, Illinois, and Michigan into the southwestern part of Canada West. This region bordering on the Detroit River and Lake St. Clair contained the counties of Essex and Kent. Many towns in the area—Windsor, Sandwich, and Amherstburg—saw a large increase in their black populace. Scholars estimate there were between 40,000 and 60,000 people of African descent living in British Canada by 1860, with some historians claiming a populace of over 100,000. Most of these people resided in Canada West, and most arrived during the 1850s.[1]

1. Noonan, *Blacks in Canada*, 531; Winks, *Blacks in Canada*, 233–40; Blackett, "Freedom," 121–22; Jason H. Silverman, "The American Fugitive Slave in Canada: Myths and Realities," *Southern Studies* (Fall 1980): 171; Fred Landon, "Amherstburg, Terminus of the Underground Railroad," *Journal of Negro History* 10, no. 1 (January 1925): 1–9; Fred Landon, "The Negro Migration to Canada after the Passing of the Fugitive Slave Act," *Journal of Negro History* 5, no. 1 (January 1920): 22; *BAP*, 2:3.

Historians have long debated this relocation of American fugitives. An older view critical of American slavery argued that Canada served as Canaan for escaped slaves. Others reject this notion of a promised land, and argue that the coming of American fugitives caused a rise in racism among white Canadians. There has also been vigorous debate over the actual numbers of fugitives who relocated to British Canada, with some scholars pointing to the propaganda purposes of inflated numbers to encourage further immigration. Finally, some scholars of the African American antebellum experience see fugitives primarily as refugees from the United States. They argue that Canada West served simply as a temporary refuge for black Americans awaiting the right conditions before they returned to their beloved homeland.[2]

The focus in this chapter is different. Debating Canadian racism and fugitive numbers can reduce black people to passive objects of the historical process. In contrast, we examine fugitives as self-emancipating actors engaged in seizing their own freedom. While grateful for the "Queen's free soil," they were neither former slaves to whom freedom had been legally granted by a benevolent state (Great Britain), nor followers of American abolitionists who maintained that slaves should await their deliverance through patience and humility (Garrisonians). They were, in the words of an editorial from their major press organ *Voice of the Fugitive* quoted in the epigraph to this chapter, "self-emancipated ones." Their mass escape provided the basis for the continental expansion of antislavery mobilization. Moreover, this chapter challenges the notion that fugitives from American slavery viewed British Canada as a temporary refuge because of a fixed national identity. This era saw the political expansion of the slave power, the civil exclusion of people of African descent in the United States, mass fugitive flight, and intra-racial tensions among black people. Such factors were hardly conducive to one national identity. Finally, racial attitudes and leadership squabbles are deemed less important than the rise and development of regional and ideological differences among people of African descent in Canada during the 1850s.

2. Much of Landon's work reflects this Canada-as-Canaan view. For its refutation, see Silverman, *Unwelcome Guests.* For the numbers debate, see Winks, *Blacks in Canada,* chap. 6; Rhodes, *Shadd Cary,* 31. For fugitives as refugees, see Horton and Horton, *Hope of Liberty,* 199; Kachun, *Festivals of Freedom,* 59, 61, 77; Pease and Pease, *Black Utopia,* 78. On the other hand, there is an important tradition of Canada serving as a haven for fugitives from American slavery to fugitives from U.S. military conscription.

It is argued here that emancipation meant something fundamentally different to fugitives because they had once been enslaved. The process of self-emancipation shaped the organizations and agenda of these fugitives. August First celebrations represented public expressions of this independent antislavery mobilization, organizational structures, and public politics. Its consequence was a constant challenge to American slavery.

THE POLITICS OF SELF-EMANCIPATION

One of the most important consequences of the fugitive exodus to Canada West was the continental expansion of antislavery mobilization. This was evident with the founding of a national antislavery organization (the ASSC) in Toronto in early 1851. But this mobilization was also very pronounced in the region of western Ontario, where many fugitives ended up relocating. Over a thirteenth-month period between January 1851 and February 1852, these fugitives played a central role in the establishment of an antislavery newspaper, a major black convention, and a new organization. One of the key individuals involved in these developments was American fugitive Henry Bibb.

Bibb was born in Shelby County, Kentucky, in May 1815, to enslaved mother Mildred Jackson and slaveholder James Bibb. As a youth, he was separated from his mother, and endured several harsh periods as a hired slave. Of this period he later wrote: "I was a wretched slave, compelled to work under the lash without wages and often without clothes enough to hide my nakedness." In 1834, he married Malinda, an enslaved woman, and they had one child, Mary Francis. After several unsuccessful escape attempts and forced returns to Kentucky between 1837 and 1841, Bibb made his final successful bid for freedom and settled in Detroit, Michigan. He attempted to find his family for the next three years, but stopped after finding out they had been sold and Malinda had become the mistress of her new owner. Bibb threw himself into antislavery work and became quite prominent. In 1848, he married Mary Miles, a free black woman and teacher involved in the Boston abolitionist movement. The following year, he published *Narrative of Life and Adventures of Henry Bibb, An American Slave.* After the passage of the Fugitive Slave Act, the Bibbs crossed into British Canada and settled in Sandwich.[3]

3. Henry Bibb, *Narrative of the Life and Adventures of Henry Bibb: An American Slave, Written by Himself* (Documenting the American South, http://docsouth.unc.edu/neh/bibb/menu.html); *BAP*, 2:109–10; Hilda A. Hill, "Henry Bibb, the Colonizer," *Negro History Bulletin* (n.d.): 148; Landon, "Henry Bibb,"; Rhodes, *Shadd Cary*, 34–35.

It was from this small town in western Ontario that Henry and Mary established the *Voice of the Fugitive,* beginning publication on January 1, 1851. This bimonthly newspaper called for the abolition of American slavery, temperance, educational reform, agricultural development, and immigration to British Canada. It published numerous articles on American fugitive cases, abolitionist meetings in the United States and Canada West, and post-emancipation conditions in the Caribbean. It also advertised and reported August First celebrations, along with articles on temperance and moral reform, together with advertisements for small businesses, including confectioners, boarding houses, clothiers, and barbers. Within one year, the *Voice of the Fugitive* claimed over a thousand paid subscribers. Many readers in British Canada first learned about major fugitives cases, like the "Shadrach" rescue in Boston and the Christiana "riot" in Pennsylvania, from the pages of this newspaper. The same journal played an important role in informing readers in the United States about the formation of antislavery organizations, the establishment and welfare of black communal settlements, and Anglo-Canadian politics. Moreover, the *Voice of the Fugitive* listed selling agents throughout Canada West, as well as in Michigan, Massachusetts, New Jersey, New York, New Hampshire, Ohio, and Pennsylvania. Martin Delaney was the Pittsburgh correspondent; James T. Holly was the agent for Burlington, Vermont. Its reach even extended to the United Kingdom: both Henry Highland Garnet and James W. C. Pennington corresponded from London.[4]

There is general agreement among scholars about the importance of the *Voice of the Fugitive.* Apart from being the first antislavery newspaper established in Canada, it also proved to be more popular than the *Provincial Freeman* during its comet-like existence between early 1851 and late 1853.[5] There were, however, several other significant and often overlooked features about the newspaper. It was, first and foremost, a newspaper founded by a fugitive and primarily dedicated to the interests of fugitive slaves in British Canada as well as the United States. This made it a rather unique black newspaper in

4. *VF,* January–December 1851; July 30, 1851, for list of agents; *BAP,* 2:111–12; Rhodes, *Shadd Cary,* 35; Roger W. Hite, "Voice of a Fugitive: Henry Bibb and Ante-bellum Black Separatism," *Journal of Black Studies* 4, no. 3 (March 1974): 274; Winks, *Blacks in Canada,* 253–57.

5. The metaphor is apt. The press offices of the *VF* were mysteriously consumed by fire in October 1853. See *BAP,* 2:112.

North America. Second, it is hard to read its columns and not be struck by the editor's insistence on self-defense, militant action, and self-determination by and for people of color. In its February 26, 1851, edition, the *Voice of the Fugitive* reported on the "kidnapping" of "Bennel" and "Tamor Williams," but also noted the armed self-defense of fugitives by black clothier James Scott and journalist E. Wright in Boston. It further reported "a thoroughly organized and armed military association is to be formed here [Boston] and called the liberty league." In one edition from early April 1851, the newspaper reprinted an extract from the *Commonwealth* on the mobilization of several hundred fugitives in New Bedford to resist federal agents under the headline: "COLORED POPULATION WIDE AWAKE!" This focus on self-emancipation no doubt drew from Henry Bibb's own refusal to remain enslaved and his multiple attempts to leave the American prison of slavery. Indeed, below the engraving of Bibb on the frontispiece of his autobiography, there is a picture of a fugitive in flight. This image, and its description, are often ignored by scholars who simply reproduce the engraving.[6]

Finally, the *Voice of the Fugitive* was an antislavery newspaper with vast scope. Like many newspapers, it was very influential locally. It appears, however, to have had limited influence in eastern Ontario and the headquarters of black loyalists. In early 1853, American abolitionist Frederick Douglass estimated "only fifteen copies of it [*Voice of the Fugitive*] are taken in Toronto, and one copy in Hamilton."[7] On the other hand, it was a transnational newspaper. Its content, editorials, columnists, and readership embraced British Canada, the United States, the Caribbean, and the United Kingdom. This crossing of national boundaries challenges the usefulness of descriptions of the *Voice of the Fugitive* as simply the "first black newspaper" or the "first antislavery newspaper in Canada."

It was through the pages of the *Voice of the Fugitive* that Henry Bibb called for a North America Convention of Colored People (NACCP) to convene in Toronto during the second week of September 1851. To hold such a meet-

6. *VF,* February 26, April 9 1851. On my preliminary reading through the *VF,* I wrote the following in my notes: "Thus far, I am struck by several things. First, the *VF* is a great source for fugitives. Second, encouraging self-defense and resistance as a duty to God. Third, encouraging emigration."

7. Rhodes, *Shadd Cary,* 77.

ing in the United States "would greatly endanger the liberty of thousands of self-emancipated persons." In contrast, Canada "bids defiance to all fugitive slave laws," while Toronto was a great commercial metropolis and central meeting place. Although the major objects would be brought before the convention, several correspondents informed Bibb what these might be, and he subsequently published them. There were four key items. First, the "immediate and everlasting emancipation of our race from slavery," together with gratitude to Great Britain, "which has so nobly protected us in the enjoyment of liberty." Second, to "become owners and tillers of the soil" through agricultural pursuits and homesteading. Third, to encourage emigration "from the United States, for the settlement of Canada land." Finally, to support "presses only as will faithfully vindicate the rights of our people."[8]

At 10:00 A.M., on Thursday morning, September 11, 1851, fifty-three delegates convened at St. Lawrence Hall, Toronto. Only four of the delegates were not of African descent: of these, John Scoble hailed from the United Kingdom and William Anderson from Jamaica. The majority of thirty-one representatives came from black communities in Canada West. Fifteen delegates attended from the United States, mostly from western New York, the Pittsburgh region of western Pennsylvania, and Ohio. In contrast to previous black conventions, no delegates represented the older African American communities of Boston, New Haven, New York City, and Philadelphia. These NACCP delegates pursued a variety of occupations, including preaching, small businesses, craftsmanship, and professional abolition. Henry Bibb was chosen as chairman pro tem. James D. Tinsley, a Virginia-born fugitive who would later immigrate to the Australian goldfields, was appointed secretary pro tem. It was his minutes that provided the basis for the convention proceedings subsequently published in the *Voice of the Fugitive* for a wider readership in the Anglo-Atlantic world.[9]

After the selection of officials, the appointment of committees, and agreement on the rules of governance, the convention got down to business. Most of this business consisted of reports from representative delegates, speeches and addresses by several delegates, and reports from various committees.

8. *VF,* July 30, 1851. This advertisement for NACCP adjoins an advertisement for an August First celebration to be held in Sandwich.

9. *VF,* September 24, 1851; *BAP,* 2:149–50, 158.

The most important committee was called the business committee. It began with five members. John T. Fisher was a black saloonkeeper in Toronto, who worked with the *Voice of the Fugitive,* pressed for united action against slavery, and called for revolutionary violence against Southern slaveholders. Hiram Wilson, a white New Hampshire-born minister and agent of the AASS, had engaged in black settlement work and antislavery activities in Canada West since 1836. Jabez P. Campbell, free-born in Delaware, had become an African Methodist Episcopal (AME) missionary to New England, and later on sponsored AME conferences in the Caribbean. George Cary, free-born in Virginia, was a businessman who became involved in black settlement work in Dresden, Canada West, and served as an important local leader in western Ontario during the 1850s. Later on, four new members were added to the business committee. William H. Topp was a free-born tailor from Albany who regularly participated in the NBC and was committed to reform activities. John Lisle, a clergyman from Syracuse, was also involved in the NBC, but was forced to flee the United States after the Fugitive Slave Act because of his participation in the McHenry rescue. Henry K. Thomas, a fugitive from Tennessee, went on to become a successful businessman in Buffalo and also worked with the NBC.[10]

It is important to identify these business committee members because they reported the most important resolutions at the NACCP. On the afternoon of the first day, the business committee reported three resolutions. The second expressed gratitude "to her Britannic Majesty's just and powerful Government, for the protection afforded us," being persuaded that Canada West "is, by far, the most desirable place of resort for colored people." The third resolution called for colored settlers to obtain "possession of uncultivated lands." Both were adopted by the delegates. This was not the case with the first resolution. In response to the recent "infamous slave enactment," it entreated "our brethren of the northern and southern states" to move northward. Four American delegates, including Martin R. Delaney, Henry F. Stanton, Payton Harris, and future committee member William H. Top, protested this resolution, considering "it to be impolitic and contrary to our professed policy in opposing the infamous fugitive slave laws, and schemes of American colonization."[11]

10. *BAP,* 2:150, 153, 157, 159–64. There is little information on the other two members, B. F. Young and F. Russel.

11. *BAP,* 2:152–53.

Over the next three days, the delegates discussed numerous resolutions in "spirited debate," including the unchristian nature of American slavery, moral improvement of temperance, education, wealth accumulation, and cultivation of the soil. Earlier calls for immigration to Canada West were repeated. It was resolved "that the convention recommend to the colored people of the U.S. of America, to emigrate to the Canadas instead of going to Africa or the West India Islands, that they, by so doing, may be better able to assist their brethren who are daily flying from American slavery."

This latter resolution emerged in response to attempts by white delegates William Anderson of Jamaica and John Scoble of England to encourage immigration of people of color to the Caribbean and South America. It is not unlikely that many delegates saw such schemes as little more than camouflage for unpopular colonization activities. In any event, the final day witnessed a resolution offered by John Fisher and amended by John Scoble for the creation of a committee of five to consider "the formation of a great league of the colored people of the North and South American continents, and of the West Indies, for the general abolition of slavery, for the protection of the common rights of their brethren throughout the world, and for their social, political and moral elevation." After its unanimous adoption, the convention met briefly in the evening for an address by Dr. Delany, after which the meeting adjourned *sine die*.[12]

The historical significance of the NACCP was several-fold. Although the NBC had been meeting since 1830, this was the first convention formed specifically in response to the American persecution of fugitive slaves. It was the consequence of draconian American law, mass fugitive flight, and political mobilization. Furthermore, it provided the seeds of an alternative black political establishment. Both black and white abolitionist elites in the United States and British Canada claimed to speak for the condition, elevation, and emancipation of the slave. This meeting offered a new challenge to an older leadership. Also, it expressed gratitude to the British Crown solely for its *present protection.* Unlike black loyalists who proudly traced their Anglo-Canadian identity, these fugitives sought the power of the British Empire for its imperial protection to fight against American slavery. This was a major reason for the convention's promotion of immigration to Canada. Finally, it is difficult to ignore the Pan-African dimensions of the NACCP in terms of its formation,

12. *BAP,* 2:153–57.

cross-national delegates, and emigration solutions. While Vincent Harding has termed it a "black government in exile," it instead represented one of the earliest attempts at fashioning an international organization of black people rooted in resistance to slavery and envisioning a new emancipation. Its organizational successors were to be UNIA after World War I, the League of Colored People during the 1930s, and Pan-African Congresses throughout the twentieth century.[13]

In the aftermath of the NACCP meeting, three of the delegates—Henry Bibb, John Fisher, and James Tinsley—issued "An Address to the Colored Inhabitants of North America" that was published in the October 21, 1851, edition of the *Voice of the Fugitive*. As one might expect from a representative address, many of the NACCP's themes and resolutions were repeated: outrage at the Fugitive Slave Act; calls for moral improvement; immigration to Canada, and the like. But there was also a more militant tone to this address anchored in the politics of fugitive self-emancipation. After outlining the unique oppression of "colored inhabitants," the hypocrisy of American Republican slavery, and the nominal freedom of free coloreds in the United States, the address turned to its main theme: abolition was in the hands of the people of color in North America. While grateful to "the true-hearted abolitionists [whites], who have stood by us in the darkest hours of adversity," the manifesto stressed that it is us who should be "standing in the front ranks of the battle, until our kinsmen, according to the flesh are disenthralled." The history of the oppressed demonstrates that they have only succeeded in liberating themselves through their own exertions. In the words of the poet (Lord Byron): "Know ye not, hereditary bondsmen? He that would be free, himself must strike the blow." The best way to accomplish this was through slave rebellion: "Three millions and a half of men, armed with the righteous cause of freedom, and the God of Justice on their side, against two hundred and fifty thousand tyrants [Southern slaveholders], could sweep them like chaff before the wind." Moreover, runaway slaves would undermine the system of American slavery. "We believe it to be an indispensable duty," read the address, "that every 'hereditary bondsman' owes to himself, first to run away

13. *BAP*, 2:149, 160; Rhodes, *Shadd Cary*, 33–34; Harding, *There is a River*, 168–69; Hite, "Voice of Fugitive," 275. Chap. 7 explores the Pan-African dimensions of West Indian Emancipation in greater detail.

from slavery, and to carry off with him whatever may be necessary to effect his escape." This latter line drew from a long history of American fugitives in Canada stretching from the Kentucky cases in the late 1830s through to two of the address writers—Bibb and Tinsley—who were themselves fugitives from American slavery.[14]

The address concluded with praise for the Refugee's Home Society (RHS) and its "noble" object of buying land and "settling fugitives in Canada." This organization was rooted in changes along the Detroit-Windsor frontier. The rapid influx of fugitives had resulted in the meeting of a local black convention at Sandwich in 1846. Its major objective was to form a new black settlement to aid fugitives through the provision of land, homes, and education. Over the next few years, the Sandwich Mission obtained about 1,200 acres, which was to be divided into 10-acre lots and resold to black settlers, with 25 acres reserved for a school and church. Although little came of this plan, the Sandwich group became the basis for the Fugitives Union Society, a black moral improvement association located in Windsor. In May 1851, a new group of white abolitionists in Detroit was moved to form a new organization whose primary object was to "extend to them [fugitives] the helping hand in their struggle to establish homes among strangers, whose laws protect them from the grasp of the American slave-hunters." The resulting body merged with the Sandwich group to form the RHS in January 1852. Its leaders included white abolitionists E. P. Benham and Horace Halleck in Detroit; American Missionary Association worker David Hotchkiss in Amherstburg; American fugitive and black settlement leader Josiah Henson; and Henry and Mary Bibb in Windsor. The RHS plan was to buy "50,000 acres of farming land, in Canada, on which to settle refugees from slavery." By 1855, it had purchased 2,000 acres and provided homes for 150 fugitives. Three years later, the RHS acquired another 290 acres along the Puce Rive east of Windsor, thus expanding the existing black community.[15]

Although the RHS fell short of its original goal, suffered from financial entanglements, and encountered fierce criticism from other black leaders like Mary Shadd and Samuel Ward, it is important not to overlook the

14. *VF*, October 22, 1851; *BAP*, 2:170–76.
15. Pease and Pease, *Black Utopia*, 109–22; *BAP*, 2:147; Rhodes, *Shadd Cary*, 41.

significance of this attempt to create independent land-based fugitive communities in western Ontario.[16] In January 1853, *Voice of the Fugitive* agent and supporter James T. Holly wrote a letter to the *Liberator* in defense of the RHS. In response to those who charged the organization with "begging," Holly pointed out that the objective was the creation of self-reliance and independence. This had been a central plank in the program of the *Voice of the Fugitive* and the NACCP. Furthermore, Holly defended the RHS's exclusive concern with fugitive slaves. Finally, in response to those who opposed "segregated communities," Holly agreed, but pointed to the educated black man of the future whose "personal sense of slavery shall be lost in a free-born generation of descendants."[17]

FUGITIVE RITES

These politics of self-emancipation by American fugitives in the western regions of Canada West were publicly demonstrated every August First throughout the 1850s. Fugitive slaves and their antislavery friends met annually to celebrate British abolition, to express thanks for the queen's free soil, and to mobilize against American slavery. Local black leaders usually organized the largest meetings, held in Sandwich and Windsor. In 1851, Mary Bibb led an organizing committee of seven black men, including Henry Brant, who would represent Sandwich as a delegate to the NACCP the following month. At the 1852 anniversary, Henry Bibb was nominated president. One of the most striking things about the fugitive August First was its cross-national dimensions. Black people in Detroit regularly attended West Indian Day celebrations in Canada West. It was reported that "the colored citizens of Detroit, at an adjourned meeting, held on Monday, the 28th of June, reconsidered a previous vote, whereby they had determined to celebrate the 1st of August in

16. This pursuit of an alternative way of life recalls Italian counselor Gonzalo's ideal commonwealth in Shakespeare's *Tempest* II;I;157–70, where "riches, poverty, And use of service none; contract, succession, Bourn, bound of land, tilth, vineyard, none . . . but nature should bring forth, Of its own kind, all foison, all abundance, To feed my innocent people." Some of these terms are suggestive. The queen's free soil was without limit or boundary ("Bourn"). Self-emancipated fugitives were no longer bound to the land. Although "tilth" or cultivation of the land was expected of the newcomers, the new land was plentiful ("all foison"), while the fugitives were "innocent."

17. Pease and Pease, *Black Utopia*, 120–21.

that city; and resolved, by a very decisive majority, to unite with their brethren in commemorating that glorious event under the British flag in Canada."
Also, many of these meetings were addressed by antislavery speakers from the
United States and elsewhere. To get a sense of these elaborate public demonstrations, let us examine those held at Sandwich in 1851 and at Windsor the
following year.[18]

On August 1, 1851, the *Voice of the Fugitive* reported that "hundreds of self-
emancipated slaves with thousands of disenthralled freemen and freewomen"
gathered together at Sandwich to give thanks for British abolition and territorial asylum "for the hunted refugees from the United States." They came
from Detroit, Amherstburg, Windsor, and Sandwich. The major purpose of
the event was "to celebrate the birthday of Liberty to the once chattelized
[*sic*] descendants of Africa on British soil." The high sheriff of Essex County
opened the meeting, followed by addresses from "several eloquent speakers"
from Ohio, Michigan, and Illinois. At 1:30, "a splendid dinner" was served.
Afterward, a "very long procession was formed, and marched through the
streets, with appropriate banners, after a delightful brass band." Many of the
visitors up from Amherstburg were "dressed in the red jacket uniform," and
marched into Sandwich after a military band "looking as bold and courageous
as 'John Bull' himself." The celebration concluded with speeches from several
school children, including the seven-year-old daughter of Kirk Jackson. Her
delivery "would have done honor to the most polished orator that ever gradu-
ated at college." Henry Bibb moved a resolution thanking the people of Sandwich together with public appreciation for the "blessings of liberty which we
so freely enjoy here under the protection of this Government." After agreeing
that the proceedings be published in the *Voice of the Fugitive*, and that next year's
celebration be held at Malden, the meeting was adjourned.[19]

The following year's event did not take place at Malden, but at Windsor. On June 28, 1852, a group of local citizens "unanimously resolved that
the day [August First] should be celebrated by a public demonstration" at
Windsor. The citizens of Detroit decided to cancel their own celebration
and join those planned for Windsor. On Monday, August 2, 1852, teams
gathered "from the surrounding settlements," while the Detroit ferry "wafted

18. *VF,* July 30, 1851; July 1, August 12, 1852.
19. *VF,* July 2, 16, 30, August 13, 1851.

boat loads of distant strangers to our shore, some of which had come many hundreds of miles from places in the States." A procession formed with the Sons of Union, a colored society of Detroit, the North American League with their members bearing badges "(N.A.L.) stamped upon them," and various other local citizens. One group carried a banner with a kneeling slave in chains on one side and on the other "a man at full length standing erect, chains with fetters lying at his feet, and broken manacles in his hands." Bringing up the rear was a "British Union Jack" floating in the breeze. The marchers proceeded to a grove and were addressed by President Henry Bibb and James Holly. After welcoming their guests from Detroit and elsewhere, nine cheers were given for Queen Victoria and the band struck up "God Save the Queen." Addresses were delivered by Mr. Carter, president of the Sons of Union, Reverend W. Munroe, and Samuel J. May of Syracuse. After dinner, several more addresses and resolutions were made, after which "the vast assemblage dispersed well satisfied with the rich intellectual feast."[20]

These August First celebrations in western Ontario during the early 1850s resembled those held in eastern Ontario. Large crowds of black people assembled for an important commemorative event. The principal streets of urban areas were occupied for the day. There were major antislavery speeches. Children were politically socialized at these events. Black veterans in red coats publicly displayed their military service to the United Kingdom. The British Crown was thanked for providing liberty from slavery in the past, as well as free soil to fugitives in the present. Indeed, West Indian Day celebrations in Canada West during the 1850s resembled those held in the Northern United States during the same period.

There were, however, some critical differences between anniversaries held in eastern and western Ontario. While some outsiders attended anniversaries in Toronto and Hamilton, a wide array of people from both sides of the national border attended celebrations held at Sandwich, Windsor, Amherstburg, and Detroit. These were borderland events, whose crowds, diversity, and social forms are not accurately described through terms like *Canadian*, *American*, *African American*, or *African Canadian*. Moreover, these events were primarily celebrations of freedom rather than public displays of colonial patriotism. The *Voice of the Fugitive* and other newspapers reported far less evidence

20. *VF,* July 1, August 12, 1852.

of formal ritual in terms of the Church of England, the drinking of tea, and the formalities of state. Unlike Toronto or the British Caribbean colonies, for instance, there was no established Anglican presence in these western Ontario towns. Instead, independent black organizations like the Baptist Church were heralded.

Furthermore, August First provided an important opportunity for the public display of self-emancipation organizations. The Fugitives Union Society marched at Sandwich in 1851 and the Sons of Union marched at Windsor in 1852; the latter event was reported as a "PUBLIC DEMONSTRATION." Finally, the hundreds of fugitives at these August First celebrations had not been freed by a benevolent state but were self-emancipated. Indeed, this Emancipation Day celebration was primarily about self-emancipation and mobilization against American slavery. As Bibb's newspaper editorialized after describing the 1851 Sandwich event: "While we shall rejoice at the noble act of the British Government in letting 'the oppressed' go free and with thousands of self-emancipated ones now protected in the enjoyment of liberty on the Queen's soil-let us not forget to sympathize with and labor for the emancipation of the three millions and a half of our enslaved brethren who are tyrannically held to labor by the American despots."[21]

Although the British government was praised in Christian terms for its abolition, there were many "self-emancipated" fugitives who enjoyed imperial protection, and American slavery was yet to be destroyed. This was a far cry from the loyalist commemoration. The social meaning of August First came primarily from the specific historical conditions of the 1850s: the territorial expansion of American slavery; fugitive self-emancipation; celebrations of past abolition; the reality of British colonial freedom; and the need to "labor for the emancipation" of others.

Not only had the social meaning of West Indian Emancipation celebrations in Canada West changed, but they also reflected a contrasting politics of identity between older and newer generations of African-descended people living in Canada. In the lakeshore cities of Toronto, Hamilton, and Brantford around southern Lake Ontario, there existed a well-established black populace, many of whom had achieved a degree of social success and stability.

21. *VF*, July 30, 1851.

TABLE 5.1. Fugitive August First, 1851–1861

1851	Stone Barracks, Sandwich
	Chatham
1852	Windsor
1853	Sandwich
1854	Sandwich
	Dawn
	Chatham
1855	London
	Amherstburg
1856	Sandwich
1857	Sandwich
	Dresden
1858	Sandwich
1859	Sandwich
1860	Chatham
1861	Drummondville

Sources: FDP, August 11, 1854; *L*, August 26, 1859; August 31, 1860; August 23, 1861; *PF*, August 19, 26, 1854; July 25, August 22, 1857; *VF*, July 2, 16, 30, August 13, 1851; July 1, August 12, 1852; McKivigan and Silverman, "Monarchical Liberty," 9; Silverman, *Unwelcome Guests*, 86.

They were Anglo-Canadians who proclaimed a loyal attachment to the British Crown and rarely missed a public opportunity to make this clear. In contrast, the Fugitive Slave Act spawned a newer generation of forced migrants from the United States. Many of them settled in areas of western Ontario like Sandwich, Windsor, and Amherstburg, which often served as terminal points on the Underground Railroad. These fugitives were not Anglo-Canadians; rather, they were escapees from American slavery whose primary connection with British Canada was freedom from slavery, and whose primary objective was the overthrow of American slavery. August First gave them an opportunity to recall a past emancipation, glorify their own self-liberation, and work toward the future emancipation of others. Let us conclude this examination of August First celebrations in Canada West with a brief look at two anniversary celebrations in 1854 whose tensions highlight some of the differences between the loyalists and fugitives.

Begun as a vocational school for training fugitives in 1842, Dawn in western Ontario soon spawned a 1,500-acre community with five hundred settlers who were self-supporting through agricultural production and lumber sales. In 1852, John Scoble, English-born Congregational minister and secretary of the British and Foreign Anti-Slavery Society (BFASS), assumed control of the school. His patronizing leadership, together with his seizure of the best lands and houses, put him at odds with many of the black settlers at Dawn. In 1855, James C. Brown, an original trustee, led a court battle for control of Dawn, which continued into the 1860s and led to the eventual demise of the settlement in 1868.[22]

On August 1, 1854, there was a "large celebration" held at Dawn. A procession formed at the school house at 12:30 P.M. and marched to the Green Lawn, whereupon the day's ceremonies began. After Reverend Josiah Henson had been appointed chairman, the speeches began. Accounts vary as to the nature and reception of these speeches. According to the reporter for the *Provincial Freeman*, Frederick Douglass "never received such a cold one [reception] as then and there." Douglass "expressed himself opposed to emigration to Canada, only as a mass, believing, it would be injurious to the present inhabitants of Canada, and their interests! and secondly, that the people of the States wanted us to emigrate, that Slavery might be extended over the entire Union." After two hours, Douglass sat down to little applause. He was followed by Scoble and King, the latter's words meeting "the approbation of the people." Despite Douglass's second speech, "the people of Dawn showed themselves to be entirely opposed to him." He stayed at Dawn for two days for want of conveyance to Chatham, only eighteen miles away. Once there, he reportedly "charged the coloured people [of Dawn] with being negligent."[23]

A rather different version of the day's proceedings, however, was reported in *Frederick Douglass' Paper*. John Scoble had invited Douglass to attend the celebration at Dawn. Douglass and his company traveled most of the 1,600 miles from Rochester to Dawn on the Western Railroad. At 10:00 A.M., "colored people," dressed "in their neatest and best," assembled at the school house.

22. Pease and Pease, *Black Utopia*, 63–83; *BAP*, 2:105–6.
23. *PF*, August 19, 1854.

An hour later, "a procession was formed under direction of elected marshals, with banners, badges and batons," making its way to a grove. John Scoble delivered a "fluent, exact, rhetorical, and sometimes truly eloquent," speech that "was listened to with delight by his sable audience." Such delight was not reported by the *Provincial Freeman*. Douglass further reported that the event was "conducted with order and decorum, and reflected credit upon the people of Dawn." He thought the afternoon had been marred by James Brown, who "seized the opportunity that the occasion afforded, to offer some objections to the plans and purposes entertained by Messrs. Scoble, Henson and others, as to the future management of the affairs at Dawn." One complaint was that the consequences of Scoble's leadership would be that Dawn would "no longer be enjoyed by Fugitives from slavery, but would be monopolized by English, Scotch and Irish [pupils]." Another complaint "was that the proceedings of Messrs. Scoble and Henson, were unauthorized, and illegal." Mr. Henson replied to Brown, and to those in the know, that "his reply, was every way satisfactory." The audience, the *Frederick Douglass' Paper* continued, "evinced much pleasure, when they found, after all that Mr. Brown had said, to the contrary, the declaration of trust, settling forth the objects of Dawn, was strictly in harmony with the declared purposes of Messrs. Scoble, Henson, Carey, and others, to whose wisdom and cooperation, the place must owe its future usefulness." This was contrary to the report provided in a letter by Mr. Brown to the *Provincial Freeman*. Also, Douglass's two speeches, and their tepid reception by the audience, went unmentioned.[24]

It is clear that there were some major tensions between organizers and participants at this 1854 anniversary in Dawn. The precise nature of these differences, however, is less urgent than our need to understand the political importance of August First. Leaders sought to use the event as a means to spread their own political messages. In addition, newspapers sought to carve the event in their own image. The point, of course, is that such actions would have been needless if August First had not assumed communal significance.

That same day, several hundred miles eastward, MASS organized its annual Emancipation Day celebration at Abington, Massachusetts. One of the invited speakers was Reverend C. H. A. Dall, who wrote a letter to his brother subsequently published in the *Liberator* that gave "a very interesting

24. *FDP*, August 11, 1854; *PF*, August 26, 1854.

account of the fugitives in that country [Canada West], and of the feelings of the white people about them." The guest speaker also commented upon relations among colored people in Canada: "There was some indifference and hardness of heart observable among those colored people who were not fugitives; but who had been there fifteen or twenty years, and might be called old settlers. They were not prompt to meet the fugitives; while the fugitives themselves were always generous." Three weeks later, a number of prominent black citizens of Toronto met at Richmond Street Chapel to consider Rev. Dall's speech. After a public reading of the speech, several attendees "addressed the Meeting in a forcible manner, taking exceptions to the speech of Rev. Dall, as being false in many particulars, and unfair towards the colored people." After further discussion, the meeting passed three resolutions. First, Rev. Dall's speech, "with regard to the disposition of the old colored settlers, in this Province, towards the newly arrived fugitives, is a serious reflection on their character" and "has a tendency to make differences between us." Second, the attempt "to divide us into two classes in Canada, by calling attention to us as free and fugitive, is a wanton invasion of our kindred and social ties." Third, "we are one people; our interests in those Provinces are the same, and that we will resist any and every attempt to sow discord amongst us." Both the proceedings of the Toronto meeting, as well as Rev. Dall's speech at the Abington anniversary, were published in the *Provincial Freeman*.[25]

Despite the alacrity with which the prominent black citizens of Toronto publicly refuted the charges of class tensions, it seems clear that social divisions had appeared as a result of British imperial emancipation, the expansion of American slavery, and fugitive flight. An older generation of black settlers resided in lakeshore cities. They pursued a policy of civic incorporation that included political participation, military service, and patriotism toward the British Crown. The annual commemoration of British abolition every August First provided them with an opportunity to proclaim these sentiments publicly. With the influx of new fugitives from American slavery during the 1850s, these older settlers assumed the role of "race leaders" for the new arrivals. In this sense, Emancipation Day celebrations took on an expanded role as public expressions for all blacks in Canada. Indeed, Thomas Smallwood played an important role in trying to heal the growing division between the

25. *PF*, August 19, 26, 1854.

two groups in Toronto. It should not be forgotten that he helped organize the Emancipation Day celebration in 1854 and attended the subsequent public meeting to consider Rev. Dall's "two classes" speech.[26]

At the same time, however, these new arrivals challenged an older agenda of civic incorporation. They had self-emancipated themselves from American slavery. They also sought freedom in this new land. This freedom was invariably pursued in smaller black communities in western Ontario largely concerned with personal and institutional efforts at self-determination. The older residents feared that past efforts to win public favor would be undermined. This difference became especially pronounced over the question of "begging." The Bibbs and the *Voice of the Fugitive* engaged in fund-raising tours as a practical means to pay for the acquisition of land and self-independence on behalf of fugitives without means. Mary Shadd and the *Provincial Freeman* criticized these schemes for their "racial segregation" policy, which they deemed detrimental to the best interests of colored Canadians.[27]

Annual commemorations of West India Day by fugitives from American slavery persisted throughout the 1850s in the towns and villages of western Ontario. Both Sandwich and Windsor continued to attract large number of celebrants every August First. In 1859, there were seven thousand in attendance for the Sandwich event, most of whom were described as "refugees from American slavery." The participants were reported to be well-dressed and well-behaved. There were several balls held in the evening at Windsor. The following year, four thousand to five thousand were present at the Emancipation Day celebration held at Chatham.[28] These celebrants were self-emancipated although they thanked Britain for its free soil. They also heralded British abolition as well as sought the overthrow of American slavery. Most important, these were large public demonstrations of past, present, and future liberation.

26. *BAP*, 2:158; *PF*, August 26, 1854.

27. *BAP*, 2:158; Hill, *Freedom-Seekers*, 74–76, 83; Rhodes, *Shadd Cary*, 53–69; *PF*, August 26, 1854.

28. *L*, August 26, 1859; August 31, 1860. Note the *Liberator's* reference to the polite behavior of colored crowds. In contrast, the *Voice of the Fugitive* was mute on such descriptions. This had to do, I would argue, with the latter's recognition that spectacles of respectability could never abolish American slavery.

August First served as an important public display of political identities among blacks in Canada. One reflected a politics of colonial patriotism and loyalty; the other represented a transnational liberation struggle against American slavery. Moreover, the social meaning of these identities must be understood within an international context of fugitive slaves, expanding American slavery, and racial tensions between fugitives and an older generation of black settlers in Canada. Most important, West India Day played an important role in mobilizing black communities in British Canada against American slavery. This mobilization resulted from imperial rivalries between the American Republic and British Canada, the continental clash over fugitives, and transnational struggles against slavery led by people of African descent.

Finally, many scholars of UNIA portray its marches and colorful regalia as unprecedented in the black historical experience. These popular August First celebrations in continental North America during the 1840s and 1850s, however, suggest otherwise. Moreover, UNIA is often credited with an unprecedented seizure of urban public space and self-defense after World War I—that was to be repeated during the urban upheavals and mobilizations of the black freedom movement during the 1960s. But its earlier expression was through the self-defense of fugitive slaves and the emergence of black militias, especially during the 1850s. It is this important mobilization, and its social expression and political significance for antislavery, that constitutes the following chapter.

Chapter 6
Rehearsal for War:
Black Militias in the Atlantic World

. . . the young blacks of the Republic are everywhere acquiring a love for martial pastimes.
Samuel R. Ward, 1855

August 1, 1851, dawned "a fine morning, though the sky looked somewhat lowering, and fleeting clouds would now and the[n], as though tauntingly, dart before the sun." A "large concourse of the citizens of Brooklyn, New York, Williamsburg and Flushing, with a number from other places more distant," had assembled. Their destination was a picnic "between the villages of Weeksville and Corsville, both colored settlements" four miles from Brooklyn, Long Island. The meeting's objectives were to celebrate "West India Emancipation," to "see a little pleasure," and to congregate "on grounds owned and occupied by our own people." In a short time, "several thousand people" were present. Much anticipation "prevailed throughout the crowd to hear the speaking commence." William Johnson of Ithaca, New York, was followed by Reverend Peter Gardner. "Just as he rose, the noise of the drum, and the shrill sound of music, announced the approach of Capt. Hackins, at the head of the Hannibal Guards. The company was taken by surprise. They marched up directly opposite the speaker's stand, and there rested for orders, which were soon given, to march round the ground. This done, they appeared opposite the stand. Again, Mr. Gardner proceeded to declare his approval of military science among our people." Why were large crowds of black people assembling? Who and what were the Hannibal Guards? Why were young black men marching and drilling during the early 1850s? Most important, what were the connections between such events and the overthrow of American slavery?[1]

1. *FDP*, September 2, 1851. For an earlier version of this chapter, see Jeffrey R. Kerr-Ritchie, "Rehearsal for War: Black Militias in the Atlantic World," *Slavery and Abolition* 26, no. 1 (April 2005): 1–33.

Although scholars have examined the role of blacks in the federal military from the Revolutionary War through the first Gulf War, few have examined black soldiers at the state and local levels. The exception is an older literature on black militias in the postbellum South.[2] Some scholars who have mentioned antebellum black militias see them as largely insignificant. William Gravely thinks these companies "added a martial atmosphere" to public parades. Benjamin Quarles argues "such outfits were largely ceremonial, parading on August 1 or at the grand opening of a church or a school." "Without state or federal support," he adds, "Negro militia companies were bound to remain small and indifferently equipped." Geneviève Fabre believes these units were largely performative, serving to attract attention and to please crowds. Other scholars acknowledge the importance of these black companies, but fail to develop the point any further. James and Lois Horton maintain these militias "readied themselves for self-defense and anticipated war," but leave it there. Patrick Rael describes an 1858 parade as an "impressive military display for Emancipation Day, which must have been typical of many." Without additional research, however, it is difficult to determine the typicality of such displays. Although Kathryn Grover explains the organization of the local company in New Bedford, the author says nothing about other black militias in Massachusetts and elsewhere. None of these scholars have explained the social meaning of black military formations during the 1850s and its political implications.[3]

Were black militias of little consequence during the ante-emancipation years? Although the evidence is scant, several antislavery and local newspapers

2. For older works, see James S. Allen, *Reconstruction: The Battle for Democracy, 1865–1877* (New York: International Publishers, 1937); Otis Singletary, *Negro Militia and Reconstruction* (New York: McGraw Hill, 1963). For more recent work on the role of paramilitary politics in the Reconstruction South, see Julie Saville, *The Work of Reconstruction: From Slave to Wage Laborer in South Carolina, 1860–1870* (New York: Cambridge University Press, 1994); David S. Cecelski, "Abraham H. Galloway: Wilmington's Lost Prophet and the Rise of Black Radicalism in the American South," in *Time Longer Than Rope: A Century of African American Activism, 1850–1950,* ed. Charles M. Payne and Adam Green (New York: New York University Press, 2003); Hahn, *Nation under Our Feet,* chap. 6.

3. Gravely, "Dialectic of Double-Consciousness," 304; Quarles, *Black Abolitionists,* 229; Fabre, "African-American Commemorative Celebrations," 85; Horton and Horton, *Hope of Liberty,* 263; Rael, *Black Identity,* 63; Grover, *Fugitive's Gibraltar,* 61, 247–48, 327.

reported the formation of independent black companies from the late 1840s onward. The establishment, personnel, and equipment of these military units, together with their importance for local black organization, have largely escaped scholarly attention. Furthermore, these companies marched annually in dozens of public parades for many years. There were probably other units: one newspaper account referred to "all the colored military companies" at a Brooklyn parade in 1858, but named only one.[4] The remarkable scene of armed companies of young black men marching in public at a time when they were not officially sanctioned by federal and state authorities has also not been explained.

Moreover, these militias and their public parades take on an added significance once they are placed within broader temporal and spatial frameworks. The antebellum and Civil War years are traditionally divided at 1861. In contrast, this chapter takes a longer approach, linking up fugitive slaves, vigilance committees, black militias, and Union soldiers from the 1830s through the 1860s. The question of fugitive slaves is usually addressed in terms of its contribution to the origins of the Civil War. In contrast to this nationalist narrative, we examine imperial rivalries between the American Republic and British Canada, the continental clash over fugitives, and transnational struggles against slavery by people of African descent in North America.

This chapter makes three arguments. First, there was a trajectory toward militarization from vigilance committees to independent companies to enrollment in Union armies. Black communities did not wait to be told by politicians or abolitionists to wage armed resistance against slavery during the Civil War. Rather, they pursued informal and formal expressions of self-defense and national liberation *before* the official opening armed hostilities in April 1861.[5] Second, links between self-defense and rights of citizenship were already being struggled over at local and state levels before the more famous

4. *BDE*, August 3, 1858.

5. The traditional narrative is that abolitionist leaders like Frederick Douglass led the way for enrolling black troops. For example, Donald, Baker, and Holt, *Civil War and Reconstruction*, 340, write: "Since 1861 Douglass, along with other black northerners, had been demanding that the war be carried 'into Africa. Let the slaves and colored people be called into service, and formed into a liberating army to march into the South and raise the banner of Emancipation among the slaves.'" In contrast, this chapter argues that "Africans" had already carried the war into the Northern states.

national expression in black Union soldiers fighting for the Union. Finally, national narratives concerning the origins of the American Civil War, African American slavery, and British Canadian history obscure the multiple roles played by people of African descent during this period. It is only through cross-national approaches toward fugitives, military formation, and antislavery mobilization that we can appreciate the role of blacks in challenging American slavery in the Atlantic world.[6]

This trajectory shapes the structure of the chapter. We begin with fugitives and the organization of vigilance committees of self-defense in North America. We then turn to state rights of self defense, the exclusion of black men from these rights, and the resulting organization of independent companies. The public parade of these black militias on West India Day in the United States and British Canada is the heart of the following section. We conclude with the continental destruction of American slavery and its consequences for the post-emancipation era.

This chapter has several objectives. First, it seeks to unearth military companies because they represented an important black institution yet to be seriously examined. Furthermore, it aims to broaden the temporal and spatial dimensions of the Civil War era through linking black militias with Union troops and political-legal relations between the American Republic and imperial Canada in the Atlantic world. The third, and most ambitious task, is to reveal the limitations of nationalist narratives by seeking out connections among people of African descent, as well as the ways in which individuals and organizations provide alternative means for comparison.[7]

SELF-DEFENSE

Scholars usually examine fugitive slaves in one of several ways. One concerns causes of the Civil War: the tensions between the slave South and the free North wrought by runaway slaves resulted in the passage of the 1850

6. There is an old historical literature on links between black troops and national citizenship during the Civil War. The first major account was George Washington Williams, *A History of the Negro Troops in the War of the Rebellion, 1861–1865,* published in 1888. The most recent work has been produced by the Freedmen Southern Society Project, especially Berlin et al., *Freedom's Soldiers.*

7. Two works on transnationalism I have found useful are Tyrrell, "American Exceptionalism," and Gregg, *Inside Out, Outside In.*

Fugitive Slave Act, contributing to the nation's inexorable slide toward sectional conflict. Another is the abolitionist crusade: the defense of fugitives and the Underground Railroad were part of a glorious chapter in interracial solidarity. A third approach depicts fugitives as evidence of slave resistance: runaway slaves point to rebelliousness rather than acquiescence to American slavery. A final way links fugitives with slaves and free blacks as part of an emerging African American nation.[8]

The focus in this opening section is different. It examines fugitive slaves within the context of American slavery, British abolition, and imperial rivalries. It seeks to answer the following question: To what extent did collective self-defense around fugitive slaves constitute an informal expression of military preparedness *led* by black people in North America?

We have already seen the divergence of continental slavery in post-revolutionary North America between expansion in the American South and contraction in the northern states and British Canada. By the 1820s, plantation slavery in the American border states was increasingly giving way to the southwest expansion of slavery through the development of a booming internal slave trade. It has been estimated that three-quarters of a million slaves were transported from the Upper South to the Lower South between 1820 and 1860. Despite federal and state laws for returning runaways, however, slaves continued to pursue their freedom continent-wide. Although the exact numbers will never be known, most historians agree that around a thousand fugitives annually escaped American slavery from the Revolution through the Civil War. Some headed south for Spanish Florida; others crossed the Mexican border, especially after the abolition of slavery in that independent nation in 1829, while others mingled with free black populations in southern towns and cities.[9]

Many fugitives, especially from the Upper South, headed north. Sometimes they received support from unusual sources. Thomas A. Emmet (1764–1827), a radical Irish nationalist who fled to New York City in 1804 to escape the British government, became a lawyer specializing in defending fugitive

8. Donald, Baker, and Holt, *Civil War*, 83; Horton and Horton, *Hope of Liberty*; Franklin and Schweninger, *Runaway Slaves*; Harding, *There Is a River*.

9. Hahn, *Nation under Our Feet*, 18; Freehling, *Road to DisUnion*, 502–4; Franklin and Schweninger, *Runaway Slaves*, 160.

slaves. More often, antislavery activists in the northern states responded with vigilance committees organized to intercept fugitive slave catchers and protect fugitives. In 1835, local black activist David Ruggles and others started the New York Committee of Vigilance "for the rights and safety of Blacks." Two years later, this vigilance committee used the celebration of the third anniversary of British colonial abolition at Broadway Hall, New York City, to proclaim "vigilance should be the watchword and rallying cry." It has been estimated that over the next several years, this self-defense organization rescued 1,373 people from American slavery. The following year, local black activist Robert Purvis began his decade-long leadership of the Philadelphia Vigilance Committee. Other vigilance committees were formed in Pittsburgh, Detroit, Boston, and Albany in the late 1830s and early 1840s. In 1842, blacks in New England organized the Freedom Association to support and aid fugitive slaves; the following year, this organization played a prominent role in Boston's August First.[10]

In the aftermath of the victorious American war on Mexico, Southern slaveholders demanded federal support for returning runaway slaves. The continental expansion of the American Empire brought with it the spread of slavery and demands for federal protection of personal property, especially fugitive slaves. Authored by Virginia senator and slaveholder James M. Mason, the Fugitive Slave Act was debated, passed, and finally signed by President Millard Fillmore on September 18, 1850. It empowered federal marshals to support Southern slaveholders' efforts to "pursue and reclaim" their fugitives "from service and labor" through either a warrant or legal seizure "without due process." It essentially beefed up the pursuit, capture, and return of fugitives by buttressing state rights with federal legislation. It further betokened a legal assault on the pursuit of freedom by slaves, a massive new threat to fugitives living in free states, and the potential for kidnapping those people of African descent who had never been enslaved.[11]

10. Foster, *Modern Ireland*, 265; *BAP*, 3:26–27, 179; Jane H. Pease and William H. Pease, *They Who Would Be Free: Blacks' Search for Freedom, 1830–1861* (New York: Atheneum, 1974), 207–12; *E*, August 24, 1837; Horton and Horton, *Black Bostonians*, 99, 110–13; *L*, August 11, 1843.

11. Junius P. Rodriguez, ed., *Historical Encyclopedia of World Slavery* (Santa Barbara: ABC-CLIO, 1997), 1:465–68; Horton and Horton, *Hope of Liberty*, 252–53; Pease and Pease, *They Who Would Be Free*, 206–32.

Scholars have examined at length the response of Northern communities to the Fugitive Slave Act.[12] Rather than repeat this important but familiar history, we emphasize two points. First, black people defended themselves in traditional ways. Many fugitives and free blacks left the United States for the comparative safety of British Canada as was the case after 1834. Some fled, while others left with resolution. Days after the passage of the law, around two hundred blacks from Pittsburgh departed carrying guns and swearing that "they would die before being taken back into slavery."[13] This was a large group of armed black people engaged in their own self-defense. Second, in extending the legal assault on slaves to free blacks in the Northern states, the Fugitive Slave Act linked the interests of slaves, fugitives, and free blacks against American slavery. One consequence was a collective determination to resist the new draconian slave law. On October 2, 1850, some 1,500 black people crowded into the Zion Chapel, New York City, to protest the new law. One week later, blacks met to protest in Elmira, New York, as well as in Pittsburgh, Pennsylvania. From Oswego, New York, it was reported that blacks had "organized and armed themselves to resist any attempt that may be made against them declaring they would fight to the last, if need be, to defend the liberty of themselves or friends." At Belknap Street Church—a prominent meeting place for August First commemorations from the late 1830s onward—the assembly agreed, "we will not allow a fugitive slave to be taken from Massachusetts." Samuel Ward, a thirty-three-year-old fugitive, Congregational minister, and prominent abolitionist, declared that the act "throws us back upon the natural and inalienable right of self-defense and self-protection."[14]

Fugitive battles became central to the political mobilization against American slavery from the early 1850s onward. Major conflicts broke out between federal agents, slaveholders, and self-defense mobs. Thomas Campbell calculates 156 fugitive slave cases involving 300 slaves during the 1850s. The Hortons count over 80 well-publicized fugitive slave rescues and attempted rescues. These rescues were often carried out by armed vigilance groups

12. See the works of Quarles, Pease and Pease, and Horton and Horton.

13. Harding, *There Is a River*, chap. 8.

14. Quarles, *Black Abolitionists*, 201–3; Herbert A. Aptheker, ed., *A Documentary History of the Negro People in the United States* (New York: Citadel Press, 1951), I:305–6; *HS*, October 10, 1850.

engaged in the self-defense of fugitives. In 1851, the attempt to capture fugitive slaves in Christiana, Pennsylvania, by slaveholder Edward Gorsuch and company was successfully repulsed by dozens of black men and women armed with guns, corn cutters, scythe blades, staves, clubs, and stones. These self-defense acts were reminiscent of earlier border skirmishes in support of fugitives from Kentucky.[15]

Newspaper reports of these fugitive battles contributed to this political mobilization. These fugitive causes célèbres were extensively reported in black and abolitionist newspapers. The press industry had taken off during the 1830s due to technological improvements, cheaper print, and educational advances. It has been estimated that by 1850 two-thirds of black adults in six Northern U.S. cities had rudimentary reading skills. Many must have shared the news with those who could not read. By the early 1850s, these readers had learned of a series of spectacular fugitive cases. This press coverage undoubtedly served to fire abolitionist and antislavery imaginations. Every fugitive struggle placed the issue of slavery directly in the hearts and minds of literally thousands of people in North America. Reports of these incidents propagated continental struggles over slavery. The Boston *Liberator* reported on fugitive escapees from Southern slavery. Many readers first learned of Fredrick Wilkins's rescue from Boston as the "Shadrach" case in the *Voice of the Fugitive*, printed from Sandwich, Canada West. In an article headlined "Colored Population Wide Awake," this fugitive abolitionist newspaper informed readers that "six and even seven hundred colored citizens, many of whom are fugitives, are here, and are determined to stand by one another, and live or die together."[16]

Indeed, it is sometimes hard to work out which was the most effective for mobilizing in the name of self-defense: reports of successful rescues, such as those of "Shadrach" and "Jerry," or failed attempts, including those of Thomas Sims and Anthony Burns? A state marshal on a visit to New Bedford, Massachusetts, on truancy business was thought to be a slave catcher. "The

---

15. Horton and Horton, *In Hope of Liberty*, 254–57, 321; Quarles, *Black Abolitionists*, 206–15; Pease and Pease, *They Who Would Be Free*, 219–27; Horton and Horton, *Black Bostonians*, 103–11; Grover, *Fugitive's Gibraltar*, 221–23; Harding, *There Is a River*, 169–70. In the image on the dust jacket, the freed slave is bearing a scythe blade in his right hand.

16. *VF*, February 26, April 9, 1851; *DG*, February 25, 1851.

rumor," wrote local citizen Joseph Ricketson, "spread like wild fire among the colored people," who "commenced arming themselves, determined to maintain their freedom with their lives." From some parts of Pennsylvania, it was reported that "armed negroes prowled around in search of slave catchers." In 1852, a Baltimore policeman arrested an alleged fugitive in Columbia, Pennsylvania. After being surrounded by an angry black crowd, the officer was bitten by the captive, whom he shot, and barely escaped back to Maryland.[17]

It is clear that the battle over fugitives played a critical role in sowing sectional divisions between Southern and Northern states during the 1850s. It is no less evident that the decade of violence against people of African descent created solidarity among people of African descent as well as between some blacks and whites. But we should not take our eyes off of the fugitives themselves. Nearly two generations ago, radical scholars W. E. B. Du Bois, Herbert Aptheker, and C. L. R. James pointed to the transformative role fugitive slaves played in mobilizing antislavery feeling.[18] It is clear that these fugitives brought forth self-defense groups. Moreover, these fugitives and vigilance committees took on a continental significance after 1834—and especially after 1850. Fugitives had been escaping for decades, especially after slavery was abolished in the British Empire. Meanwhile, individuals, vigilance committees, and mobs engaged in armed self-defense to protect fugitives from the laws of American slavery as well as the ambiguities of British colonial law. What made the 1850s *qualitatively* different was the need for collective defense against an expansionist Slave Power that was inexorably moving west (Kansas, Dred Scott), north (Fugitive Slave Act), and south (Mexico, Cuba).[19] The self-emancipation of slaves, together with their protection by arms-bearing crowds and spontaneous mobs, constituted a continental means of self-defense, preparing the way for the establishment of independent military companies.

17. Horton and Horton, *In Hope of Liberty*, 206–7; Pease and Pease, *They Who Would Be Free*, 219–27; Grover, *Fugitive's Gibraltar*, 215–16; Edward R. Turner, *The Negro in Pennsylvania: Slavery-Servitude-Freedom, 1639–1861* (New York: Arno Press, 1969), 243–44; Herbert Aptheker, *Essays in the History of the American Negro* (New York: International Publishers, 1964), 133.

18. W. E. B. Du Bois, *Black Reconstruction in America, 1860–1880* (New York: Atheneum Press, 1992), 9–13; Aptheker, *Essays*, 124; C. L. R. James, *American Civilization* (Oxford: Blackwell Press, 1993), 85–98; Franklin and Schweninger, *Runaway Slaves*, chap. 1, 233.

19. For a persuasive linking of slavery expansion and calls to reopen the African slave trade during the 1850s, see Sinha, *The Counterrevolution of Slavery*, chap. 5.

INDEPENDENT COMPANIES

The right to armed self-defense against external aggression emerged as one of the central planks of natural rights philosophy in the new American Republic. This right, however, quickly became restricted to white men only. Although men of African descent protested their exclusion almost immediately, it was not until the 1850s that they sought alternatives, including independent organization. In 1855, John Snow of London published the *Autobiography of a Fugitive Slave: His Anti-Slavery Labors in the United States, Canada and England*, written by visiting abolitionist Samuel R. Ward. Readers might have been struck by Ward's observation that "the young blacks of the Republic are everywhere acquiring a love for martial pastimes." "Their independent Companies of military," he added, "are becoming common in many of the large towns." How do we explain this love for martial pastimes, the timing, and its political significance?[20]

The denial of the legal right to self-defense to men of African descent was established very early on at both federal and state levels. Although over five thousand slaves and free blacks served the patriot cause during the War of Independence, the price of nation-building and the making of independent states was the exclusion of blacks from citizenship rights, including the right to armed self-defense. The U.S. Congress limited naturalization to white aliens in 1790. Two years later, the federal militia was formed with membership restricted to able-bodied white men. Despite their service in the War of 1812, African American men were still denied entrance to the federal militia. Some state constitutions initially enrolled members regardless of race, but this practice was quickly overturned. Pennsylvania's constitution of 1776 was amended the following year, restricting service to "every male white person"; subsequent state militia acts repeated the restriction. Eligibility for private elite companies as well as public militias in Pennsylvania was restricted to white men. Ohio's first constitutional convention in 1802 did not limit male membership to the state militia, but in the act of December 30, 1803, only whites were declared eligible. The state constitution of Indiana, passed in 1816, excluded blacks, men of mixed heritage, and Indians from the militia. Even those blacks who had temporarily served in state militias usually served

20. *NYDT*, August 2, 1855; Hill, *Freedom-Seekers*, 183; Ward, *Autobiography*, 99.

in a secondary capacity and did not bear arms. This was to be a white man's republic defended by white arms.[21]

African Americans, however, continued to struggle for the right to join state militias from which they had been excluded. At the Ohio constitutional convention of 1850–51, the motion to strike out "white" in military service to the state was defeated by a margin of sixty-two to twenty-two votes. The most ardent struggle was conducted in Massachusetts. The state had banned black men from its state militia. One response by African Americans was to seek official support for an independent organization. In 1852, sixty-two Boston blacks led by prominent activists and abolitionists Robert Morris and Charles Lenox Remond petitioned the state legislature to organize their own militia company. They were unsuccessful but resubmitted the petition on February 24, 1853. In his presentation to the legislative assembly on the militia, machinist and abolitionist William J. Watkins argued for the right to form an independent company because the petitioners "are law-abiding, tax-paying, liberty-loving, NATIVE-BORN, AMERICAN CITIZENS; men who love their country, despite its heinous iniquities." Watkins added that their request was reasonable, was morally correct, and deserved to be met since "colored men fought for the Independence of this country." These committee members, he reported, requested "us to hurry," while one committee member "took leave to withdraw." In mid-April, the committee withdrew the petition. Watkins expressed his disgust in a letter to the *Boston Herald:* "the colored citizens of Massachusetts are still arrayed among the lunatics, paupers, and common drunkards." We were "treated as men" when it came to crimes, but denied the right to "show ourselves as men"

---

21. Quarles, *Black Abolitionists,* 229–30; Litwack, *North of Slavery,* 31, 35, 60; Turner, *Negro in Pennsylvania,* 179, 182; Davis, *Parades and Power,* 49–51; David A. Gerber, *Black Ohio and the Color Line, 1860–1915* (Urbana: University of Illinois Press, 1976), 3–4; Frank U. Quillin, *The Color Line in Ohio: A History of Race Prejudice in a Typical Northern State* (1913; New York: Negro Universities Press, 1969), 22; Emma Lou Thornbrough, *The Negro in Indiana: A Study of a Minority* (Indianapolis: Indiana Historical Bureau, 1957), 21, 120; John K. Mahon, *History of the Militia and the National Guard* (New York: Macmillan, 1983), 22, 54. Although some black companies were eventually organized, it was not until 1936 that the word *white* was removed from the militia article in the Indiana constitution. See Thornbrough, *Negro in Indiana,* 250.

in self-defense. "We have colored lawyers, physicians, and teachers; why not colored soldiers?"[22]

It was from this combination of legal exclusion, the need for self-defense, and the expansion of American slavery that young black men began to organize their own militias in the Northern states. In 1848, a "company of colored young men" established the Hannibal Guards "to learn military tactics." The *Brooklyn Daily Eagle* reported that a "military corps" was "in the full tide of successful experiment in the city of Albany," during the summer of 1850. In response to the 1850 Fugitive Slave Act, black paramilitary companies were set up in Cleveland and Cincinnati, Ohio. After the failed rescue of fugitive Anthony Burns in Boston, and rumors of the seizure of a fugitive from New Bedford, local black activists formed the Union Cadets "to hold themselves in readiness at all times for the protection of the civil rights of the community." In late 1855, this "colored military company" was renamed the New Bedford Independent Blues. After their petition for an independent black company was rejected by the Massachusetts legislature in 1855, Boston blacks organized the Massasoit Guards. In 1857, a new company was formed in Boston called the Liberty Guard. In 1855, the National Guards of Providence, Rhode Island, was formed. Unlike Massachusetts, the National Guards gained state approval for independent organization. During the mid-1850s, several independent companies were established around New York City, including the Independent Cadets, the MacFarian Guard, the Hall Guard, the Independent Village Guard, and the Independent Attee Guard. In 1857, Cincinnati blacks organized the Attucks Blues to study military tactics and proficiency "in the use of arms." Other independent black militias were established in Reading and Harrisburg, Pennsylvania; Paterson, New Jersey; and Detroit, Michigan.[23]

Who constituted the leadership and rank-and-file of these black militias? Captain J. J. Simmons led the Attucks Guards of New York; Capt. Hackins headed the Hannibal Guards of New York; and Capt. Dorrell commanded

22. William J. Watkins, "Our Rights as Men. An Address Delivered in Boston, Before the Legislative Committee on the Militia, February 24, 1853," in *Negro Protest Pamphlets: A Compendium*, ed. Dorothy Porter (New York: Arno Press, 1969), 2–21.

23. See sources for Table 6.1.

the National Guards of Providence. Capt. Ferguson led New York's Attic Guard. The officers for the Union Cadets of New Bedford in 1854–55 were Captain Henry Johnson from Virginia, First Lieutenant Issac Guinn from Virginia, Second Lieutenant James Fairweather from Rhode Island, and Orderly Sergeant Robert Gibson from Georgia. By 1858, Captain Robert Gibson had assumed command of the black company in New Bedford. Captain Lewis Gaul, a hackman (horse cabby), commanded the Liberty Guard of Boston. There appears to be little information, unfortunately, on the rank-and-file of these militias. According to one report, the Attic Guard of Brooklyn "was some sixteen strong, including four formidable pioneers." The Liberty Guard of Boston was made up of fifty-five men who worked a variety of occupations, including laborers, printers, and saloon keepers.[24]

During earlier displays by black militias in New England, uniforms and weapons were often borrowed from slave owners or paternal whites. By the 1850s, equipment and clothing were being provided by private and communal contributions. Uniforms were probably put together by African American women and girls. The Henry Highland Garnet Guards wore gray coats, pants, and fatigue caps, with white belts. The Liberty Guard wore black pants, tops, and caps, with white gloves. Members of the Attic Guard marched with "enormous bearskin hats," "cockades," and "other paraphernalia." The Sons of Liberty, a company of young lads in Boston, were "neatly and uniformly dressed." Such uniform dress provided a sense of discipline and martial solidarity. It is also possible that the dress and colors were deliberately chosen to contrast with the functional "Negro cloth" usually distributed to slaves.[25]

Although some companies reportedly marched with broomsticks, many were armed with weapons. Members of the Attic Guard bore "sanguinary looking axes" during public parades. Boston's Liberty Guard marched with guns, while the Henry Highland Guards bore "new muskets." The black militia of New Bedford always carried muskets during their public parades. Moreover, companies in Boston, Pittsburgh, and Detroit had their own

24. Horton and Horton, *Hope of Liberty*, 263; *FDP*, September 4, 1851; August 10, 1855; *BDE*, August 3, 1858; Grover, *Fugitive's Gibraltar*, 327; Rael, *Black Identity*, 62.

25. Piersen, *Black Yankees*, 137; Quarles, *Black Abolitionists*, 116; *L*, August 5, 1859; *BDE*, August 3, 1858; Grover, *Fugitive's Gibraltar*, 262; Martha Brown, "Clothing," in *Dictionary of Afro-American Slavery*, ed. Randall M. Miller and John David Smith (Westport, Conn.: Greenwood Press, 1997), 117–21.

TABLE 6.1. Organization of Black Militias, 1848–1863

1848	Hannibal Guards, Brooklyn, Long Island, N.Y.
1850	Independent Company, Albany, N.Y.
1851	Independent Company, Cleveland, Ohio
	Independent Company, Cincinnati, Ohio
	Independent Cadets, N.Y.
1854	Union Cadets, New Bedford, Mass.
1855	New Bedford Independent Blues, New Bedford, Mass.
	Massasoit Guards, Boston, Mass.
	National Guards, Providence, R.I.
	MacFarian Guard, New York City, N.Y.
	Hall Guard, New York City, N.Y.
	Independent Village Guards, New York City, N.Y.
	Independent Attee Guard, Brooklyn, N.Y.
1856	Queen Victoria's Rifle Guards, Hamilton, Canada West
1857	Liberty Guard, Boston, Mass.
	Attucks Blues, Cincinnati, Ohio
1859	Douglass Guards, Reading, Pa.
	Victoria Pioneer Rifle Corps, Victoria, Canada West
	Henry Highland Garnet Guards, Harrisburg, Pa.
1860	New Bedford Attucks Frontiers, New Bedford, Mass.
1861	Hannibal Guards, Pittsburgh, Pa.
	Independent Company, Detroit, Mich.
	Groton Home Guard, Groton, Conn.
1862	Independent Company, St. Catherines, Canada West
1863	Independent Company, Poughkeepsie, N.Y.
n.d.	Attucks Guards, New York City, N.Y.
	Independent Company, Paterson, N.J.

Sources: BDE, August 5, 1850; *FDP,* August 10, 1855; September 4, 1851; *L,* August 15, 1851; August 15, 1856; August 14, November 27, 1857; August 6, 13, 1858; August 5, 1859; *NYDT,* August 2, 1855; *PE,* August 3, 15, 1863; *WAA,* August 10, 17, 1861; *BAP,* 2: 345–48; 3: 449; Collison, "Loyal and Dutiful Subjects," 67; Grover, *The Fugitive's Gibraltar,* 248, 262; Harding, *There Is a River,* 161; Hortons, *Black Bostonians,* 91, 120; Horton and Horton, *In Hope of Liberty,* 263; McPherson, *The Negro's Civil War,* 19–20; Pease and Pease, *They Who Would Be Free,* 160; Quarles, *Black Abolitionists,* 116, 229–30; Rael, *Black Identity,* 62; Winks, *Blacks in Canada,* 153, 278–79.

armories. Most of these weapons were either independently owned or provided through community contributions. One reporter, for instance, praised the military company in Paterson for its gun manufacturing.[26]

We can get an idea of the social meaning behind these black militias through a brief examination of their names. Many units called themselves "Independent." This reflected an important duality: the lack of dependence on the state as well as self-organization in the face of official state exclusion. Other companies named themselves after prominent abolitionists like Douglass and Garnet. Some units were named after famous black heroes. The Attucks companies were named after the black revolutionary hero Crispus Attucks. It is also possible that they chose this name to declare the contradiction of dying in the service of one's country while being denied the basic right to self-defense. Indeed, many of these company names point to a corporate identity of black republicanism in which African Americans drew upon a tradition of natural rights to argue for the extension of those rights.

It would, however, be too simplistic to lump all black companies under one republican rubric. The Attic Guard recalled the greatness of Athenian independence rather than Roman republicanism. The Hannibal Guards took their name from the famous Carthaginian general who fought two successful wars against Roman colonization of North Africa, before being defeated by Scipio Africanus at Zama in 202 BC. The Massasoit Guards were named after the leader of the Wampanoag nation in Massachusetts, who helped rescue starving English pilgrim emigrants during the 1620s. And it should not be forgotten that Attucks was reportedly a runaway slave of African American and Native American origins, with familial roots in the Bahamas.[27]

The significance of independent companies can best be illustrated by the inaugural parade of the Liberty Guard. On the afternoon of November 16, 1857, the people of Boston witnessed the first public parade of a new military unit. The company had been formed three months earlier on August First. A few months before their formation, the U.S. Supreme Court's decision on the Dred Scott case had confirmed that black people "can be noth-

26. *BDE*, August 3, 1858; Grover, *Fugitive's Gibraltar*, 61, 247–48, 327; *FDP*, August 10, 1855; *L*, August 15, 1856; August 6, 13, 1858. For a negative reference to the "Broomstick Guards," see *CR*, March 7, 1863.

27. See sources for Table 6.1; Linebaugh and Rediker, *Many-Headed Hydra*, 232.

ing but an alien, disfranchised and degraded class."[28] The fifty-five soldiers, dressed in black and led by Capt. Gaul, left their armory and marched up Cambridge Street to the martial sounds of Bond's brass band, followed by black men, women, and children. Boston whites proceeded to heckle the Liberty Guard: "Turn out your toes niggers," "look out for your heels," "hold your gun up, colored man," "keep step with the brass band," and "look out for the eagle on the flag staff." The military company ignored the taunts and concluded their march with a dress parade greeted by three cheers from the crowd. The militia marched to William T. Pinhall's barber shop, where refreshments were served. The company proceeded to march to the mayor's residence on Rice Street. On reaching Dover Street, an altercation broke out opposite the orphan asylum between white onlookers, who hurled paper bags filled with flour and pebbles, and black onlookers who retaliated. The air was filled with "clubs, stones, howls, curses." The white crowd was driven back. Meanwhile, the Liberty Guard marched on "without taking any notice of the fight." There was a further clash on Warren Street, where the black followers were eventually bettered; they rushed to the protection of the militia, where they remained "unmolested." The white attackers hurled a volley of brickbats at the Liberty Guard. This attack proved to be too much for some company members who, ignoring Capt. Gaul's orders, charged the rowdies, "fleshing their bayonets in the posteriors of their assailants." The Liberty Guard returned to their armory in Cambridge Street and concluded their parade.[29]

After the parade, a banquet was held at Faneuil Hall, Boston, attended by the Liberty Guard and members of the "fair sex." From 9:00 P.M. to 12:00 midnight, there was a grand promenade led by Bond's brass band, with the waltzing of many "belles" costumed in "sylph-like forms." At 11:15, Miss Sarah Hill presented the military company with its silk standard of a spread eagle with an American shield, with Liberty Guards on one side and on the reverse a pine tree. This standard had been presented to the "colored citizens" of Boston during the American Revolutionary War. In her speech, Hill commended the company for its independent formation in spite of not being granted a charter by the state legislature. While they had been provoked today, she said, they showed great restraint, being "true and brave soldiers."

28. Litwack, *North of Slavery*, 63.
29. *L*, November 27, 1857.

They would take the standard, if called, and fight behind their country. To a round of cheers, Bond's brass band struck up "The Girl I Left Behind," and the evening's festivities continued into the early morning hours.[30]

There are several important points about this inaugural parade of Boston's Liberty Guard. First, ordinary black working men had formed a military company by themselves with the support of the local community. This link was suggested both by their equipment as well as events during the parade itself. Second, this was a communal event, with many in the black community drawing a great deal of pride in watching these black soldiers drill, march, and act. Third, these black soldiers insisted on their manhood, independence, and self-defense. The unit remained disciplined until it was physically attacked. Fourth, the flag presentation and praise delivered by Sarah Hill points to the limited but important public ceremonial role of black women. Most important, this public parade demonstrated an African American willingness for self-defense and armed struggle against American slavery. The following summer, Capt. Gaul and twenty-five members of his company armed with muskets joined the Independent Blues in the West Indian emancipation anniversary at New Bedford.[31]

AUGUST FIRST REHEARSAL

One of the most striking features of public parades every August First Day was the marching of black militias. The August First Day celebration in New Bedford was attended by several different militias during the 1850s, including the Independent Cadets of New York, Providence's National Guard, Boston's Liberty Guard, as well as the town's own black company. Five military companies participated in the 1855 Clifton Park anniversary, including the MacFarian Guard, the Hall Guard, the Independent Village Guards, the Independent Atte Guard, and the Independent Cadets of New York. "All the colored military companies" were expected at the Emancipation Day parade at Morris Grove, Long Island, in 1858, including the Attic Guard. The Fort Pitt Cadets provided annual escort service for the Emancipation Day parade in Pittsburgh from the mid-1850s through the early 1860s. Numerous other

30. Ibid.
31. *L*, August 13, 1858.

black militias regularly participated in Emancipation Day parades in Ohio, New Jersey, Michigan, Pennsylvania, and Connecticut.[32]

The attendance and marching of these black militias on West India Day made quite an impact. Frederick Douglass's reaction to the participation of military companies in the 1855 commemoration at New Bedford deserves quoting at some length since it is one of the few extended descriptions we have. "A novel and striking feature of the procession," he wrote,

> was the presence of two colored military companies, the "NA-TIONAL GUARDS," of Providence, and the "UNION CADETS," of New Bedford. Each company had its band of music, so that there was no lack of the thrilling "concord of sweet sounds." But how did these companies look and act, you will ask? I answer, for all the world, just like soldier[s]? They marched, halted, wheeled, and handled their arms just as you have seen well-drilled white soldiers do. I never saw colored soldier[s] before, and before I saw them I had serious doubts of the wisdom of their coming out on that day. It is so easy to be ridiculous, or to seem so; and we, as a people, have been so much the objects of ridicule, that I felt averse to given [*sic*] cause for anything further in that line. But the companies quite surpassed me by their soldierly bearing, and compelled my admiration. CAP-TAIN DORRELL, of the National Guards, may well be proud of his company of fine looking men, and of their conduct of [*sic*] this occasion and the officers of the Union cadets need not be ashamed for their appearance and performance that day. Both companies deported themselves handsomely, and attracted much attention. Of the propriety of forming such companies, it is unnecessary to speak at length here. It is enough to say, that if a knowledge of the use of arms is desirable in any people, it is desirable in us.[33]

This is a very revealing account. Douglass found these militias novel, yet the contemporary press reported that military companies had been organiz-

---

32. See sources for Table 6.2.
33. *FDP*, August 10, 1855.

ing, drilling, and parading since at least the late 1840s. Furthermore, Douglass was struck by their professionalism. These two companies both looked and acted like soldiers in terms of their appearance, drilling, and marching to martial music. Indeed, Douglass paid them his highest racial compliment: they performed like "well-drilled" white soldiers.

Moreover, these companies impressed the skeptical and self-conscious propagandist. His fears of ridicule, for instance, were well-grounded. During the 1820s, "bobalition" broadsides mocked black celebrations as feeble imitations of American public festivals. In 1850, the *Brooklyn Daily Eagle* reported the public parade of the Independent Company of Albany under the subheading "Black-Guards," concluding sarcastically: "We will wager a peck of Jersey clams that these brave fellows will never turn *pale* in the presence of the enemy." Douglass's skepticism, however, abated once confronted with the sight of "real" black soldiers. One can almost feel the pride swell in Douglass's chest. Finally, Douglass, much like Samuel Ward the same year, and Reverend Peter Gardner at the 1851 Brooklyn celebration, acknowledged the importance of military science for African Americans in their fight against American slavery.[34]

Black sailors marched in some of these Emancipation Day parades. According to New Bedford's most recent historian, the maritime commerce and whaling industry of this southeastern Massachusetts town provided an international context, even crossroads, for its inhabitants. This cosmopolitan world was on view during the transnational celebration of West India Day with the marching of visiting seamen. In 1851, a fraternity of seaman marched in the New Bedford parade. Five years later, Capt. Webquise led a company of "colored seamen." Thomas Price headed a procession of "colored" sailors in 1858.[35]

There are three major points to make about these sailors and their participation in Emancipation Day parades. First, together with fugitives, vigi-

34. Rael, *Black Identity*, 74; *BDE*, August 5, 1850. Compare with Douglass's comments of February 6, 1863: "The colored man only waits for honorable admission into the service of the country.—They know that who would be free, themselves must strike the first blow." McFeely, *Frederick Douglass*, 218.

35. Grover, *Fugitive's Gibraltar*, 6–8, 10, 56; *L*, August 15, 1856; August 6, 1858.

TABLE 6.2. West India Day Militia, 1850–1861

1850 Independent Corps, Albany, N.Y.

1851 Independent Cadets of New York, New Bedford, Mass.
   Hannibal Guards, Brooklyn, Long Island, N.Y.

1855 National Guards of Providence, New Bedford, Mass.
   Union Cadets of New Bedford, New Bedford, Mass.
   MacFarian Guard, Staten Island, N.Y.
   Hall Guard, Staten Island, N.Y.
   Independent Village Guard, Staten Island, N.Y.
   Independent Attee Guard of Brooklyn, Staten Island, N.Y.
   Independent Cadets of New York, Staten Island, N.Y.

1856 Independent Blues of New Bedford, New Bedford, Mass.
   Fort Pitt Cadets of Pittsburgh, Pittsburgh, Pa.

1857 Attucks Blues of Cincinnati, Ohio

1858 Independent Blues, New Bedford, Mass.
   Liberty Guard of Boston, New Bedford, Mass.
   Colored Militia, Paterson, N.J.
   Attic Guard, Morris Grove, Long Island, N.Y.

1859 Liberty Guard of Boston, Boston, Mass.
   Henry Highland Garnet Guards of Harrisburg, Pa.

1860 New Bedford Attucks Frontiers, New Bedford, Mass.
   Liberty Guard of Boston, New Bedford, Mass.

1861 Fort Pitt Cadets of Pittsburgh, Pittsburgh, Pa.
   Colored Military Company of Detroit, Mich.
   Groton Home Guard, Groton, Conn.

Sources: *BDE*, August 5, 1850; August 2, 3, 1858; *FDP*, September 4, 1851; August 10, 1855; *L*, August 15, 1851; August 15, 1856; August 14, 1857; August 6, 13, 1858; August 5, 1859; *NYDT*, August 2, 1855; *WAA*, August 10, 17, 1861; *BAP*, 2:76–83, 95–96; Grover, *Fugitive's Gibraltar*, 230, 248, 262; Hill, *Freedom-Seekers*, 182–83; Quarles, *Black Abolitionists*, 116–17; Rael, *Black Identity*, 62–63.

lance committees, and independent companies, black seamen belonged to a broader network of self-defense. Ever since the failure of freedman Denmark Vesey's plot to seize and burn Charleston, South Carolina, in 1822, black sailors faced incarceration when on leave in southern ports. Emancipation Day parades reminded participants of their common racial oppression and the need for collective self-defense. Second, these sailors were identified with a dissenting tradition. It was sailors who spread the news of the proposed rebellion led by former mariner Vesey. The Boston-based African American clothes merchant and rebel David Walker used sailors to help circulate his 1829 incendiary pamphlet *Appeal to the Colored Citizens of the World* from ships visiting southern ports. Black sailors often assisted vigilance committees in forcibly deterring potential slave catchers and kidnappers. Third, black sailors served as international conduits of what some scholars have identified as an incipient Pan-African politics.[36]

It is clear that black militias who marched on West India Day resembled white militias who marched on American Independence Day. Led by military bands, they often marched to the fife and drum in uniform and in order to the sounds of cheering crowds. Furthermore, they acted out the ceremonial duty of military service and self-defense with the rights of man in an emerging order of public male-centered politics. But these black companies were also very different from their white counterparts. These colored companies instilled black pride in onlookers. Uniformed, disciplined, and self-organized groups of young black men compelled the admiration of Douglass, Gardner, the followers of the Liberty Guard, and countless others. It is hard to think of white militias serving such a function given their legal countenance and axiomatic respectability.[37]

36. Grover, *Fugitive's Gibraltar*, 98; David Walker, *Appeal to the Colored Citizens of the World*, ed. Peter P. Hinks (University Park: Penn State University Press, 1996), 100–103; *BAP*, 3:38; Aptheker, *Essays*, 119; Horton and Horton, *Hope of Liberty*, 235; Linebaugh and Rediker, *Many Headed Hydra*, chap. 7.

37. It is difficult to determine exactly what abolitionists like Garrison thought of these black militias. The evidence is contradictory. The *L* opposed armed struggle against American slavery, yet it regularly reported these black militias. These companies represented black self-determination, but the Garrisonians were firmly committed to leading a biracial antislavery movement.

Moreover, by drilling, marching, and bearing arms, these black militias reminded spectators of imminent racial violence from slave catchers, federal agents, and white terrorists, as well as providing some protection in their military escort and large numbers. This explains why most of these companies were established *during* the 1850s, especially in the middle of this decade of racial violence. Much like "bloody Kansas," the formation, marching, and propagation of military science by black militias represented a rehearsal for war.

Finally, fugitives, large gatherings, militant speakers, and young men drilling offered a spectacle of militancy to deter would-be aggressors. At the Clifton Park, Staten Island, celebration in 1855, there were five independent black militia companies. As Miss McQ asked rhetorically, "Who dare molest, or make us afraid?"[38] This was a performative politics of the street designed to display resistance, militancy, and power. The spatial defense of communities, the projection of militancy through parades and guns, and political mobilization anticipated the quasi-military displays of UNIA during the 1920s, the Black Panther Party for Self Defense in the 1960s, and the Nation of Islam in the 1990s. By the 1850s, images of militant fugitives and marching soldiers rendered increasingly obsolete older images of the prostrate slave with outstretched hands pleading for his (or her) emancipation and the grateful slave thankful for his freedom.

WAR AGAINST SLAVERY

If blacks were so serious about military science, it might be objected, then how do we explain the failure of John Brown's recruitment efforts in his war against slavery in 1859? This question can only be fully answered from a continental perspective with a focus on recruitment, fighting for freedom, and the power of American slavery.

Radical abolitionist John Brown arrived in Chatham, Canada West, on April 29, 1858, seeking support from fugitives for an uprising against American slavery. The place was carefully chosen. In 1851, there were over 350 black people in Chatham (one-sixth of the population), of which 43 percent were married. Over 50 percent of those men twenty-one years old and over were either skilled or semiskilled. It was also the base for prominent black lead-

38. *WAA*, August 17, 1861.

ers and intellectuals: Isaac Shadd and his influential antislavery newspaper, the *Provincial Freeman;* Martin Delany, black nationalist leader originally from Pittsburgh; and Harriet Tubman, fugitive and antislavery activist. In addition, there were numerous black institutions: Baptist and Methodist churches; the Victoria Reform Benevolent Society; two literary groups, the Dumas Literary Society and the Chatham Literary Society; and a fireman's company. Chatham also had a long tradition of West India Day celebrations stretching back to the early 1840s. The August First Day meeting in 1855 drew a crowd of three thousand.[39] Brown and those interested met at the First Baptist Church on May 8–10, 1858, for "a very quiet convention." Thirty-four black men and twelve white men were in attendance. The former included William C. Munroe, Martin Delany, Isaac Shadd, J. H. Kagi, Thomas M. Kinnaird, and Osborne P. Anderson. Although there were disagreements over whether to fly the American flag and the return of fugitives, there was little dispute over the basic right to bear arms in self-defense and the need to overthrow American slavery.[40]

John Brown's raid on the federal armory at Harpers Ferry on October 16, 1859, failed, but had important reverberations in the U.S. North and British Canada. Around a thousand people met in Montreal, Canada East, during Brown's show trial in Charleston, Virginia. On the day of his execution, a memorial service was held in New York City. Henry Highland Garnet delivered the eulogy: "Often have I indulged the hope of seeing slavery abolished without the shedding of blood; but that hope is clouded." The "dreadful truth" of Jehovah came forth: "For the sins of this nation there is no atonement without the shedding of blood." Pennsylvania-born printer Osborne P. Anderson, the only black attendee at the Chatham meeting to join Brown, situated the raid within a historical framework of black soldiers fighting for freedom in

39. Walton, "Blacks in Buxton and Chatham," 62–89; Louis A. De Caro Jr., *"Fire from the Midst of You": A Religious Life of John Brown* (New York: New York University Press, 2002), 248–51.

40. Winks, *Blacks in Canada,* 267–69; De Caro, *"Fire from the Midst of You,"* 258–61; Hill, *Freedom-Seekers,* 20–23; Dorothy Sterling, *The Making of an Afro-American: Martin Robison Delany, 1812–1885* (New York: Da Capo Press, 1971), chap. 16, esp. 172; Rhodes, *Shadd Cary,* 129–31; *BAP,* 2:425–29; Anderson, *Voice from Harpers Ferry,* chaps. 2 and 3. The Dumas Society was probably named after French novelist Alexander Dumas, whose African ancestry was often trumpeted by black leaders to dispute claims of racial inferiority.

North America. Having escaped back to Chatham, Anderson sought funds to publish an account of the raid. Toward the end of his speech at the Colored Regular Baptist Church in Toronto, on April 9, 1860, it was reported:

> He said that it is known to all that colored men shared the perils of the Revolutionary War, as well as that of 1812, '14, and '15; and even here, in suppressing the Canadian Rebellion [1837], colored men took an active part. But is there anything in history to prove it? It was for this reason he urged the colored people to aid him in snatching from oblivion the heroism of the colored men who so nobly seconded the efforts of the immortal John Brown.

Colored men had played an "active part" in fighting against colonial oppression and enslavement. Their record, however, was underappreciated. The heroism of colored men and freedom fighters like Brown—much like the abolition of the Anglo-American slave trade and British colonial slavery—had to be remembered. Numerous readers first learned about John Brown's raid and Anderson's account in the *Weekly Anglo-African* of April 29, 1860. A year later, the memoir was published in pamphlet form as the first unofficial history of John Brown's raid.[41]

One possible explanation why Brown failed to raise black militias in British Canada was that he waited too long, allowing eighteen months to elapse between the Chatham convention and the Harpers Ferry raid. Potential followers lost interest given the lengthy wait. This seems unlikely, though, since past plots against slavery—King Court's in 1736 (Antigua), Gabriel Prosser's in 1800 (Virginia), Denmark Vesey's in 1822 (South Carolina), Nat Turner's in 1831 (Virginia), and Samuel Sharpe's in 1831 (Jamaica)—all took much longer in their preparations. Indeed, part of the initial success of Turner's revolt in Southampton County in August 1831 can be attributed to the time the slave rebels spent in drilling, marching, and practicing in military forma-

---

41. Silverman, *Unwelcome Guests,* 119; Gary Collison, "'Loyal and Dutiful Subjects of her Gracious Majesty, Queen Victoria': Fugitive Slaves in Montreal, 1850–1866," *Quebec Studies* 19 (1994–95): 65–66; Garnet, "Eulogy of John Brown," 186; *BAP,* 2:426–27; *WAA,* April 29, 1860; Anderson, *Voice from Harpers Ferry,* 76–77. This first account remained out of print until 1974.

tion. A more persuasive argument was the perfidy of the English abolitionist and mercenary Hugh Forbes, whose clashes with Brown successfully undermined the plan and the commitment of its supporters.[42]

But this still does not explain why blacks fond of military science did not flock to Brown's standard to fight against slavery. The explanation has to do with the armed might of American slaveholders. African-descended people had always challenged New World slave regimes; they rarely embarked upon suicidal attacks on powerful slave regimes. The social and political order of American slavery was enforced through a network of white paramilitary organizations, including slave patrols, local police, volunteer companies, and state militias.[43] This helps to explain the lack of major slave revolts in the American South, as well as limited support for armed forays from the U.S. North and beyond. Whenever cracks in the political structure appeared, however, the consequences were challenges to the slave regime. Scores of African slaves in Virginia rebelled during Nathaniel Bacon's rebellion against British colonial rule in 1676. The American Revolutionary War witnessed the revolt and self-emancipation of tens of thousands of African slaves against colonial slavery. The slave masses of St. Domingue rose during the crisis of the French state after the revolution, while thousands of slaves rose against colonial slavery in Jamaica during the crisis of British rule in the early 1830s.[44] It would take a major crisis in the U.S. political system, together with the potential for an overthrow of the slaveholding regime, for people of African descent to commit fully to armed struggle against the might of American slavery.

Black communities were already challenging American slavery prior to the official outbreak of armed hostilities in the spring of 1861. Fugitives and vigilance committees engaged in continental armed struggles against American slavery. There were even attempts to overthrow slavery through armed uprisings. In 1844, steamboat operator Moses Dickson along with eleven other black

42. DeCaro, *"Fire from the Midst of You,"* 244; Hill, *Freedom-Seekers,* 21; Sterling, *Making of an Afro-American,* 173.

43. Hahn, *Nation under Our Feet,* 266–72.

44. Morgan, *American Slavery,* 256–58; Fick, *Making of Haiti;* Craton, *Testing the Chains,* chap. 22; Blackburn, *Overthrow of Colonial Slavery,* chap. 11.

men met to form an organization for the overthrow of American slavery. Two years later, they met in St. Louis, Missouri, and began a secret society called the Knights of Liberty.[45] Moreover, blacks began to organize independent military companies during the decade of racial violence. They participated in communal activities, especially West India Day, the largest annual antislavery demonstration among free people of African descent and their supporters in North America. It was this preparation that helps to explain why free blacks enthusiastically enrolled in the official fight against slavery after the outbreak of the Civil War. In other words, armed blacks had already *anticipated* the rallying cry of "men of color, to arms" issued by prominent abolitionists in 1861.

Their enthusiasm was palpable during the earliest weeks of the war. On April 17, 1861, a black militia unit in Pittsburgh wrote to the militia commander of western Pennsylvania wishing to "tender to the state the services of the Hannibal Guards." One week later, African American Jacob Dobson wrote to the secretary of war, informing him "of some three hundred of [*sic*] reliable colored free citizens" in Washington, D.C., who wished to defend the city. In early May, the New York City–based *Anglo-African* reported that "a party of colored men made their appearance on Broadway," and, "with fife and drum, and bearing the American flag," attempted to march up the street. "They were dispersed by the crowd, their drum and flag taken away, and were informed that 'niggers could not be allowed to carry that flag.'" Over the next several weeks, blacks in Massachusetts repeated earlier efforts to persuade the state to remove discriminatory militia laws. An assembly of Cleveland blacks resolved: "we are ready to go forth and do battle in the common cause of the country." An independent company had been established in that city at least ten years earlier. Other new black militias were reportedly raised in Boston, New York, and Cincinnati.[46]

Such efforts were replicated in British Canada. On February 19, 1860, a group in Montreal, Canada West, submitted a petition requesting permission to form a militia unit called "The Colored Company of Montreal Volunteer Rifles." It would consist of fifty members led by a captain, a lieutenant, and an ensign together with three noncommissioned officers. The idea for the

45. Work, "Secret Societies," 343–44.

46. *AA*, May 4, 1861, in Jackson, "Anglo-African," 350–51; McPherson, *Negro's Civil War*, 19–22.

company seems to have emanated from the city's respectable tradesmen: many of the petitioners were barbers, tobacconists, carpenters, and dyers. Moreover, the petitioners were international: of the twenty-four signatories, only one had not been born in the United States, while non-signers included those born in the United Kingdom and the British West Indies.[47]

Many of these black militia efforts were rebuffed. In Montreal, the petition to form a company was apparently rejected because of the large number of existing companies as well as there being too few people of color. Northern states continued their traditional opposition to the formation of black companies and integrated militias. The militia commander in Ohio rejected the offer by Cleveland blacks as impermissible by state law. The New York City chief of police halted drilling by black men, fearing racial violence. The Massachusetts legislature postponed acting on black petitions. The federal government was no less intransigent. The secretary of war informed Dodson that the department "has no intention at present to call into the service of the Government any colored soldiers." During the first years of the conflict, President Lincoln refused to enlist black volunteers because the war was about Unionism and he felt the need to placate those border slave states (Delaware, Maryland, Missouri, Kentucky) that were still in the Union. This has led some historians to dismiss the early enthusiasm of blacks for enlistment as an "erroneous judgment [that] stemmed from misperceiving the nature of the war." As the war progressed, however, events suggested it was Lincoln who had erred about the true nature of the war—the fight over American slavery.[48]

By the war's end, large numbers of blacks had fought and died in the Union army. The leading authorities on black enrollment during the Civil War estimate that voluntary enlistment and conscription accounted for 178,975 black men in the Union army. The majority—nearly 150,000—were self-emancipated slaves, with the remaining number consisting of free blacks representing Northern states. It is important to remember, however, that some of the latter were drawn from the Atlantic world. It has been estimated that two-thirds of all young adult men from the rural black communities of Elgin

47. Collison, "Loyal and Dutiful Subjects," 66–67.
48. Ibid., 66; McPherson, *Negro's Civil War*, 21–22; Walton, "Blacks in Buxton and Chatham," 131–32, 152.

and Buxton in Canada West enlisted in the Union army. Seventy settlers at the Elgin Association settlement returned to fight for Union forces during the war. Black men from Chatham, Raleigh, and other towns and cities in British Canada served in the New York, Michigan, and Massachusetts regiments. An older authority estimates that "thousands" returned to "assist in winning liberty" for their enslaved brethren. While the 55th Massachusetts included recruits from three other countries, the 23rd U.S. Colored Infantry had members from the British colony of Jamaica. It was this continental ferment of slaves, fugitives, and free blacks that played a vital role in eventually destroying American slavery.[49]

Moreover, there were connections between black Union soldiers and independent black companies. Some former militia members ended up enrolling in the United States Colored Troops. From New Bedford, with its tradition of independent militias, it has been estimated that some fifty "men of color" served in the 54th and the 55th Massachusetts regiments. Moreover, some militia members became recruiting agents for the Union army. Robert Jones, first sergeant of Queen Victoria's Rifle Guards, returned to Philadelphia in 1863 to urge blacks to join the Union war effort. Finally, black enrollment occurred in Northern states with a tradition of Emancipation Day. Of the 37,723 black soldiers who served from Northern states, 8,612 were credited to Pennsylvania, 5,092 to Ohio, 4,125 to New York, and 3,966 to Massachusetts. Black people in these four most populous Northern states had been commemorating August First and challenging American slavery for decades. It is likely that these communities provided freedom's soldiers.[50]

Between 1834 and 1865, slavery was legally abolished and militarily destroyed in the Anglo-American world. Nearly 800,000 slaves of African provenance were freed by colonial law throughout the British Empire. Some 3.9 million slaves of African extraction were freed in fifteen slave states after a four-year

49. Green, "Upper Canada's Black Defenders," 390; Walton, "Blacks in Buxton and Chatham," 158–59; Pease and Pease, *Black Utopia*, 107; Winks, *Blacks in Canada*, 152–53; Hahn, *Nation under Our Feet*, 14, 94; Landon, "Anti-Slavery Society of Canada," 40. According to Berlin, *Freedom's Soldiers*, 126, some 36,000 black soldiers died "serving their country." I would add they gave their lives to destroy American slavery.

50. Grover, *Fugitive's Gibraltar*, 278; *BAP*, 2:348; Berlin et al., *Slaves No More*, 203.

bloody civil war. Despite their obvious differences, these processes of abolition were interconnected. The battle over fugitives was a continental struggle from the 49th Parallel to the Mexican border. Many young black men, such as the Chatham militia during the early 1840s and the Brooklyn Hannibal Guards in 1851, sought knowledge of military science in order to combat American slavery and its territorial spread. They paraded their enthusiasm during the most celebrated annual event among black people in North America. These ceremonial endeavors represented important forms of self-organization and political mobilization against slavery, resulting from a long tradition of legal and civil exclusion. Out of the ferment of state repression and protest, black people embarked on the spatial defense of communities, the projection of militancy through parades and guns, and political mobilization. Most important, they demonstrated an important link between bearing arms and rights of citizenship. Their self-defense and antislavery mobilization constituted a rehearsal for war.

Chapter 7
Emancipation in Pan-African Perspective

On August I, 1848, thirty-year-old former fugitive and abolitionist Frederick Douglass addressed a crowd of hundreds assembled in Washington Square, Rochester, New York. The "grand object" of the meeting, explained the speaker, was to "congratulate our disenthralled brethren of the West Indies on their peaceful emancipation; to express our unfeigned gratitude to Almighty God, their merciful deliverer; to bless the memory of the noble men through whose free and faithful labors the grand result was finally brought about; to hold up their pure and generous examples to be admired and copied; and to make this day, to some extent, subservient to the sacred cause of human freedom in our own land, and throughout the world." Douglass's five stated points—nonviolent emancipation, abolition as God's work, noble British activists, models for American abolitionists, and universal freedom—defined the Anglo-American abolitionist framework. Underlying these points was the view that emancipation represented progress in world history. The young antislavery activist went on to become one of the most prominent abolitionists in the United States.[1]

This framework has shaped the way many scholars interpret the antislavery struggle during this era.[2] It has a number of problems. First, people of African descent are represented as objects rather than historical agents. They are liberated by everyone else—British abolitionists, American abolitionists, "God"—but not by their own actions. Second, Douglass is chosen by scholars to represent black abolitionist thought and actions. His voice drowns out those of others. He is included in the noble band of transatlantic brothers, while other antislavery leaders and activists in the black Atlantic world are reduced in significance, deemed radically irrelevant, or ignored

1. *NS*, August 4, 1848. For a dated but superb biography, see McFeeley, *Frederick Douglass.*

2. The works of David B. Davis have been especially influential. For its institutional expression, see the Gilder Lehrman Center at Yale University, now directed by Douglass's biographer David Blight.

altogether. Third, abolition is seen in universal rather than particular terms. This reflects the Christian aspects of some abolitionists, together with the multicultural aspirations of some modern scholars. One unfortunate consequence has been the dismissal of alternative representations of slavery and emancipation engaged in a contemporary international politics of national liberation and revolutionary emancipation. Finally, this framework ignores the spatial and temporal dimensions of antislavery work, especially its interaction with the shifting world of expanding American slavery, emancipation in the British Empire, and the cross-national movement of fugitives and black abolitionists.[3]

This concluding chapter argues that West Indian emancipation politicized people of African descent around slavery and in support of emancipation and greater consciousness of the fate and aspirations of people of African descent in the Atlantic world. It draws upon a three-part Pan-African methodology. The first component examines the dispersal/movement of people, intellectuals, and activists of African descent against slavery and for emancipation. The second component explores interactions at centers and peripheries between slave and free people in transatlantic cities, towns, and villages. Both components are the subject of the chapter's first section. The point both these components seek to make is that antislavery speakers and popular anniversaries functioned as conduits of Pan-African communication. The third component of this Pan-African methodology is consciousness of this movement and interaction. Its most important aspect concerns the universal place of Africa in world history and politics during the past, present, and future.

The second part of this chapter provides an alternative analysis of West Indian emancipation orations in search of this Pan-African consciousness rooted in slavery, abolition, and post-emancipation. It challenges key ideas of Anglo-American abolition and African American nationalism with alternative ideas drawn from international politics as well as changing social conditions. The argument here is that ideas around slavery, emancipation,

---

3. I critique Douglass not to demean him, but to challenge his embodiment of how African Americans conceived liberty and freedom during this period. This explanation failed to satisfy one white neo-abolitionist at a Douglass Conference in Rochester who accused me of being ideological not scholarly. I told him I guess I was being radical and irrelevant!

and liberation formed the basis for a racial politics of identity grounded in being African in the modern world.[4]

The major objectives for this final chapter are threefold. First, we examine August First speeches, addresses, and orations for an alternative set of antislavery ideas based on racial identity and common consciousness as an important part of the cultural and geographical dimensions of the black Atlantic world. Second, we situate this alternative framework within a broader context of expanding American slavery, Caribbean emancipation, and transnational movements of fugitives and black abolitionists. Third, we shed new light on old models of transformation in the collective identity of people of African descent by focusing on the cross-national dimensions of these Emancipation Day orations.[5] The key research question is the following: to what extent do the movements of black antislavery activists, the intellectual and political content of their emancipation orations, and the popular nature of these events contain the seeds of what later became known as Pan-Africanism?[6]

FREE ETHIOPIANS

Anniversaries of West Indian Emancipation Day served to highlight the transnational dimensions of slavery and abolition in the Atlantic world. The expansion of American slavery brought with it a corresponding expansion of antislavery mobilization. This involved the movement of slaves, fugitives, free blacks, activists, abolitionists, and intellectuals during the middle decades of the nineteenth century. Their travels took them both around the Atlantic

4. I have found the following Pan-African studies useful: Gomez, *Exchanging Our Country Marks*, 1–16; Joseph E. Harris, ed., *Global Dimensions of the African Diaspora* (Washington, D.C.: Howard University Press, 1993); Sweet, *Recreating Africa*; Gilroy, *Black Atlantic*; James, *Holding Aloft*.

5. For important works on this collective transformation, see Jones, *Blues People*; Sterling Stuckey, *Slave Culture: Nationalist Theory and The Foundations of Black America* (New York: Oxford University Press, 1987); Gomez, *Exchanging Our Country Marks*.

6. In a recent web site discussion on Pan-Africanism, the various contributors defined it as spanning the eighteenth through twentieth centuries, encompassing western and southern Africa, the Caribbean, and Afro-America, and involving intellectuals, anti-colonial activists, slaves, sailors, emigrationists, and so on. The definition was so all-inclusive, one was left wondering who and what exactly was not Pan-African! See *History-Africa Discussion Network*, August 2005. This chapter simply argues that Pan-Africanism must *begin* with both the historical conditions of enslavement, abolition, and post-emancipation, as well as the consciousness of those conditions.

world as well as between the Caribbean and the mainland. The following section begins with these various movements. It then turns to the impact that such cross-national travels had on the antislavery politics of these black travelers. It concludes with a brief comment on the attendance of these black travelers at August First celebrations in the black Atlantic world.

Let us begin with a sketch of the international dimensions of slavery and emancipation in the modern world. Recent research estimates that between 9.6 million and 10.8 million African slaves survived the transoceanic slave trade, reaching the Americas between 1450 and 1870. After the abolition of the Atlantic slave trade by the British and Americans in 1807 and 1808 respectively, new slave trading routes were established between Caribbean islands, from the American Upper to Lower South states, and from the northeast to the southeast of Brazil. As a result of the successful slave revolt and war of independence in Haiti, many slave owners and their slaves moved to Cuba, Louisiana, and elsewhere. The new black Republic was the destination for six thousand African Americans alone during the 1820s. As a result of the American Revolution, thousands of African American slaves were moved to the British Caribbean, Canada, and coastal colonies in West Africa. Sierra Leone, created in 1787 as a haven for African-descended people in the British Empire, began with London's black poor, then Nova Scotia blacks seeking land, and finally recaptives by the British navy. These recaptives, or liberated Africans, also settled Libreville on the coast of Gabon in 1849. It has been estimated that the British navy captured 1,635 ships and freed just over 160,000 slaves during the nineteenth century, many of whom were settled in Sierra Leone and the Caribbean. Black soldiers who served in the British army received land and ended up in Trinidad. Liberia was first settled by freed slaves from the United States in 1822; it gained its independence in 1847. This was the swirling world in which black abolitionists operated during the ante- and post-emancipation decades.[7]

Between 1830 and 1865, it has been estimated that at least eighty-three black abolitionists visited the United Kingdom. Travelers over the first two

---

7. Lovejoy, "Atlantic Slave Trade," 368; David B. Gaspar and David P. Geggus, *A Turbulent Time: The French Revolution and the Greater Caribbean* (Bloomington: Indiana University Press, 1997); Chris Dixon, *African America and Haiti: Emigration and Black Nationalism in the Nineteenth Century* (Westport, Conn.: Greenwood Press, 2000); Walker, *Black Loyalists;* Illife, *Africans,* 148, 155; Rodriguez, *World Slavery,* 2:410, 543–44.

decades included Nathaniel Paul (1832–36); James McCune Smith (1832–37); Robert Purvis (1834); Moses Roper (1835–44, 1846); Peter Williams (1837); Henry Watson (ca. 1840); Robert Douglass Jr. (1840–41); Charles Lennox Remond (1840–41); Madison Jefferson (1841–42); Moses Grandy (1842–43); James W. C. Pennington (1843); Frederick Douglass (1845–47); J. R. Bailey (1846); Molliston M. Clark (1846–47); John Joseph (1847); Stephen Glouster (1847–48); Josiah Henson (1849–50); and Jeremiah Asher (1849–50). Some left with a specific objective: to fund a black church or school; to raise money to help emancipate enslaved family members; or to find a publisher for their slave autobiography. Others pursued more general tasks relating to antislavery activism: consciousness-raising, fund-raising, and building an antislavery wall around American slavery. Charles Remond, for instance, attended the World's Anti-Slavery Convention in London, after which time he spent eighteen months on an important antislavery lecture tour in Great Britain.[8]

The passage of the Fugitive Slave Act in 1850, however, turned this trickle into a flood of black abolitionist visitors. Indeed, many black abolitionists who visited the United Kingdom went as fugitives from American slave law. Baltimore-born Alexander Duval fled slavery in 1849 and settled as a cooper in New Bedford. Spying his owner in early 1851, he left for England, where he remained until 1858. His companion on the ship to Liverpool was fellow fugitive Francis Anderson, who stayed until 1855. Born in Maryland, Henry Garnet escaped slavery with his family in 1824 and pursued church, antislavery, and Liberty Party politics in New York for the next two decades. In 1850, he relocated to Britain, addressing Scottish and English audiences on the woes of American slavery. Along with fellow fugitives Josiah Henson and James Pennington, Garnet served as English subscription agent for the Canada-based *Voice of the Fugitive*. Maryland fugitive Samuel Ward spent a busy two-and-a-half years in the United Kingdom between 1853 and 1855. Serving as a lecture agent for the ASSC, he embarked upon antislavery lecture tours to Scotland, Ireland, Wales, and England. These activities were subsequently described in his *Autobiography of a Fugitive Slave*, published in 1855 by John Snow of London. William Wells Brown escaped Kentucky slavery in January 1834

8. *BAP*, 1:3, 79, 571–73; William Andrews, ed., *North Carolina Slave Narratives: The Lives of Moses Roper, Lunsford Lane, Moses Grandy, and Thomas H. Jones* (Chapel Hill: University of North Carolina Press, 2003), 24, 136.

and became involved in antislavery activities in western New York and the border areas with British Canada. In October 1849, he left for Britain, where he stayed until 1854. Although there were numerous personal and political reasons for the length of his visit, he also faced re-enslavement after the passage of the Slave Act. Indeed, while sharing the specific and general objectives of fellow abolitionists noted above, it should be emphasized that a number of these fugitives sought sanctuary from American slavery, potential kidnapping, and Northern racism.[9]

The British Empire also provided a safe haven for African Americans. As noted in earlier chapters, Canada West had long been identified as a relatively safer realm compared to a United States of slavery and prejudice. Virginia-born Austin Steward escaped slavery and pursued a variety of antislavery activities in upstate New York during the 1820s. In 1831, Steward left Rochester to run the Wilberforce colony of free blacks in Canada West between 1831 and 1837. It was the Fugitive Slave Act, however, which really increased the number of black abolitionists in Canada West. As a result of their helping William "Jerry" McHenry escape federal agents in Syracuse in October 1851, former slaves Samuel R. Ward and Jermain Wesley Loguen were forced to relocate to Canada West. Baltimore-born William Watkins escaped the city's worsening racial climate in 1852 and settled in Toronto, where he opened a grocery business. Abner Hunt Francis, businessman and activist in Buffalo, moved to Oregon Territory in mid-1851, and by the end of the decade had settled in Victoria, Vancouver Island. Philadelphia-born Mifflin Wistar Gibbs, a successful businessman and activist involved in the city's Underground Railroad, moved to San Francisco. Despite his success, Gibbs relocated to Vancouver Island in 1858, to escape California's racism.[10]

Moreover, a number of black abolitionists who moved to Canada West joined the burgeoning antislavery movement. Ward worked as a very successful agent for the ASSC. Virginia fugitive and Ohio activist Hezekiah Ford Douglas became an agent for the *Voice of the Fugitive* and co-owner of the

---

9. *BAP*, 1:3, 153–54, 227, 256–57, 300, 571–73; Burke, *Ward*, 54–55; *VF*, July 30, 1851. Rice, *Scots Abolitionists*, 151–62, describes the activities of some of these black abolitionists, but his focus is upon ideological squabbles between British and American abolitionists.

10. *BAP*, 1:300; 2:53, 198, 420; 3:97; 4:78–79, 106–7, 155; *The Montreal Star*, April 21, 1963.

Provincial Freeman in 1856. Peter H. Walker became an agent for the Haytian Emigration Bureau in Canada during 1861. Gibbs spent a decade on Vancouver Island, where he joined the first volunteer militia on the Pacific Coast. It should not be forgotten that in 1858, Chatham was home to over a thousand fugitives from American slavery; it was also the residence of a number of prominent black leaders, including *Provincial Freeman* publisher Isaac Shadd and physician, scholar, and nationalist Martin Delany.[11]

The British colony of Jamaica was another important part of this black Atlantic world. Some African Americans ended up either working or relocating there. James G. Barbadoes, a clothier, barber, and prominent abolitionist in Boston, moved his family to Jamaica in the spring of 1840. Malaria killed two of his children, and he died of the same disease a year later. In 1845, Pennington visited Jamaica to examine missionary stations, as well as the potential for African American emigration. During the early 1860s, Virginia-born Alexander Thomas Augusta spent some time in the West Indies, after which he returned to become the Union army's first black physician. The governing board of the Scottish Presbyterian Church designated Garnet as its official missionary to Jamaica in October 1852. Garnet, along with his wife, adopted daughter, and infant son, left in December. The Garnets were posted to Stirling in the southwest parish of Westmoreland. Over the course of the next two years, the Garnets provided religious services together with daytime, industrial, and Sabbath schooling. After his successful antislavery activities in the United Kingdom, Ward decided not to return to either Canada West or the United States, but instead moved to Jamaica. John Chandler, a Quaker from Chelmsford, U.K., owned property in the parish of St. George, Jamaica. After hearing Ward speak at Chelmsford, Chandler gifted fifty acres of land to Ward. The transaction was overseen by William W. Anderson, a Scottish immigrant and legislative member, who had represented Jamaica at the NACCP held in Toronto in 1851. Ward became pastor at Kingston's Baptist Church until 1860, after which time he settled down to a life of farming some land in the parish of St. Thomas-in-the-East, where he lived out the rest of his days until 1866. Although there is some debate about Ward's reasons for going to Jamaica—one of which entailed a financial dispute with London

11. *BAP,* 1:300; 2:53, 198, 420; 3:343; 4:78–79, 106–7, 155; *The Montreal Star,* April 21, 1963; De Caro Jr., *"Fire from the Midst of You,"* 248.

tradesman William Baynham—it should not be forgotten that Ward faced potential incarceration under the Fugitive Slave Act should he return to the United States. In his acceptance of the Scottish Presbyterian Church's designation, Garnet also noted that the recent American law prevented his return.[12]

Moreover, Afro-Americans and Afro-Jamaicans established important antislavery connections in the struggle against the expansion of American slavery. In early 1853, while visiting Jamaica, white Tennessean Thomas J. Adams enticed fourteen-year-old Alexander Hendrickure to come to work for him. On arriving in Pittsburgh, a vigilance committee liberated Hendrickure and drove Adams off. On May 31, 1853, Martin Delany, John C. Peck, William Webb, and Thomas Burrows wrote to the Kingston *Morning Journal* describing the kidnapping case and referring to other instances in which "almost every American steamer which touches the island bring[s] away some colored youths to the United States, always predicated upon great promises of doing great things for them." The letter writers condemned this new "species of the slave trade," and sought to warn their fellow Afro-Jamaicans of "a regular system of decoying, kidnapping and selling into hopeless bondage, in the United States," Jamaican boys and girls.[13]

Black women also traveled, worked, organized, and protested in this Atlantic world. During the 1850s, several African American women pursued antislavery activities in the United Kingdom. Clarissa and Josephine Brown, daughters of William Brown, accompanied their father during the early 1850s to Britain, where they taught school and pursued various antislavery activities. Fugitives Ellen and William Craft were forced to flee Boston to escape slave catchers and resettled in the United Kingdom. During the 1850s, they worked the antislavery circuit, welcomed visiting black abolitionists, and published their joint autobiography *Running a Thousand Miles to Freedom* in 1860. Throughout the 1860s, Ellen continued her activism with freedmen's aid societies and women's rights. Fugitive Harriet Brent Jacobs visited Britain in 1845–46 and 1858, eventually publishing her autobiography *Life of a Slave Girl.* In 1868, Jacobs returned to fund-raise for a freed people's orphan asylum in Savannah, Georgia. In 1859, Sarah Parker Remond conducted a year-long antislavery speaking tour of the United Kingdom. She stayed in England

12. *BAP,* 2:150, 164, 379; 3:306–7, 337, 343–44, 476; *MRUPC,* November 1852–June 1853; Schor, *Garnet,* 125–33; Ward, *Autobiography,* 404–6; Burke, *Ward,* 57–58.

13. *BAP,* 4:157–63.

for the next seven years, taking education courses, criticizing the Confederate States of America, and working for the London Emancipation Society.[14]

African American women also pursued antislavery work in Canada West. After accepting a post with the Maine Anti-Slavery Society in 1854, Frances Ellen Watkins Harper addressed audiences in Canada as well as Northern states for the remainder of the decade. As noted earlier, Mary Ann Shadd, born in Wilmington, Delaware, and raised in the mid-Atlantic region, immigrated to Canada West in 1851. Over the next decade, she taught school in Windsor and Chatham, wrote an important immigration tract *Notes on Canada West*, published in 1852, and edited the influential *Provincial Freeman* between 1854 and 1857. She returned to the United States in 1864 to teach school.[15]

There was also a Caribbean connection to these activities. The owners of Mary Prince brought her to the United Kingdom in 1828, but she left after being abused. Seeking to return to Antigua to join her husband, but fearing a return to slavery because her owners would not manumit her, she wrote *The History of Mary Prince, A West Indian Slave, Related by Herself*, published in 1831. Henry Garnet's wife Julia accompanied her husband first to Britain and then to Jamaica, where she directed two elementary schools and a female industrial school for children over a three-year period. Their adopted daughter, Stella Weims, was a fugitive from Maryland who assisted in these activities. She died of bilious fever at age twenty-four while at the Stirling post. Her life, according to Garnet's eulogy, was embittered by an "atrocious system of American Republican despotism." Although it is easy to exaggerate the political and intellectual significance of such movements and activities, we should not dismiss evidence of the stirrings of an early black sisterhood. A common struggle against institutionalized slavery, against the patriarchal order, and for alternative understandings of womanhood was directly informed by the international nature of slavery and antislavery.[16]

14. *BAP*, 1:168–69, 243, 251, 440–41, 571–72; Jean Fagan Yellin, "Harriet Ann Jacobs," *Legacy* 5, no. 2 (1988): 55–61.

15. *BAP*, 2:192; 4:405; Rhodes, *Shadd Cary*.

16. Prince, *History of Mary Prince*; Blackburn, *Overthrow of Colonial Slavery*, 442–43; *MRUPC*, March 1856, vol. 11, p. 36; Schor, *Garnet*, 129–30; Swift, *Black Prophets*, 281; *BAP*, 3:337. Abolitionist women in the Atlantic world were the subject of a conference at Yale, "Sisterhood and Slavery," Gilder Lehrman Center Conference, October 25–27, 2001. Both the conference and Anderson, *Joyous Greetings*, pay insufficient attention to black abolitionist women, their antislavery sisterhood, and its implications for gender alliances.

There were additional cross-national dimensions to this movement of black abolitionists. In the immediate aftermath of emancipation in British South Africa, North Carolina slave fugitive Moses Roper sought land in Cape Good Hope. The failure to get this land encouraged Roper to move from Britain to Canada in 1844 with his English wife Ann Stephen Price and their child. Isaac N. Cary lived in Haiti for several years, along with stints in Toronto and Washington, D.C. After antislavery and emigration activities in Canada West and the United States during the 1850s, James T. Holly led 111 black people from New Haven, Boston, and Canada West to settle in Haiti in 1861. Although forty-two settlers, including four members of Holly's family died within nine months, Holly resided there until his death in 1911.[17]

Although it is important to trace these international travels, we must also examine how such movements *transformed* the antislavery consciousness of black abolitionists in the Atlantic world.[18] James G. Barbadoes vehemently opposed colored emigration. After working to recruit free black settlers to British Guiana, however, he ended up relocating to Jamaica. Samuel Ward's views changed in several ways because of fund-raising visits to the United Kingdom. One thing that attracted his attention "was the comfort and cleanliness, not to say the elegance of appearance, presented by the working classes." Along with British parliamentary interest in working people, these were "two truths which the pro-slavery portion of the Americans did at all like to tell." Furthermore, unlike his experience in the United States and Canada West, Ward was struck by the almost universal commitment to the cause of abolitionism in the United Kingdom. Rather than fashionable statement, he found "in every part of England, Ireland, Scotland, and Wales, that abolitionism is not a mere abstract idea, but a practical question of grave importance." Finally, antislavery tours of Scotland and Ireland caused him to later remark that his travels abroad had taught him about the universality of human suffering and the need for emancipation. In no part of the United States where "Negroes are nominally free, much less where they are really free," remarked Ward, "did I ever see such degradation as abounds not only in the towns, but in the rural districts, of Ireland." "I have seen Ann Street," he continued,

17. Andrews, *North Carolina Slave Narratives*, 24; *BAP*, 2:142, 380.
18. Gilroy, *Black Atlantic*, 17, raises this important issue.

"the worst haunt of the most debased coloured population of Boston—the Five Points, the Aceldama of New York—the Moyamensing District, the incomparable slough of Philadelphia's indecency; but never saw so large a proportion of a population so utterly degraded, as that in the neighbouring island." Although the Irish were not enslaved, their poverty and oppression resembled that of enslaved people.[19]

R. C. Henderson served as a black catechist in the Anglican Church of British Guiana. An African American freeman touring Demerara to raise funds to help support fugitive slaves in the United States persuaded Henderson to visit Canada, where he was ordained in the Independent Methodist Episcopal Church. Henderson returned to Demerara, preaching for black ministers and against white ministers of black congregations. During the early 1850s, Henderson returned to Canada, where he was designated bishop. Much to the chagrin of white missionaries, he proved to be very popular with black congregations. One source reported with distaste: "he panders to the prejudices, passions, and depraved tastes of the creoles, who will readily listen to such a man, especially if he has plenty to say against the whites, and particularly white ministers. These he represents as tyrants and oppressors of the people, whose aim is to enrich themselves and keep the creoles in a state of darkness, servitude, and ignorance." While it is clear that this view reflected the deep disdain white preachers had for black preachers and their increasing control over congregations, the major point is the cross-national transformation experienced by Henderson.[20]

Henry Garnet's four-year stint as an antislavery activist in the United Kingdom and missionary to Jamaican freed people certainly had an important impact on changing his consciousness. "Such an audience I had never had before," wrote Garnet about his Kingston congregation. Once at Stirling post, he was welcomed by older members who "never thought [they would] live to see a black minister." Close to this colonial post of former slaves,

19. Lydia McNeil, "James G. Barbadoes," *EAACH*, 1:263; Ward, *Autobiography*, 237–40, 301–2, 379–380; Burke, *Ward*, 55–56. The Aceldama was the field of bloodshed from Acts 1:19. For contemporary fashionable statements, one only has to peruse the pages of the *New Yorker*, where the bourgeois reader can read about the Rwandan massacres and feel temporarily outraged, while sipping coffee made by poor peasants in Brazil or Vietnam.

20. Green, *British Slave Emancipation*, 343–44.

there were 150 liberated Africans, whom the British navy had delivered to Jamaica. Garnet tried to convert them to Christianity, but failed. Instead, the Africans seem to have converted Garnet. After his return to the United States from Jamaica, Garnet positively embraced black emigration and moved toward a transnational consciousness. These new views were institutionalized through the formation of the African Civilization Society (ACS), an organization dedicated to the proliferation of black missionaries and business to Africa.[21]

Many of these black abolitionists addressed antislavery audiences at West Indian Emancipation Day celebrations in the United Kingdom. In early August 1836, the Glasgow Emancipation Society held its second annual meeting in the Scottish city. James McCune Smith, the son of former slaves and a graduate student in the medical school of Glasgow University, was an active participant in the society. It is quite likely that he was in attendance. "In various parts of England and Scotland," noted the *Colored American* referring to the 1838 abolition, "has the day of freedom to the negroes been celebrated." It is probable that black abolitionists resident in Britain attended these momentous antislavery celebrations. In 1843, James Pennington addressed antislavery audiences in the English cities of Leeds and Birmingham in celebration of British emancipation. Nearly a thousand people attended an antislavery meeting at the Hall of Commerce in London on August 1, 1851. The meeting was organized and directed by fugitive slaves to celebrate the anniversary of West Indian emancipation and the return of veteran British abolitionist George Thompson from his antislavery tour of the United States. In attendance were the Browns, Duval, Anderson, Benson, and several other black abolitionists. Three years later, the Anti-Slavery and India-Reform League held a "great" antislavery meeting at the Athenaeum in Manchester to celebrate the twentieth anniversary of West Indian emancipation. In attendance were the Browns, Ward, South Carolina fugitive William North, and William P. Powell, "a colored gentlemen of Liverpool." Sarah P. Remond and Ellen Craft were also reported to have attended a public meeting at the Music Hall, Bedford

21. *MRUPC*, May 1853, vol. 8, p. 294; May 1854, vol. 9, p. 85; Schor, *Garnet*, 156; *BAP*, 2:440; Horton and Horton, *Hope of Liberty*, 261. For the transformative travels of a later generation of black women, see Ula Y. Taylor, "Intellectual Pan-African Feminists: Amy Ashwood-Garvey and Amy Jacques-Garvey," in *Time Longer than Rope*, ed. Payne and Green, 179–95.

TABLE 7.1. August First Day Commemorations and Speakers in Black Atlantic World, 1838–1861

1838	Port of Prince, Haiti
	Stellenbosch, Cape of Good Hope, South Africa
1843	James W. C. Pennington, Leeds, United Kingdom
1847	Cinnamon Hill, Jamaica
1849	Port Maria, Jamaica
1850	Savannah Grande, Trinidad
1851	William Wells Brown, London, United Kingdom
	Josephine Brown, London, United Kingdom
	Clarissa Brown, London, United Kingdom
	Alexander Duval, London, United Kingdom
	Francis S. Anderson, London, United Kingdom
	Benjamin Benson, London, United Kingdom
	Kingston, Jamaica
1852	Samuel R. Ward, Toronto, C.W.
1854	Frederick Douglass, Dawn, C.W.
	William Wells Brown, Manchester, United Kingdom
	Samuel R. Ward, Manchester, United Kingdom
	William P. Powell, Manchester, United Kingdom
	William North, Manchester, United Kingdom
	Josephine Brown, Manchester, United Kingdom
	Clarissa Brown, Manchester, United Kingdom
	Port Maria, Jamaica
1857	Martin Delany, Chatham, C.W.
1859	Sarah P. Remond, London, United Kingdom
	Ellen Craft, London, United Kingdom
	Monroe, Liberia
1861	Spafields Chapel, London, United Kingdom

Sources: AA, October 15, 1859; *ASB,* August 30, 1851; September 10, 1859; *CA,* September 22, 1838; *L,* August 17, 1849; August 19, 26, 1859; August 23, 1861; *MRUPC,* August 1847, 120–21; *NS,* October 27, 1848; *PF,* August 26, September 2, 24, 1854; *BAP,* 1:256–57, 285, 398, 571–73; Blackett, *Beating against the Barriers,* 28; Brereton, "Birthday of Our Race," 73; Fabre, "African-American Commemorative Celebrations," 85; Scully, *Liberating the Family?* 64; Taylor, *British and American Abolitionists,* 355.

Square, London, held in commemoration of the twenty-fifth anniversary of British colonial emancipation.[22]

Some of these black abolitionists from the United States also addressed antislavery audiences at August First celebrations in Canada West. Fugitive Samuel Ward from Syracuse spoke at the anniversary in Toronto in 1852. Rochester-based Frederick Douglass addressed the assembly at Dawn, western Ontario, in 1854. Peter Humphries Clark, Cincinnati-based teacher and abolitionist, delivered an antislavery lecture in the colored Baptist church in Chatham in April 1857. Three months later, Martin Delany spoke at that city's antislavery anniversary.[23]

Moreover, the antislavery press provided local readers with international information. African American readers and listeners regularly learned about the activities of black abolitionists in the Atlantic world, along with developments in the British Caribbean and occasionally West Africa, from the pages of the *Liberator.* The *Provincial Freeman* and the *Voice of the Fugitive* constantly reported on American slavery and antislavery to readers in Canada West, the Northern United States, and the United Kingdom. The latter newspaper also had regular subscription agents—Henson, Garnet, and Pennington—in England during the early 1850s. Robert Hamilton, the editor of the important New York–based black newspaper, the *Anglo-African,* introduced a new issue in July 1861, with the explanation: "we commence to-day the publication of a weekly journal which shall be devoted specially to the best interests of the colored people in this and other countries."[24]

Although our focus concerns the movement, activities, and transformation of black abolitionists, we should not ignore some additional intriguing aspects of West Indian Emancipation Day celebrations in the Atlantic world. On August 1, 1838, there was an Emancipation Day festival in Port au Prince, Haiti. It opened with church services followed by a "splendid banquet." In attendance were high-ranking public officials, including the French and British consuls, together with M. Courtois, editor of the *Feuille du Commerce* and

22. *L,* August 6, 1836; September 5, 1851; August 25, September 1, 1854; August 19, 26, 1859; *CA,* October 13, 1838; *PF,* August 26, September 23, 1854; *BAP,* 1:58, 256, 285, 398; *ASB,* September 10, 1859; Webb to Quincy, August 2 1854, in Taylor, *Abolitionists,* 355; Blackett, *Beating against the Barriers,* 29–30.

23. *L,* August 20, 1852; *FDP,* August 11, 1854; *PF,* April 25, 1857; *BAP,* 2:206.

24. *VF,* July 30, 1851; *AA,* July 27, 1861, in Jackson, "Anglo-African," 332.

president of the day's proceedings. Numerous toasts followed. The British official used the occasion to celebrate "a day so glorious in the annals of my country." The French ambassador toasted the day of happiness "to the confraternity, then, of colors!" The newspaper editor toasted the French monarch: "A great king, the most liberal and well-qualified monarch who has honored civilized Europe." The remaining several toasts were made to those "Friends of Liberty and universal emancipation," including British and American antislavery politicians and abolitionists. There was no comment on the attendance of ordinary people and what they thought of the occasion. This was clearly a respectable emancipation celebration a generation after Haiti's bloody entrance into the modern world.[25]

Other scholars have identified the ship and music as conduits of Pan-African communication during the eighteenth and twentieth centuries respectively.[26] Their nineteenth-century counterpart was the black abolitionist who traveled widely, linked up scattered communities, and spoke and wrote about "our" struggles as slaves, fugitives, and freed people. Their antislavery activism constituted a human and political dispersal that mirrored older forms of the African Diaspora such as the transoceanic slave trade, transcontinental slave trades, and transnational antislavery struggles. The spoken and written word at West Indian Emancipation Day celebrations around the Atlantic world were important sites for this communication, and it is to these that we now turn.

AUGUST ADDRESS

Antislavery speeches by black abolitionists provided the main intellectual fare at August First celebrations. Organizers would invite prominent speakers to deliver an antislavery harangue or discourse of the ceremonial kind. Although the content varied, orations usually commented on the passage of British abolition, the ills of American slavery, and how best to bring about emancipation. Sometimes one main orator was featured; other times, there were several speakers on the platform. These speeches could last from thirty minutes to three hours. Although the antislavery press often identified the major speakers of the day, many of the addresses are lost to us. The *Poughkeepsie*

25. *CA*, September 22, 1838.
26. Linebaugh and Rediker, *Many-Headed Hydra*, chap. 5; Gilroy, *Black Atlantic*, chap. 3.

Eagle provides the best explanation: "We regret that want of room renders it impossible for us to publish it." Some speeches by prominent abolitionists like Garrison, Douglass, and Watkins, however, were considered important enough to be printed subsequently in the abolitionist press. Other orators had their speeches published as separate pamphlets upon popular demand. On August 1, 1856, James Pennington delivered an address at Gillette's Grove in Hartford, Connecticut. "At the repeated solicitation of a number of those who heard it," wrote Pennington, "I have consented to put it to press."[27]

As noted earlier, scholars have interpreted these speeches in terms of either Anglo-American abolition or African American nation-building. The richness, diversity, and contradictions of these speeches, however, transcend such frameworks. Anglo-American abolitionism, with its juxtaposition of American republican slavery and British monarchical freedom, focuses on antislavery strategies at the expense of freedom for slaves of African descent and their common racial politics of identity. Furthermore, abolition is primarily seen in terms of a boon bestowed by well-meaning abolitionists rather than a demand by slaves, fugitives, and abolitionists. An emphasis on African American liberation theology trumpets Christian orations at the expense of their secular and political content. (Hence the preference by such scholars for the term *oration* over *speech, address, talk,* etc.) More important, a contemporary analysis of national liberation struggles and revolutionary emancipation is ignored for a primary emphasis on homiletics and how the Bible was manipulated to explain existing conditions. The notion of double-consciousness freezes people of African descent into normative categories like "free," "Northern," "American," when August First suggests their experiences were much more labile/complicated/transient—"fugitive," "continental," "diasporic." Finally, these frameworks trap emancipation orations in hermetically sealed time and space. One has no sense of how these speakers and their talks changed over time as a consequence of shifting historical conditions. Instead, we are left with a-historical categories like republican hypocrisy, biblical counter-memory, and double-consciousness, approaches that can be used to explain just about anything that ever happened over the past two centuries.

27. *PE,* August 7, 1858; James W. C. Pennington, *The Reasonableness of the Abolition of Slavery at the South: An Address Delivered at Hartford, Connecticut, August 1856* (Hartford, Conn.: Case Tiffany, 1856), 2.

TABLE 7.2. August First Speeches, 1838–1860

1838	William Douglas,† Philadelphia, Pa.
	William L. Garrison,† New York City, N.Y.
1839	Robert Banks,* Detroit, Mich.
	James W. C. Pennington,* Newark, N.J.
	Henry Highland Garnet,† Troy, N.Y.
1840	Abraham D. Shadd,† Wilmington, Del.
	James W. C. Pennington,† Hartford, Conn.
1842	Josiah Jones,* Chatham, C.W.
1843	Jehiel C. Beman,† Boston, Mass.
1847	Amos Gerry Beman,* Hudson, N.Y.
1848	Frederick Douglass,† Rochester, N.Y.
	H. W. Johnson,† Rochester, N.Y.
1849	Abner Hunt Francis,† Buffalo, N.Y.
	John I. Gaines,† Cincinnati, Ohio
	J. H. Perkins,† Cincinnati, Ohio
1851	William Wells Brown,† London, U.K.
	Alexander Duval,† London, U.K.
1852	Samuel R. Ward,† Toronto, C.W.
	Samuel J. May,† Windsor, C.W.
1853	William J. Watkins,† New Bedford, Mass.
1854	William W. Brown,† Manchester, U.K.
	William J. Watkins,† Columbus, Ohio
	James C. Brown,† Dawn, C.W.
1855	William J. Watkins,† Adams, N.Y.
	William L. Garrison,† Brooklyn, N.Y.
1856	James W. C. Pennington,* Hartford, Conn.
1857	Frederick Douglass,* Canandaigua, N.Y.
	William Whipper,† Dresden, C.W.
1858	Frederick Douglass,* Poughkeepsie, N.Y.
1860	Frederick Douglass,* Geneva, N.Y.

Sources: ASB, August 18, 1855; *Chatham Journal*, August 6, 1842; *CA*, August 18, 25, September 1, 1838; August 22, 26, 1840; *FDP*, August 18, 1854; August 10, 1855; *HS*, August 6, 1852; *HF*, November 1, 1839; *L*,

(*continued*)

TABLE 7.2. continued

August 11, 1843; September 5, 1851; August 20, 1852; August 19, 1853; August 25, September 1, 1854; *NE,* August 23, 1855; *NS,* August 4, 21, 1848; August 17, September 7, 1849; *PF,* August 26, 1854; August 22, 1857; *VF,* August 12, 1852; Banks, *An Oration, Delivered at a Celebration in Detroit, 1839;* Beman, *Address Delivered at the Celebration of the West Indian Emancipation, 1847;* Pennington, *West Indian Emancipation Address;* Pennington, *An Address Delivered at Hartford, Conn., on the First of August, 1856; BAP,* 1:285–89, 290–92, 398–406; 2:95–96; Blackett, *Beating against the Barriers,* 29–30; *Frederick Douglass Papers,* 3:183–208, 214–42, 366–87; Schor, *Garnet,* 21–22.

*Published in pamphlet.

†Published in newspaper.

Moving away from these dialectics—British/American, memory/counter-memory, race/nation—we pursue an alternative dialectic between the enslavement and emancipation of people of African descent within an international context. This is done through identification and examination of six different aspects of August First addresses. Thus, instead of the biblical exodus from Egypt to Canaan with the American Republic as modern Egypt, our focus in the speeches is on the African origins of man, the greatness of Egypt, and its place in Africa. Second, rather than the universality of human liberation, the natural rights of man, and July 4 against August 1, why not begin with the proposition that August 1 was a common celebration of racial identity uniquely befitting people of African descent? Third, we replace the notion of emancipation as a boon from dedicated British and American abolitionists with an emphasis on the black heroic tradition with African-descended leaders in the vanguard of the struggle for their people's liberation. Fourth, instead of abolition as a peaceful process, our focus is on those speakers and parts of their speeches praising slave revolt and calls for revolutionary violence against American slavery. Fifth, rather than focus on the debate over abolition's success or failure, we view the emancipation of Afro-Caribbean slaves as racial vindication of all people of African descent. Finally, the notion of Anglo-American abolition as evidence of progress is replaced by a focus on the more complicated notion of the role of progress in enslaving and dehumanizing people of African descent in the modern world. Although the major sources are West Indian Emancipation Day speeches listed in Table 7.1, these will be supplemented by additional ideas and references in contemporary letters, pamphlets, poems, books, and other speeches.

Before we examine this alternative dialectic, let me anticipate three objections to the argument. First, can one downplay the Christian content of these antislavery speeches, since many of the speakers were ministers? Many of these preachers, however, did not limit themselves to biblical references, but often commented upon political and social changes in the world in which they found themselves. Also, not all antislavery speakers were of the cloth. Second, how could newspapers and publishers that were clearly not concerned with cross-national racial identification propagate such ideas and arguments? The antislavery press often published speeches that contained ideas and arguments that were directly contradictory. Thus, we learn about slave revolts from newspapers adhering to peaceful emancipation, while organs promoting the universality of abolition reproduced arguments for racial particularism. Besides, it is important not to forget that these antislavery articles and pamphlets were originally independent speeches beyond editorial control. Finally, does not a focus on some aspects of these antislavery speeches at the expense of others run the risk of distorting their overall meaning? Although it is a question of scholarly emphasis (when is it not?), the most important point to bear in mind throughout the subsequent discussion is the way in which the words and ideas of these August First speakers provided alternative views of people of African descent as *historical subjects*—not objects—of slavery, abolition, and post-emancipation.

Black Egypt

As Albert Raboteau, Eddie Glaude Jr., and other scholars of African American religious history have pointed out, the black experience in the United States has often been cast in terms of the biblical Egypt. This was no less true of orations at August First events. William Watkins castigated those popular speakers, chief priests, and rulers "down among the flesh pots of Egypt," rather than attending the 1854 commemoration in Columbus, Ohio. Furthermore, speakers sometimes equated Egypt with tyrannical regimes. In his address at the 1848 Rochester celebration, Douglass depicted the recently overthrown French monarch as one "who had arrayed himself against freedom, [and] found himself, like the great Egyptian tyrant, completely overwhelmed."[28] This notion of Egyptian bondage is evident in the image on the book's dust jacket.

The antislavery writings and speeches of black abolitionists, however, contained an important alternative intellectual and political genealogy with regard to Egypt. In 1799, French colonial forces in Egypt unearthed the Rosetta stone. This massive boulder, with its three engraved writings in Greek, Demotic script (popular form of ancient Egyptian writing), and hieroglyphics, allowed scholars to translate the hitherto unknown language of ancient Egypt for the first time in modern history. Jean Francois Champollion provided the first thorough examination of the translation in *Précis du systèm hiéroglyphique des anciens Egyptiens*, published in 1823. Although there appears to be little direct evidence that black abolitionists drew upon Champollion's work, it is clear that intellectual links between ancient Egypt, the African world, and black identity were being forged during this period.[29]

Some black abolitionists, for instance, turned the notion of biblical Egypt on its head by arguing for the African origins of civilization in which Egypt lay at the center. David Walker, a prominent black community activist in Boston, made this point in his 1829 *Appeal to the Coloured Citizens of the World.* "When we take a retrospective view of the arts and sciences," he wrote, "—the wise legislators—the Pyramids, and other magnificent buildings—the turning of the channel of the river Nile, by the sons of Africa or of Ham, among whom learning originated, and was carried thence into Greece, where it was improved upon and refined." In his *Textbook of the Origin and History of the Colored People*, published a year after he became pastor of the Talcott Street Congregational Church in Hartford, James Pennington argued that "the arts and sciences had their origin with our ancestors, and from them have flown forth to the world." In his lecture, "The Past and the Present Condition And The Destiny of the Colored Race," delivered in Troy in 1848, Garnet preached: "These people [ancient Egyptians] astonished the world with their arts and sciences in which they reveled with unbounded prodigality." White abolitionist

28. Raboteau, *Fire in the Bones;* Glaude Jr., *Exodus; FDP*, August 18, 1854; *NS*, August 4, 1848.

29. Wilson, *Understanding Hieroglyphics*, 10.

Reverend F. Freeman, in a book called *Africa's Redemption,* published in 1852, wrote that the lights of Greece, Rome, and Christianity had been "kindled on the dark shores of Africa."[30]

This concept of the African origins of man also found expression in antislavery speeches delivered at August First celebrations. At the 1849 Cincinnati event, J. H. Perkins explained the idea of "the natural inferiority of the colored race" to his audience. After referring to the "Book of books" as the basis for the notion of universal man, Perkins proceeded to give a history lesson on the African origins of man. "History informs us," he said, "that the sciences were partial to the sable children of the sun, and made their abode among them ere they had condescended to look upon the rest of mankind." Based on Egypt's "20,000 cities, her brazen towers and eternal pyramids," Perkins was "prepared to prove, that the Africans can boast of more greatness than any other people on the face of the globe, under the same circumstances. They were the first in wisdom and policy; the first in philosophy and letters. None will dispute that we are indebted to Africa for the very language that we speak: and now, her children are the first in meekness and humility, patience and long suffering." At the Buffalo commemoration the same year, speaker Abner H. Francis discussed the ingratitude of modern-day tyrants who "have repaid us for the light of science and letters which dawned upon their benighted visions from our Egyptian ancestors." Without such ancestors, Francis asked his audience, what would "a horde of naked savages have had today to boast of in their Anglo Saxon or Caucasian origin?" "I stand here today," he told the audience,

> a representative of those who were the benefactors of that noble blood of which you love to contemplate. The pure ills of science, from which you my white fellow countrymen now drink had their origin in Egypt and Ethiopia, and in their wanderings have fertilized all succeeding generations. I know efforts have been made to throw discredit upon these precious relics of history, but it has now become an almost universally admitted truth. Those who desire information only need

---

30. Walker, *Appeal,* 21; James W. C. Pennington, *A Text Book of the Origin and History, &c. &c. of the Colored People* (Hartford, Conn.: L. Skinner, 1841), 47–48; *BAP,* 3:477; Garnet, "Past and Present," in Ofari, *Garnet,* 162; Howe, *Afrocentrism,* 38.

to trace back civilization and knowledge through their European ancestors, and from them through the Greeks, the Romans and the Jews directly to Africa, and they will find their benefactors to be Egyptians and Ethiopians.

Three years later, in his August First address at the Toronto celebration, Samuel Ward lectured his audience of a hundred black men, women, and children on the source of world civilization as being Africa, Egypt, and Ethiopia. William Whipper wrote to the *Provincial Freeman* regretting his absence at the forthcoming commemoration at Dresden, Canada West, in 1857. In his letter of apology, he remarked on the likelihood of great expectations from people of African descent based on their past achievements. "Every age and almost every nation," wrote Whipper, "from the most flourishing period of Egyptian history down to the present moment, have been enlightened by the contributions of African genius, and flourished by their industry." In short, Egypt in the past had been great and virtuous, while modern America was corrupt and tyrannical.[31]

Moreover, many black abolitionists insisted on a racial identification with Africa and Egypt. In his *Appeal to the Coloured Citizens of the World*, Walker wrote:

> Some of my brethren do not know who Pharaoh and the Egyptians were—I know it to be a fact, that some of them take the Egyptians to have been a gang of *devils*, not knowing any better, and that they (Egyptians) having got possession of the Lord's people, treated them *nearly* as cruel as *Christian Americans* do us, at the present day. For the information of such, I would only mention that the Egyptians, were Africans or coloured people, such as we are—some of them yellow and others dark—a mixture of Ethiopians and the natives of Egypt—about the same as you see the coloured people of the United States at the present day.

In Pennington's 1841 textbook, he wrote: "Many will seek to evade this fact by saying that we are not of Egypt; but I have shown from Herodotus that

31. *NS*, August 17, September 7, 1849; *L*, August 20, 1852; *PF*, July 25, 1857.

the Egyptians were black people, and from other facts that they are one with the Ethiopians in the great events of history." In Garnet's 1848 "Past and Present" lecture, he noted: "We learn from Herodotus, that the ancient Egyptians were black, and had wooly hair." One of Martin Delany's most popular lectures in the United Kingdom was called "Africa and the African Race," in which he directly linked the depiction of animals and reptiles on chiefs' houses in Central Africa with those on statues brought from Egypt. He also argued that the Egyptian monarchs Ramses, Osiris, and Sesostris "were of the negro and not of the Caucasian race." Reverend F. Freeman agreed: in a book called *Africa's Redemption*, published in 1852, he wrote that "Egyptians were in fact black and curly-headed." That same year, Ward explained to his Toronto audience that Euclid was black. After describing various social conditions of blacks in San Francisco and Brooklyn, anonymous writers to *Frederic Douglass' Paper* signed off as "Nubia" and "Ethiop."[32]

The idea of black Egypt was not popular among those who sought to defend American slavery. Much proslavery thought in the antebellum South rested on biblical justifications for human slavery and avoided any mention of Egypt beyond its traditional biblical depiction as the land of bondage. Some Southerners were disturbed enough by the idea to provide a refutation. In an article headed "The Ancient Negro," the editors of a Southern journal sought to expose an "old error that has been recently revived and is now going the rounds of the newspapers," that the modern Negro is the descendant of the ancient Egyptians. Not only had the Negro been a slave in ancient Egypt, but "the long braids of silken hair which yet remain on [the mummies of Egyptians]" attest to their "freedom from negro blood." But the idea of a link between Africa and Egypt was hard to break in the minds of numerous contemporaries. In a large freedmen's school of 145 pupils in the post-emancipation South, the class was asked questions on government and citizenship. One of the Q and A's recorded by the visiting Freedmen's Bureau official was the following: "What was the wisest country of old times? The Answer: Egypt

32. Walker, *Appeal*, 10; Pennington, *Text Book*, 47–48; Garnet in Ofari; *FDP*, September 22, 1854; August 17, 1855; Robert S. Levine, ed., *Martin R. Delany: A Documentary Reader* (Chapel Hill: University of North Carolina Press, 2003), 363–64; *PF*, July 25, 1857; Howe, *Afrocentrism*, 38. Nubia was an ancient civilization encompassing the lower reaches of the Nile Valley, and is considered by historians of Africa to be one of the earliest recorded African states outside Egypt. See Iliffe, *Africans*, 26–30.

in Africa." In Russian novelist Fyodor Dostoyevsky's *Crime and Punishment*, published in 1866, the great antihero Raskolnikov kills an old woman for her wealth. Afterward, he has feverish day-dreams: "in one, that kept recurring, he fancied he was in Africa, in Egypt, in some sort of oasis." Indeed, Martin Bernal's recent work *Black Athena* is especially persuasive in its argument that nineteenth-century racism sought to break the tie between Egypt and Africa in the name of new imperial projects.[33]

Much of the recent debate over Egypt's relationship to Africa has more to do with the contemporary politics of race than the specific historical conditions in which such subjects were broached in earlier periods. It is quite clear, for instance, that numerous writers of the early nineteenth century wrote of Africa as uniquely history-less. In his *World History*, German political philosopher George W. F. Hegel had written that Africa had no history because it had no modern state. In 1831, the French scholar G. Cuvier had written that the "Negro hordes" have "always remained in the most complete state of Barbarism." Two decades later, the French father of scientific racism, Arthur Gobineau, noted the animal character of blacks, which "never leaves the most restricted intellectual zones." In response, black abolitionists insisted that Africa had a glorious past; that this past was basic to human civilization; and that Egyptians were the ancestors of *all* Africans in the modern world. One of the critical points that is often overlooked by scholars is that this debate occurred within the context of struggles over slavery and abolition in the mid-nineteenth-century Atlantic world. Moreover, if one of the key ideas of Pan-Africanism is black Egypt in world history, we can see this argument clearly in the writings and orations around West Indian Emancipation Day during this period. Finally, these black abolitionists were conscious of their intellectual and political mission. According to George Shepperson, "Whether they [early nineteenth-century writers] knew it or not, they disputed the view that Africa had no place worth considering in world history—and the destruction of this view is an essential element in the study of the African

---

33. Faust, ed., *The Ideology of Slavery: Proslavery Thought in the Antebellum South, 1830–1860* (Baton Rouge: Louisiana State University Press, 1981); Robin W. Winks Collection, Reel 4; Morris, *Reading, 'Riting, and Reconstruction*, 174–75; Fydor Dostoyevsky, *Crime and Punishment* (1866; New York: Everyman's Library, 1977), 63; Bernal, *Black Athena*.

diaspora." I agree with Shepperson that the view of writers—and I would add orators—was absolutely vital, but I am also persuaded that black abolitionists knew it.[34]

Our Emancipation

One of the most important arguments made by antebellum abolitionists was that the struggle against American slavery was a universal one. On the one hand, slaves and slaveholders were God's children. On the other hand, the abolition of slavery offered the prospect of a liberty affecting all of mankind. August First Day recognized no immediate boundaries. Having described the joyful commemoration at Marlboro Chapel in Boston in 1839, the *Liberator* lectured its mostly black readership: "The first of August is not a colored anniversary, and we must not suffer our dark-skinned friends to monopolise its pleasures." "The occasion is not one of color, but of universal man," Frederick Douglass informed his Rochester audience at the 1848 commemoration. He went on to express his happiness at the mixed crowd, "for though this is our day peculiarly, it is not so exclusively." Indeed, one of the objects for the Rochester assembly was to make Emancipation Day "subservient to the sacred cause of human freedom."[35]

Numerous black abolitionists, however, pointedly disagreed with the idea of emancipation as being everyone's liberation in a number of important ways. First, modern slavery was a condition uniquely experienced by people of African descent. For "three fourths of a century [slavery] crushed us as a race," explained Abner H. Francis in his address at the 1849 Buffalo celebration. A year earlier, Henry W. Johnson had reminded his Rochester audience that slavery existed in the United States to such an extent that "there is not one spot upon which a colored man can rest his feet, and declare that he is free." (This criticism of continental slavery was uttered three years *before* the Fugitive Slave Act.) There was "no protection upon American soil," for either "the nominally free man of color" or the "panting fugitive." Indeed, it was

---

34. Bernal, *Black Athena*, 240–46; Shepperson, "Concept and Context," in *Global Dimensions*, ed. Harris, 42. The otherwise interesting discussion in Howe, *Afrocentrism*, chap. 4, ignores this antislavery context altogether.

35. *L*, August 9, 1839; *NS*, August 4, 1848.

the "spirit of slavery," according to Theodore S. Wright's oration "Prejudice against the Colored Man," that was responsible for "that prejudice" that treats colored people "irrespective of their morals or intellectual cultivation."[36]

Moreover, if slavery was the burden borne by the "race," then emancipation represented that group's peculiar liberation. In his 1849 speech, Abner Francis referred to this moment, "when the shackles are falling from hundreds of thousands of our race." It was fellow African slaves freed in the British West Indies in 1834 as well as the French West Indies in 1848, not simply the inevitability of human progress, which inspired the speaker. A year after the termination of the apprenticeship system in the British West Indies, Garnet told his audience that "if these blessings are not immediately ours, they are remotely." This racial bonding among people of African descent in the black Atlantic world was in marked contrast to Douglass's 1848 sentiment.[37]

Indeed, what is striking about many of these orations is the extent to which speakers not only insisted that August First was *our liberation*, but that its historical memory *belonged* exclusively to people of African descent. In his 1839 oration at the Newark commemoration, James Pennington pointed out the calamity that black people had no great event to excite and celebrate compared to others. The Egyptians had the overflow of the Nile. The English had their Charter of Rights. New England had the Pilgrims' landing. America had July Fourth. August First, "a triumph of the principles of human liberty," represented our moment. It was a soothing thought, said Robert Banks in his oration at the Detroit commemoration the same year, that this was a place "where he [the colored man] can stand erect and feel himself a man." According to one report of the celebrants at Goodale Park, Columbus, in 1854: "They all seemed happy in view of the emancipation of their West Indian brethren, whole [whose?] jubilee of freedom they had met to glorify." A large meeting of "Colored Visitors" at the Bannaker House, Cape Island, on Wednesday, August 1, 1855, resolved: "That we hail with delight the

36. *NS*, August 21, 1848; August 17, 1849; Theodore S. Wright, "Prejudice against the Colored Man," in *Negro Orators and Their Orations*, ed. Carter G. Woodson (Washington, D.C.: Associated Publishers, 1925), 93; Schor, *Garnet*, 21.

37. *NS*, August 21, 1848; August 17, 1849.

anniversary of the day which gave freedom to 800,000 of our brethren in the British West Indies."[38]

The racial nature of the commemoration was clearly articulated by Jehiel C. Beman at the 1843 August First celebration organized by the New England Freedom Association, a black vigilance committee operating in Boston. "B.F.R.," an unidentified contributor to the *Liberator*, reported that Beman began by linking West Indian suffering with American slaves and the free coloreds' nominal freedom. "He insisted that the colored man, as he was the injured party, could alone *feel* on this occasion." While acknowledging white sympathy, Beman "considered they *could not*, having never been placed in the same circumstances with the colored people, feel as they do in celebrating this event. Who were the slaves in the West India Islands? Colored Men. Who were rejoiced in the great jubilee? Colored Men. Who ought now, above all others, celebrate this day? Colored Men." This was decidedly different from the *Liberator*'s view that the celebration was not a colored anniversary![39]

A number of prominent abolitionists, both white and black, celebrated August First as a true moment of human liberation. Many of them went further to suggest that British abolition was greater than American independence because of the latter's connection with slavery and tyranny. This has led numerous scholars to argue that Emancipation Day was an African American July Fourth, or what one recent scholar of freedom festivals has referred to as a "borrowed day."[40] In contrast, the argument here is that August First was not a national surrogate, but a critical commemoration and forecast of international liberation for all people of African descent. These West Indian Emancipation Day speeches bespoke the notion of racial unity based on the particular enslavement and emancipation of African-descended people in the modern world. The implication is that recent scholarly debates over questions of authenticity, racial representation, and identity politics have a much older lineage traceable to antislavery struggles in the black Atlantic world.

38. J. W. C. Pennington, *West Indian Emancipation Address at Newark, August 1, 1839* (Newark: Aaron Guest, 1839), 9–10; Robert Banks, *An Oration Delivered at a Celebration in Detroit of the Abolition of Slavery in the West Indies, Held by Colored Americans, August 1, 1839* (Detroit: Harsha and Bates, 1839), 3; *FDP*, August 18, 1854; August 24, 1855.

39. *L*, August 11, 1843. Italics in the original.

40. Kachun, *Festivals of Freedom*, chap. 2.

African Brotherhood

As Douglass's 1848 Rochester speech makes clear, one of the central ideas of Anglo-American abolition was that a small group of dedicated activists had won British abolition. On the same Rochester platform, Johnson proclaimed that British abolition "was a glorious day for that noble band of noble-hearted philanthropists who for years had breasted the storms and tempests of an adverse public opinion." Three years later, William Brown told his London audience: "This act was the commencement of a long course of philanthropic and Christian efforts on the part of some of the best men that the world ever produced." Douglass's invitation to the Rochester crowd to give three cheers for the indefatigable British abolitionist and parliamentarian George Thompson was met with great enthusiasm. The names of these noble men—Thomas Clarkson, William Wilberforce, Thomas Fowell Buxton, George Thompson—were frequently honored on August First.[41]

British colonial missionaries also received fulsome praise, especially their stewardship of abolition through the chapel watch night. On the "first of August, 1838, at twelve o'clock, at midnight, the hoary-headed monster died, at his late residence, in the British West Indies," Garnet informed his listeners at the Troy celebration in 1839. Eight years later, Beman recalled the moment for his listeners at Hudson: "Hark! Twelve O'Clock, their freedom's natal hour is tolled." "Midnight passed and they were free," Judge Stephen Myers informed his five thousand listeners at Staten Island in 1855. J. Underwood, president of the commemoration in Flushing, Ohio, in 1849, opened the day's events with a selection from Thome and Kimball's influential book. At the Columbus celebration in 1854, Watkins read out to his audience "that most thrilling account of the service in the Wesleyan chapel, Antigua," with an "extract from 'Thome and Kimball's Emancipation in the West Indies.'" After the clock struck twelve, read Watkins:

> a moment of profoundest silence passed then came the burst they
> broke forth in prayer—they shouted, they sung "glory," "alleluia";
> they clapped their hands, leaped up, fell down, clasped each other in
> free arms, cried, laughed, and went to and fro, tossing upward their

41. *NS*, August 4, 21, 1848; *NYDT*, August 2, 1855; *L*, September 5, 1851, in *BAP*, 1:286; *FDP*, August 4, 1848.

unfettered hands; but high above the whole there was a might [*sic*] sound which ever and anon swelled up; it was the utterings in broken negro dialect of gratitude to God.[42]

Moreover, this band of brothers deserved emulation by American activists in order to terminate slavery in the United States. Visiting activists like Garrison and Phillips, together with scores of black abolitionists, were often greeted with tremendous enthusiasm in their antislavery tours. "It was with the greatest delight," recorded Ward, "that I found, in every part of England, Ireland, Scotland, and Wales, that abolitionism is not a mere abstract idea, but a practical question of grave importance." In his speech at the August First anniversary in London in 1851, William Brown reminded his large audience of that "band of fearless men and women in the city of Boston," who constituted a "noble and heroic class." Indeed, it is unlikely that the United Kingdom would have been so frequently visited without such a warm reception.[43]

This concept of Anglo-American abolitionist brotherhood has rarely been challenged, but it is problematic for several reasons.[44] To begin with, it uncritically assumes that black abolitionists were anglophiles. This makes some sense, given the paucity of critical comments about the United Kingdom by these travelers. This seems hardly surprising, however, given the British commitment to imperial emancipation and the importance of the pursuit of freedom to black abolitionists. Besides, black abolitionists needed antislavery funding, support, and pressure from the United Kingdom. It would harm their cause to attack the very country and institutions from which they sought help in the monumental struggle against American slavery.

Moreover, the notion of black anglophiles ignores the British racism black abolitionists encountered in their antislavery travels. Alexander Duval,

42. Schor, *Garnet*, 22; Beman, *Address Delivered at the Celebration of the West India Emancipation, in Davis' Hall, Hudson, New York, on Monday, Aug. 2, 1847* (Troy, N.Y.: J. C. Kneeland and Co. Steam Press, 1847), 6; *NYDT*, August 2, 1855; *ASB*, August 18, 1849; *FDP*, August 18, 1854; August 10, 1855.

43. Rice, *Scots Abolitionists*, 150–62; Ward, *Autobiography*, 301; *BAP*, 1:287.

44. The exception, of course, are those writings on women abolitionists referred to earlier: Jeffrey, *Great Silent Army*; Anderson, *Joyous Greetings*; Kathryn Kish Sklar, *Women's Rights Emerges within the Anti-Slavery Movement, 1830–1870: A Brief History with Documents* (Boston: Bedford/St. Martin's, 2000).

after his stirring speech at the 1851 commemoration in London, found it hard to obtain employment and was forced to beg on the streets. There is little doubt that his poverty would have provided useful evidence of the failure of emancipation to proslavery ideologues; it might also have earned the stern disapproval of anti-begging people like Shadd and Ward. Henry Garnet wrote a letter to the Mission Board of the United Presbyterian Church stating health concerns should he continue as missionary in Jamaica. The board responded that Garnet had "lost interest in the Jamaica mission." Garnet rebuked the committee: "of my own actual experience and feelings, no one can so well judge as myself." Some black abolitionists were caught in the ideological divisions within the Anglo-American abolitionist movement. Prominent Garrisonian Maria Weston Chapman opposed the speaking efforts of Pennington, the Crafts, and William Brown in Edinburgh. Fellow abolitionist Parker Pillsbury, while on a British antislavery tour in 1854, attacked several black abolitionists. "The thing which troubles me most here," Pillsbury wrote to Samuel May, "is to find so many of all sorts of creatures travelling in the name of the American Anti-Slavery, and picking the people's pockets for *vigilance Committees, Canada Missions, Chaplain funds, colored schools* in the West, & colored churches in Canada." He went on to describe "Pennington, Garnet, Ward, Hemming, Henson, Gloucester, & that fry," as being "an outrage on all decency, & a scandal to the name of anti-slavery," and "published a long letter about their deeds in several papers."[45]

Most important, the antislavery travels, writings, speeches, and activities of black abolitionists encouraged the development of an alternative narrative around an African band of brothers that has drawn considerably less scholarly comment.[46] On the one hand, there were the sorts of racial encounters by

45. *BAP,* 1:88, 257, 404; *MRUPC,* January 1857, vol. 12, p. 8; Rice, *Scots Abolitionists,* 155–56; Pillsbury to May, October 5, 1854, in *British and American Abolitionists: An Episode in Transatlantic Understanding,* ed. Clare Taylor (Edinburgh: Edinburgh University Press, 1974), 412. This white liberal insistence on defining black identity and protest bedeviled abolitionist and neo-abolitionists movements. It continues to stalk academic corridors.

46. Many abolitionists were no doubt familiar with the rallying cry of Shakespeare's Henry V on St. Crispen's day: "We few, we happy few, we band of brothers; For he to-day that sheds his blood with me Shall be my brother." *Henry V* 4, iii, 60–62. It should be recalled, however, that this rally to arms was even more relevant for black abolitionists calling for revolutionary emancipation.

Garnet in Jamaica and Bibb in Canada West noted earlier. On the other hand, there was the making of a black heroic tradition around slavery and abolition. Freedom fighters of African provenance were celebrated for their resistance toward racial oppression and colonial slavery, as well as providing a noble example for putting down American slavery. This black heroic took several forms. African leaders were celebrated. After noting black Egypt, Walker invoked "that mighty son of Africa, HANNIBAL, one of the greatest generals of antiquity who defeated and cut off so many thousands of the white Romans or murderers, and who carried his victorious arms, to the very gate of Rome." Several black militias were named after the victorious North African general. In addition, Americans of African descent were praised for their exploits. In his 1843 "Address to the Slaves," Garnet called on the slaves to rise against their masters: "Rather die freemen than live to be slaves." On the Rochester platform in 1848, Johnson referred to past "revolutionary heroes," including "Benjamin [Crispus] Attucks, from whose veins flowed the first drop of blood that mingled with American soil." Twelve years later, Johnson was still singing the praises of Crispus Attucks. This black revolutionary hero was also a popular name for black militias.[47]

Another expression of this black heroic concerned slave rebels and the international consequences of their actions. In his 1843 "Address," Garnet evoked a black revolutionary pantheon of "Noble Men" like Denmark Vesey, Joseph Cinque, Madison Washington, and Nathaniel Turner to put down American slavery. Even though Douglass opposed Garnet's 1843 call for revolutionary emancipation, he praised Nat Turner in subsequent speeches. "About eighteen years ago," Douglass informed his Rochester audience, "a man of noble courage, rose among his brethren in Virginia. 'We have long been subjected to slavery. The hour for our deliverance has come. Let us rise and strike for liberty. In the name of a God of justice let us slay our oppressors.'"

A decade later, Douglass told his Canadaigua audience that "abolition followed close on the heels of insurrection in the West Indies, and Virginia was never nearer emancipation than when General Turner kindled the fires of insurrection at Southampton." The speaker was aware that slave revolt was due to abolitionists' discussions, but he also knew that "the slaves of the West

47. Walker, *Appeal*, 22; Woodson, *Negro Orators*, 157; *NS*, August 21, 1848; Grover, *Fugitive's Gibraltar*, 262; *ASB*, August 14, 1852.

Indies did fight for their freedom, and that the fact of their discontent was known in England, and that it assisted in bringing about that state of public opinion which finally resulted in their emancipation." He added: "What Wilberforce was endeavoring to win from the British Senate [House of Commons] by his magic eloquence, the Slaves themselves were endeavoring to gain by outbreaks and violence . . . abolition followed close on the heels of insurrection in the West Indies." The following year, at the Abington celebration arranged by MASS, visiting Barbados missionary Bleby recounted to an American audience his interview with Samuel Sharpe, the head of the Jamaican slave rebellion of 1831–32.[48]

Finally, there were slave fugitives and self-emancipation. August First orators increasingly referred to fugitives and their escapes in the United States, Canada West, and the United Kingdom. In his 1857 Emancipation Day speech, Douglass discussed the "honorable" Margaret Garner, the "noble William Thomas at Wilkesbarre," "Parker and his noble band of fifteen at Christiana," "noble Krooman," Joseph Cinque, and the "worthy" Madison Washington. The latter proved of special concern to Ward. In his 1855 *Autobiography*, Ward narrated the dramatic story of Washington's escape from slavery and his relocation to Canada West. Part of the narrative was how Madison, along with Pompey Garrison and Ben Blacksmith, seized the slave ship *Creole* and took it to Rhode Island. "What lacked these men," concluded Ward, "of being Tells, Mazzinis, and Kossuths, in their way, except white or whitish skins?" The comparison is a telling one. Ward and others were well aware that revolutionary heritage was reserved for the Italians, Hungarians, Irish, and the like, but not people of African descent. When the former rebelled, they were heroes; when the latter revolted, they were savage beasts moved by instinct rather than ideas of freedom. These were among the earliest attempts to construct a pantheon of black heroes around issues of enslavement and revolutionary emancipation.[49]

Anglo-American abolition represented an important transatlantic movement against American slavery. This involved cross-national travel, organizing,

48. *BAP*, 3:409–10; *Frederick Douglass Papers*, 3:200, 207, 205–8; *NS*, August 4, 1848. See also Scott Andrew French, "Remembering Nat Turner: The Rebellious Slave in American Thought, 1831 to the Present" (Ph.D. diss., University of Virginia, 2000), chap. 2; Williams, *Capitalism and Slavery*, 208.

49. *Frederick Douglass Papers*, 3:204–6; Ward, *Autobiography*, 166–68.

and fund-raising. It should not be forgotten, however, that black abolitionists involved in such activities also developed a racial consciousness of themselves as past and present leaders. Indeed, August First addresses represented a pioneering intellectual and political expression of black leadership that was insufficiently appreciated by many contemporary abolitionists as well as their scholars.[50]

Revolutionary Emancipation

One of the most frequent representations of West Indian emancipation in North America was its peaceful nature. Alongside Douglass at the Rochester celebration, Johnson explained that abolition brought "none of those frightful evils—none of those awful scenes of blood and butchery, which we were told would be the inevitable consequences of this measure." Six years later, in 1854, Watkins informed his Columbus audience that West India emancipation "had been attended with most happy results." There had been no "rebellion, no cutting of throats, non-pillaging of houses!" The following year at an anniversary event held in Adams, New York, Watkins repeated his earlier point. "To the cutting of their masters throats, to the indiscriminate slaughter of women and children? Not at all; not one drop of blood was shed, not one house was pillaged." One of Douglass's opening points at Rochester concerned peaceful emancipation.[51]

There were several reasons for this view of British abolition. Many supporters of abolition in the British colonies were unsure what exactly would happen when emancipation came. When race war did not break out—relief all around—this became a vindication for the policy of abolition. Thus, numerous travel accounts and missionary reports described the coming of British abolition in glowing terms. Furthermore, the specter of the Haitian revolution and racial chaos haunted emancipation. For a generation after the founding of the independent black republic in 1804, American slaveholders pointed to the bloody consequences of abolition. Their power in federal

50. The subtitle of this section was chosen to evoke comparison with the African Blood Brotherhood of the World War I era. This was a secret organization of leading black radicals who combined nationalism, Marxism, and Pan-Africanism in an eclectic ideological mixture. See Kelly, *Freedom Dreams*, 45–46; James, *Holding Aloft*.

51. *NS*, August 21, 1848; *FDP*, August 18, 1854; August 10, 1855.

government ensured the pariah-status and subsequent isolation of Haiti for decades. Their antislavery rhetoric increased with Turner's slave revolt in 1831. Meanwhile, the burgeoning abolitionist movement could point to an important peaceful emancipation process during the early 1830s. Without saying as much, this presentation of quiet abolition was designed to assuage fears of the repetition of the revolutionary emancipation of Haiti. The legal and orderly transition from slavery to emancipation in the British Caribbean was trumpeted as a means to counteract the bloody image in the minds of many contemporaries. Finally, British abolition provided a peaceful model for the abolition of American slavery. This massive experiment had occurred without "those frightful evils"; there was no reason why American slavery could not be likewise terminated.[52]

There are several problems, however, with this representation of peaceful British abolition. First, it is historically inaccurate. Henry Bleby and others pointed to heroic slave rebels initiating emancipation. At his 1858 speech, Bleby quoted Sam Sharpe's final words: 'I, for one, am ready to die, in order that the rest may be free."[53] Furthermore, although the passage of British abolition had not been violent, neither was it quite the peaceful process propagated by British and American abolitionists. As noted in chapter I, there had been numerous protests, marches, and arson attacks on sugar plantations by former slaves disgruntled with the conditions of emancipation. And colonial authorities, Christian missionaries, and former slave owners had worked *very hard* to ensure a peaceful transition through the organization of official processions, chapel services, and estate feasts. Indeed, the emergence of "other" freedom festivals suggests the degree to which these attempts to subordinate and control the transition from slavery to emancipation in the West Indies were not entirely successful.

Moreover, the scholarly focus on quiet emancipation in the British West Indies has brushed aside the topic of revolutionary emancipation in the

52. For the impact of Caribbean events on Southern slaveholders, see David B. Davis, *Challenging the Boundaries of Slavery* (Cambridge, Mass.: Harvard University Press, 2003), chap. 3; Wilkins, "Window on Freedom."

53. Bleby, "Speech," 11. Compare Nelson Mandela's words from the dock at the 1964 Rivonia trial: "It is an ideal [freedom] which I hope to live for and to achieve. But if needs be, it is an ideal for which I am prepared to die." Kathadra, *Memoirs*, 177.

Caribbean. In February 1848, the monarchy of Louis Phillipe was overthrown, leading to the establishment of the French Second Republic. The provisional republican government legally emancipated around 150,000 slaves in the Caribbean islands of Guadeloupe and Martinique. At the Rochester celebration the following August, Douglass praised the coming of abolition to the French West Indies. "Among the first of its [republican provisional government's] acts," observed Douglass, was to decree "the complete, unconditional emancipation of every slave throughout the French colonies." After the antislavery speeches, there was a public reading of the 1848 French emancipation act and the 1834 British emancipation act. The following year, William Brown spoke at a peace congress in Paris. "By the revolution of 1848," Brown told the assembly, "France not only set her inhabitants free, but also emancipated the slaves in Martinique and Guadeloupe. Now I wish to see the same thing done in the United States." After the antislavery speeches had been delivered at the Columbus commemoration in 1852, the brass band struck up the "La Marseillaise," presumably in celebration of the international dimensions of revolutionary abolition.[54]

Indeed, the first historical example of revolutionary emancipation in Haiti had more of an impact on African-descended people than thought by scholars. Mitch Kachun expresses little surprise "at the absence of any organized public demonstrations commemorating the Haitian revolution." He argues the Haitian revolution was not publicly celebrated because the fears of "bloody slave rebellion and revolution would only alienate and infuriate the very people they [black Americans] needed to convince of African American respectability." This view is limited in several ways. Most obviously, it confines all black abolitionists to one respectable straitjacket. Not all black Americans expected the boon of abolition from white Americans. Furthermore, the primacy of public celebrations and demonstrations of British abolition makes historical sense. The coming of British abolition coincided with the early mobilization of the antislavery movement. British and African American antislavery efforts complemented one another. The British state, not the French or Haitian states, had the power of economic demand and control of the high seas to weaken American slavery.

54. *BAP*, I:155, 160; *NS*, August 4, 1848; *ASB*, August 14, 1852.

This view also overlooks numerous examples of Haiti's revolutionary emancipation celebrated by black abolitionists. In his 1829 *Appeal,* Walker praised "Hayti, the glory of the blacks and terror of tyrants." In his 1838 speech comparing slave abolition in the French and British colonies, Smith noted France's "first, most glorious example" of revolutionary republicanism followed by "immediate and entire emancipation" and acknowledged "the independence of Hayti." In a letter to the *North Star* published in July 1849, Delany called upon the colored races of Cuba to recall the Haitian example: "Let them but remember the masterly and noble reply of Henry Christophe, one of the oppressed of St. Domingo, who in answer to general Leclerc, the able Captain and brother-in-law of the emperor Napoleon, said, 'It is needless to count on numbers of means. My determination to be a man and *freeman,* is the sum of my arithmetic.'" In an address published in the *Provincial Freeman,* J. W. Johnson praised the freedom of Hayti's patriots:

> In seventeen hundred and ninety-one
> Beneath the rays of the West Indies sun,
> A spark of patriotism through Hayti ran
> That caused a shout through all the land.
> The Haytian patriots walked the soil,
> And planted freedom by their toil;
> Long many their banner wave o'er the spoil,
> And keep the noble hand in coil.

An editorial in the *Liberator* published in the first year of its existence praised the black republic: "If there be a republic worthy of universal admiration, it is the republic of Hayti. Her independence was effected solely through the almost matchless valor of her citizens." Toussaint L'Ouverture, one of the major leaders of the Haitian revolution, was often praised by antislavery speakers. Some organizations bearing his name were reported participating in West Indian Emancipation Day celebrations.[55]

Finally, an emphasis on peaceful abolition and its model for American slavery was rendered increasingly obsolete by a decade of violence during the

55. Kachun, *Festivals of Freedom,* 57; Walker, *Appeal,* 23; Smith, "Abolition," in Woodson, *Negro Orators,* 120; Levine, *Delany,* 167; *PF,* July 12, 1856; *L,* August 6, 1831.

1850s. In the international arena, there were week-long riots against British colonial rule in Guiana in early 1856. From April 1856 through the end of 1857, the colonial rule of the East India Company in south Asia was challenged by mutinous Sepoy troops, disgruntled local elites, and elements of the peasant masses, culminating in the First Indian War for Independence. In early October 1857, the *Liberator* reported on the "wholesale massacre" of "400 persons" by "satan" at Cawnpore and the reoccupation of the garrison town by British forces. One month later, the *Liberator* reported that "the Queen's 78th Regiment put to death no fewer than *ten thousand* people; or, according to another version, killed all the natives they could get at, *whether men, women, or children.*"[56]

Meanwhile, fugitive battles raged in the Northern United States. The continuing freedom of fugitives was based on self-defense throughout the Atlantic world. During the mid-1850s, American states were embroiled in conflict: Northern states opposed the imposition of federal fugitive law; western states battled over the free/slave status of new territories; slaves continued to escape slavery in the Southern states. Meanwhile, slaveholders were seeking more land and slaves. It simply did not make sense to argue for peaceful emancipation in such a warlike climate.

The same year Douglass delivered his Rochester address saw the twin publication of Walker's *Appeal to the Colored Citizens of the World* and Garnet's "Address to the Slaves." In 1851, John Fisher, black storekeeper in Toronto and contributor to the *Voice of the Fugitive*, called for armed struggle against Southern slaveholders because they were at war with black people. In his oration at the Columbus anniversary the following year, H. F. Douglass eulogized the "powerful victory" of Clarkson and Wilberforce through the "weapons of love." "But when necessary," he added, "we shall imitate Washington, Hancock, Adams etc." During the mid-1850s, James Smith called for the celebration of Denmark Vesey and Nat Turner to inspire blacks to rise

56. Craton, *Testing the Chains*, 325–26; Judd, *Empire*, chap. 7; *L*, September 25, October 7, November 27, 1857. The British Victorians' description of the rebellion as the "Indian Mutiny" was an attempt to deny its popular support as well as to delegitimize armed struggle. Southern slaveholders did the same with their references to "mad Nat" and "crazy Brown." Its modern echoes can be heard in official Anglo-American references to "terrorists" in Iraq, lumping together various Sunni groups, anti-Saddam nationalists, Islamist groups, foreign nationalists, and criminal gangs.

against American slavery. In his 1857 Emancipation Day speech, Douglass compared Indian anticolonial and American antislavery struggles. "We may fight," he noted, "but we must fight like the Seapoys [*sic*] of India, under white officers. This class of Abolitionists don't like colored celebrations, they don't like colored conventions, they don't like colored Anti-Slavery fairs for the support of colored newspapers. They don't like any demonstrations whatever in which colored men take a leading part." During the late 1850s, Martin Delany began work on his novel *Blake.* The novel describes an attempt at slave insurrection in Cuba and the United States. In one section, Blake discusses recruitment in West Africa for his slave revolution in the Americas: "I am well acquainted with the native Krumen on the coast, many of the heads of whom speak several European tongues, and as sailing master, I can obtain an many as I wish, who will make a powerful force in carrying out my scheme on the vessel." In 1859, the *Anglo-African* began serial publication of the novel. This was one year after Johh Brown's attempted mass slave uprising.[57]

Racial Vindication

Many supporters of American slavery opposed British abolition because emancipation had resulted in a reduction in sugar production. In his *Letter to an English Abolitionist,* published in 1845, South Carolina governor and proslavery advocate James Henry Hammond condemned the "injurious effects" of emancipation "in your little sea-girt West India islands." Quoting from the *London Quarterly Review* of 1840, Hammond noted: " 'The wild rashness of fanaticism has made the emancipation of the slaves equivalent to the loss of one-half of the West Indies, and yet put back the chance of negro civilization.' " In an 1849 Address of Southern Delegates, forty-eight proslavery congressmen representing twelve slave states rejected British abolition because it had ruined the British West Indies. That same year, prominent British essayist Thomas Carlyle published his "Occasional Discourse on the Nigger Question," which declared West India emancipation to be a failure because of the indolent and lazy habits of "Quashee." In the *Case of the British West Indies Stated,* published by the Glasgow-based West India Association in 1851, the Abolition Act was

---

57. Walker, *Appeal;* Garnet in *BAP,* 2:403–12; Fisher in *BAP,* 2:157; H. F. Douglass in *ASB,* August 14, 1852; Smith in Sweet, "Fourth of July," 270–71, and *Frederick Douglass Papers,* 3:200; *Frederick Douglass Papers,* 3: 203; Levine, *Delany,* 297–312.

described as a mistake because it had been passed without "safeguards" for the British sugar industry. The consequence was not only economic decline, but "the emancipated negro" was "rapidly lapsing into barbarism in the British colonies." By the end of the 1850s, this view of economic decline and lazy blacks had become commonplace among supporters of American slavery. The *Brooklyn Daily Eagle* made the connection in its account of an Emancipation Day celebration in 1860: "the darkeys of the West Indies have since [abolition] been leading a life of masterly inactivity, and if they are not generally libeled they are about as lazy and useless a sett [*sic*] of free darkeys as get a living anywhere without earning it." The comparative point was clear: do not abolish American slavery because it will result in a similar economic decline and return to barbarism on the part of former slaves in the United States.[58]

Anglo-American abolitionists fundamentally disagreed. Not only had West Indian emancipation been successful, but it had also demonstrated *improvement* in the condition of the Negro. At the 1854 August First celebration in Columbus, Watkins quoted one Dr. Ferguson that emancipation "is working most admirably, especially for the planters. It is infinitely better policy than slavery or the apprentice ship either." At Rochester, Douglass called attention to common press statements that "'emancipation has been a failure.'" His reply was to quote Lord John Russell, the English prime minister, in a speech reported in the *London Times* of June 17, 1848. As a result of the 1834 act, "I believe a class of laborers more happy, more in possession of all the advantages and enjoyments of life than the negro population of the West Indies, does not exist." In short, British abolition had been successful and thus served as a model for American abolition. Antislavery speeches propagated this message as a means of convincing Emancipation Day audiences, as well as readers of the abolitionist press, of the efficiency of slavery's abolition and its positive effects.[59]

58. Hammond, *Letter to an English Abolitionist*, in Faust, *Ideology*, 200–201; Fladeland, "Emancipated Compensation," 185; Carlyle, "Occasional Discourse"; Blackett, *Divided Hearts*, 37–38; Holt, *Problem of Freedom*, 502; W. I. Association, "Case," 3, 12–13; *BDE*, August 2, 1860.

59. *NS*, August 4, 1848; *FDP*, August 18, 1854. The debate over West Indian Emancipation can also be traced in the foreign policy views of John C. Calhoun and John Quincy Adams, as well as in the polemics of George Fitzhugh, Lydia M. Child, and Wendell Phillips.

This debate—what we might call the Condition of Emancipation Question—was conducted in cross-national terms. West Indian emancipation and American slavery were clearly linked and argued over by abolitionist and proslavery ideologues. For the latter, any post-emancipation society was bound to be a failure because it refuted the fundamental premise upon which American slavery rested: slavery was good for the nation, region, and slaves. For the former, post-emancipation societies were always a success because they had begun with the abolition of slavery. The propaganda campaigns of both sides, however, served to obscure the facts on the ground. Between 1835 and 1848, sugar production in the British West Indies did decline from 159,928 to 119,155 metric tons. Over the next decade, however, it rose to 140,193 metric tons. One encounters, quite understandably, little attention to such nuance in the fierce polemics.[60]

More important, the Condition of Emancipation Question has served to obscure another important aspect of the transnational connection. Many black abolitionists endorsed emancipation not simply for polemical purposes, but because of its *racial vindication* of former slaves, fugitives, free blacks, and slaves. They refuted weighty historical charges: enslaved Africans did not want their freedom (i.e., revolts were rare); they were unable to manage their own freedom (i.e., poor post-emancipation societies); and they were eternally destined for servitude (i.e., wealthy American slave South). At stake was neither an experiment nor strategy, but the future freedom of people of African descent.[61]

After describing the peaceful nature of West Indian emancipation in his 1839 Newark address, Pennington noted our West Indian brethren were "susceptible of liberty," and "their wishes are moderate, their pretensions are modest, their aims are noble, their claims are just, and their concessions are reasonable." "The Island of Jamaica has been singled out," explained Watkins to his audience at the 1855 Adams celebration, "and held up to the world, as an illustration of the impracticality of IMMEDIATE EMANCIPATION,

60. Holt, *Problem of Freedom*, 120.

61. The dishonesty of proslavery ideologues over Haiti should be apparent: boycott the regime, watch its economic decline, then point to the failure of emancipation. It brings to mind former Premier Margaret Thatcher's dishonesty about the British welfare state: deprive it of state funding, oversee its decline, point to its failure, and then call for privatized medicine.

and the evils necessarily resulting from it." "The enemies of emancipation," the speaker added,

> have affirmed that the emancipated slaves have to improved [*sic*] their mental, moral, social, or religious condition, and that they are, indeed, much more degraded than formerly. The enemies of the colored man, believing in the truthfulness of such declarations, very readily conclude that freedom has been a curse to the country. But their assertions are wholly without foundation. In plain English, they are lies, concocted by the enemy, to promote the base purpose of despotisms.

As a result of abolition, "they [are] now free men, breathing for the firs [*sic*] time the air of freedom, and walking to and fro, in all the majesty of unfettered manhood." Such comments were about more than simply an abolitionist strategy to persuade American audiences of the efficacy of emancipation; they also sought to defend freed people of African descent from the "lies" that they were unfit for freedom and should never have been freed in the first place.[62]

This racial vindication of black liberation transcended August First speeches. In a letter published in the *North Star* in February 1848, Delany drew upon Haiti as "evidence of the capacity of the colored man for self-government." "The proud little republic of Hayti has for the last fifty years fully demonstrated this truth." In a letter to the president of Haiti, John Brown Jr. passed along his cordial greetings . He also praised the self-determination of the people:

> Haytians, brothers and sisters, here, in this land of slaves, the warmest friends of your race are watching you to observe how you refute the defamation that the African is incapable of self-government. You have given proof of your ability as soldiers. Without other assistance that that you found in your own energy and valor, you have thrown off and broken the yoke of the tyrant, and obliged him to seek refuge on the ocean.

62. *BDE*, August 2, 1860; Pennington, *West Indian Emancipation*, 5–6; *FDP*, August 10, 1855.

On October 21, 1859, the Victoria *British Colonist* republished an article written for *The Times* by Amor de Cosmos condemning British emancipation as an economic failure. Mifflin Gibbs, Philadelphia-born and recent immigrant to Vancouver Island, wrote an angry rebuttal. His opening criticism was relevant for overzealous abolitionists and ardent proslavery defenders as well as readers of the *Times:* "The idea of its measuring a great act of national righteousness, like the West India Emancipation, by the increase or diminution of a few pounds of sugar exhibits a depth of moral depravity, and a contempt for the essential principles of true national greatness, which is revolting to every friend of morality and justice." Gibbs went on to list the benefits of British abolition, including new schools, the legal bond of marriage, professional posts in church, state, and business, and reduced crime. In short, "improvement is everywhere visible." Moreover, to abolition's detractors, he insisted, "tell them that every man is now owner of himself, a recognized and protected British freeman." The writer even went so far as to explain that the reason for "disappointed planters" was because "laborers there, like mankind everywhere, refuse to work for mere nominal wages for others when they can admirably sustain themselves by the cultivation of their own soil." Although Gibbs depicted a rather roseate view of post-emancipation conditions in the British West Indies, his defense of abolition, especially the familial, educational, and work choices of former slaves, illustrated an important sense of racial solidarity in the black Atlantic world.[63]

In short, the success or failure of West Indian emancipation concerned more than just production statistics or rhetorical strategy; it was also an important vindication of racial freedom unifying people of African descent against the powerful charge that they never were, are, or will be fit for freedom. It is perhaps hard for us today to appreciate the extent of these charges. Their racist echoes can still be heard today in some so-called explanations for failed states in Africa and the Caribbean compared to Yugoslavia or the Soviet Union. In the latter, the problem is invariably presented as one of the crisis of legitimacy, totalitarian regimes, and popular unrest, while in the former, it is often seen as backwardness, the absence of civil society, and barbarous violence.[64]

63. Levine, *Delany*, 77–78; *ASB*, August 11, 1860; *BAP*, 2:417–19.

64. During the early 1990s, South Africa underwent a transition from apartheid to democracy. At the time, I was conducting research for my first book at the Danville His-

Blackened Scroll

The abolition of American slavery was inevitable—at least according to many Anglo-American abolitionists. On the one hand, emancipation was God's will. At the 1839 August First Day celebration in Newark, Pennington told the audience that West Indian emancipation had been a "triumph of the principles of human liberty," and "those principles are in the care of God." A decade later, Perkins told the assembly in Cincinnati that the "cause of universal liberty is progressing in keeping with the dissemination of the gospel." Some abolitionists, faced with obstacles to achieving the end of American slavery, believed they needed to act in order to realize divine will. "God has, in all ages, employed human instrumentality in the accomplishment of the grandest results," Watkins told his Adams's audience in 1855: "And we firmly believe that, that the intellect, and conscience, and humanity, And religion of the indignant world, will yet elaborate some mighty movement, which shall sweep into the abyss of ruin, this incarnation of Death and Hell, as though a whirlwind, red with the avenger's blood, had, in all its fury, breathed upon it." Oftentimes, the abolitionist press linked abolition with grand design through their subheadings reporting on August First Day celebrations as the "Great Jubilee."[65]

On the other hand, there was the Whig view of British history in which the past was represented as one long evolutionary tale of progress and triumph led by a benevolent state whose latest expression was British abolition. At the 1839 Detroit anniversary, speaker Robert Banks reviewed the history of the English slave trade and the notorious cases of Jonathan Strong and James Somesett in the late eighteenth century. In his West Indian emancipation oration, delivered at Columbus in 1854 and Adams in 1855, speaker Watkins provided the assembly with a historical "glance" at "British philanthropy." The 1834 act, he said, was a "capstone, placed upon the magnificent superstructure of Britain's glory." This superstructure included ending the Norman Yoke of 1066; the Mansfield decision of 1772; the settlement of Sierra

---

torical Society in Virginia. As a result of my criticism of the curator's description of the new South Africa as being savage and barbarous, I never received promised copies of documentary materials.

65. Pennington, *West Indian Emancipation*, 12; *NS*, September 7, 1849; *FDP*, August 10, 1855. For links between moral progress and antislavery in the Western intellectual tradition, see David B. Davis's oeuvre.

Leone; the abolition of the slave trade in 1807; the abolition of the internal slave trade in 1824; and the abolition of "Hottentot" slavery in 1828. According to Douglass's 1848 Rochester address, abolition simply demonstrated that "England [is] the heart of the civilized world!" One wonders if the Irish audiences Douglass addressed during his inaugural 1845–47 visit would have agreed, or, for that matter, those engaged in the First Indian Uprising against the British Empire in 1857.[66]

But August First orations contained other important concepts that contradict Christian and colonial teleological frameworks. Many speakers challenged the Anglo-American Whig narrative by arguing that the American Republic did *not* represent a shining beacon to mankind. In his 1843 Buffalo "Address," Garnet noted that "two hundred and twenty-seven years ago, the first of our injured race were brought to the shores of America." Unwilling emigrants, whose first dealings were with "men calling themselves Christians," "they came with broken hearts, from their beloved native land, and were doomed to unrequited toil and deep degradation." "Succeeding generations," he added, "inherited their chains, and millions have come from eternity into time, and have returned again to the world of the spirits, cursed and ruined by American slavery." In his 1849 Emancipation Day speech at Cincinnati, John Gaines criticized revered founding father Thomas Jefferson, "as a Virginian by birth and a slaveholder, [who] could not find it in his heart to take sides with the oppressor." Slavery was the "blackened scroll of this nation's history," according to Watkins in 1854. Sharing the platform with Douglass at Rochester in 1848, Johnson was more wordy than Watkins but no less vehement: "I will not open the black and bloody pages of my country's history, and look over that dark catalogue of crime, oppression, outrage and

66. Banks, *An Oration*, 1839, 4–7; *FDP*, August 4, 1848; August 18, 1854; August 10, 1855. A memorable definition of Whig history was once provided by British historian A. J. P. Taylor, *Essays*, 44: "It is the story of English liberty, founded by Magna Carta, consolidated by the Glorious Revolution, expanded by the great Reform Bill, and reaching its highest achievement with the Labour government . . . It is the doctrine of history as progress: men always getting wiser and more tolerant; houses more comfortable, food more plentiful; new laws always better than old laws; new ideas always better than old ideas; new wives, I suppose, always better than old wives (this last much practiced by the Whig aristocracy)." The equivalent for American whig history is not too hard to fathom.

wrong, of which she has been guilty, from the earliest stages of her existence down to the present moment."[67]

Moreover, some speakers recognized the ugly side of colonial settlement and slavery in which the New World represented a living hell for indigenous peoples as well as people of African descent. David Walker noted a strange juxtaposition in a South Carolina newspaper of runaway slave advertisements, "the cuts of three men, with clubs and budgets on their backs," and the declaration that the "'Turks are the most barbarous people in the world.'" "I declare," wrote Walker, "it is really so amusing to hear the Southerners and Westerners of this country talk about *barbarity*, that it is positively, enough to make a man *smile*." Abner Francis replaced irony with bluntness in his message to the 1849 Buffalo audience: "From that hour when the Pinta touched down at St. Salvador, and those daring marinors [*sic*] of Columbus' fleet fell prostrate and kissed the newly discovered continent, a portentous cloud of slavery and death has hung over the new world."[68]

Indeed, the catalogue of crimes described in these West Indian Emancipation Day speeches contributed toward the making of a transnational counter-argument to modernity. In the *Communist Manifesto* published in 1848, Marx and Engels challenged the glories of the capitalist epoch, opening with the lines: "The history of the world is the history of class struggle." Three years later, fugitive Alexander Duval explained to his London audience at an August First celebration: "The history of the negroes in America is but the history of repeated injuries and acts of oppression committed upon them by whites."[69] Rather than a history of the slow and gradual advance of mankind, these critiques of colonial settlement, racial slavery, and the obstacles to American abolition suggest an early recognition that the path to the modern world was soaked in the blood of exploited colored people. What is really

67. *NS*, August 21, 1848; August 17, September 7, 1849; *BAP*, 3:405; *FDP*, August 18, 1854. Compare with the reasoned skepticism of Edward Gibbon's famous definition of history as "little more than the register of the crimes, follies, and misfortunes of mankind." Gibbon, *Decline and Fall*, 106.

68. Walker, *Appeal*, 15; *NS*, August 17, 1849.

69. Alexander Duval, "An Appeal to the People of Great Britain and the World," August 1, 1851, in *BAP*, 1:290. See also Kerr-Ritchie, "Emancipation from *The Communist Manifesto*."

underneath this catalogue of crimes is a refusal to accept moral progress as the foundation of Western civilization, based as it was on extermination, colonization, enslavement, and racial oppression. This social critique provided a pioneering challenge to the notion that Western civilization was inherently better, together with a questioning as to who was making such a judgment in the first place.[70]

This chapter provides an international view of black antislavery orators and orations during West Indian Emancipation Day celebrations. Through an examination of the cross-national travels of black orators, an alternative focus on key ideas in their antislavery speeches, and the popular nature of the event, it challenges the notion that West Indian emancipation can be understood simply in terms of Anglo-American and African American frameworks. Without underestimating the context of imperial emancipation and British slavery, this chapter makes the case for a politics of African diasporic identity around common issues of origins, enslavement, and liberation. This racial unity lay *beyond* the biblical injunction that Ethiopia shall stretch forth her hands for the purpose of Christian civilization and racial uplift. Moreover, the travels of these orators, their common struggles, and the notion of universal Africa points to an earlier provenance for the politics of racial identity. West Indian emancipation and American antislavery politicized people of African descent around slavery and in support of emancipation, and provided a greater consciousness of the fate and aspirations of people of African descent. These were the rites of August First.

70. For cultural, materialist, and intellectual expressions of this critique respectively, see Gilroy, *Black Atlantic*; Blackburn, *New World Slavery*; Coury, "A New Aryanism?"

Epilogue

For some three decades, August First served as an important cross-national anniversary linking people, ideas, and organizations throughout the Atlantic world. With the legal abolition of U.S. slavery in 1865, the age of Anglo-American emancipation came to a close. The international dimensions of emancipation and its commemoration, however, were too entrenched to simply disappear overnight.

The American Civil War and its outcome had an important impact on black people in Canada West. As noted in chapter 6, numerous young black men joined regiments in Northern states to fight against American slavery. Some crossed the border for the first time; others were returning; still others went back to the slave South from which they had self-emancipated years earlier. After the overthrow of American slavery, there emerged the promise of reconstruction, especially under the guidance of congressional Republicans. This prospect of making freedom in the United States proved attractive to numerous black residents from Canada. Some stayed after serving in the Union army. Others like Mifflin Wistar Gibbs relocated from Vancouver Island to Arkansas and became a local judge. The same year as the U.S. Reconstruction Acts were passed, Canada West was granted independent dominion status by the British government.

This black exodus and independence, however, did not stop public celebrations of August First in Canada. Although these appear to have been less prevalent in eastern Ontario, this was not the case in the west of the province. Commemorations of August First were regularly reported from Amherstburg in western Ontario during the 1890s. In 1902, Booker T. Washington was invited as guest speaker to an anniversary of British abolition. These annual events appear to have been both commemorations of an important past event, as well as important community affairs. Their regional influence was indicated by mass annual meetings in Windsor organized by local black businessman Walter Perry from the 1930s through the 1960s. These events were important enough civic affairs to attract major politicians: the Windsor anniversary of 1952 was endorsed by city Mayor John Wheelton, while the 1997 Toronto event was supported by Mayor Barbara Hall. These official endorsements clearly reflected a degree of new Afro-Caribbean immigration to Canadian cities. They also recall an older form of civic exchange.[1]

In 1876, the American Republic celebrated its centennial. Coming as it did a mere decade after the bloody defeat of secession, this proved an important moment to trumpet national reunification. There were hundreds of meetings, commemorations, and speeches across the reconstructed nation. Some of these speeches talked of American emancipation and compared it with British abolition. While the former was a noble business, the latter smacked of a shady deal. "Our National Influence," an address delivered at the YMCA in New York City by Reverend Thomas Armitage on July 4, 1876, was eloquent on this point. Since 1776, noted the speaker,

> the American Republic has done more for liberty and against bondage than all other people had done before. Britain is entitled to great credit for her West Indian emancipation. But it cost her half a century of bitter agitation before she could adopt that high policy, as well as great treasure. Even then, she adopted it merely as a policy and paid for it as a bargain, failing largely to bring down the doctrine of freedom to the question of man's rights as the root of his humanity.

Of course, the reverend neglected to point out the contradictions of American freedom and American slavery, and the fact that American abolition had cost over a half century of agitation, culminating in a bloody civil war forcibly ending slavery. Nonetheless, Armitage maintained that American abolition was part of a unique national crusade for the spread of freedom globally.[2]

This view of republican emancipation was hardly endorsed by the British. Reverend James Phillippo believed that it was monarchical emancipation that had been exceptional. "When a century shall have passed away," he wrote a

1. Alvin D. McCurry Papers, F2076, Ontario Archives; Flyer Commemorating Emancipation Day in Windsor, Canada, June 9, 1952, in Winks Papers, Reel 10, Box 12, Folder 4, Doc. 121; Hall letter, August 1, 1997, in Edwards, *Emancipation Day.*

2. Saunders, ed., *Centennial,* 352–53. This is an excellent collection of speeches.

decade after the event, "the greatest honour England ever attained was when, with her Sovereign at her head, she proclaimed THE SLAVE IS FREE, and established in practice what even AMERICA recognises in THEORY: *that all men are created equal—that they are endowed by their Creator with certain unalienable rights—that among these are life, liberty, and the pursuit of happiness.*" Eight years after the U.S. centennial, the British celebrated the semi-centennial of abolition. It served as a forum for trumpeting Great Britain's progressive role in world affairs, especially its leadership in the abolition of bondage. At the Guildhall in the City of London, on Friday August 2, 1884, an auspicious gathering of the Establishment assembled to commemorate. according to *The Times*, "no nobler chapter in the history of English freedom." The prince of Wales led the chorus, explaining amid loud cheers "that the chief object of this jubilee meeting is to rekindle the enthusiasm of England and to assist her to carry on this 'civilizing torch of freedom' until its beneficent light shall be shed over all the earth." It was left to *The Times* to outline the real significance of the occasion. "The duties imposed on us for the future by the ennobling memories of the past" required finishing the abolitionist work begun in England to end slavery especially in the Spanish Caribbean, Brazil, and Africa.[3]

This progressive role fit snugly with England's global imperial stewardship. The British led the way with the emancipation of 750,000 slaves, providing the basis for a global crusade against slavery. This began a defining moment in Britain's dealings with the wider world. It was also fictitious. The United Kingdom had once led the world in slave trading during the eighteenth century. During the first half of the nineteenth century, British factory owners had relied almost exclusively on cotton made by American slaves, while ordinary British people consumed the products of plantation slavery—tobacco, sugar, coffee—with little thought for their bloody roots. In addition, Thomas Armitage was partly correct in ascribing an economic motive for British abolition: it paid to emancipate slaves and pursue antislavery policies on the high seas.[4] The echoes of this hypocritical Anglo-American crusade for global freedom can currently be heard in the Arab world, much to the anger of many of that region's inhabitants.

3. Phillippo, *Jamaica*, 70; *Times* (London), August 2, 1884, 9–10. See also *Times* (London), July 31, 1884, 9.

4. Walvin, *Slavery*, 165; Williams, *Capitalism and Slavery*.

During the 1880s in the United States, African Americans participated in numerous Emancipation Day celebrations. Many of these commemorated fusion between Unionism and abolition during the Civil War: January 1 (Lincoln's Emancipation Proclamation of 1863); July 4 (Independence Day after 1863); and Juneteenth (the emancipation of slaves in Texas in 1865). But August First continued to be commemorated by African Americans. Richard White has written about Emancipation Day celebrations in upstate New York in 1886 and 1887, as responses to the local and national backlash to Reconstruction's civil rights agenda. He does not note that these commemorations took place on August First—as part of a longer regional commemorative tradition stretching back into the ante-emancipation decades—and that they belonged to an older tradition of political mobilization.[5]

In my own search for ante-emancipation celebrations, I discovered a couple of reports of August First celebrations in the post-emancipation era. On August 2, 1887, "great throngs" attended "Freedmen's day" in Meadville, Pennsylvania. The social forms were familiar: the public parade, prominent speakers, a large banquet, and a dance. But there were also some differences: in the parade marched black veterans who had helped *win* the war against American slavery. A year earlier, "4000 and 5000" people had attended the "annual celebration of the emancipation of slaves in the West Indies" in Nicodemus, Kansas, an all-black town founded in 1877. Without additional research, it is hard to be precise about the social meaning of this latter anniversary. But it was obviously a major communal event, which probably emerged as a consequence of black emigration from the southern states during the late 1870s. One generation later, the same stream of emigrants would attend UNIA meetings held on August First.[6]

The centennial of British abolition does not appear to have been celebrated by African Americans in 1934. There were, however, mass celebrations and commemorations in the United Kingdom and the British West Indies in August. Surface similarities existed with events of a century earlier:

5. White, "Civil Rights."

6. *Cleveland Gazette*, August 6, 1887; *Western Cyclone*, August 5, 1886. At the same time, older traditions were being lost. The Jamaican festival of Jonkunno, celebrated at Christmas by both enslaved and free African Americans in North Carolina during the nineteenth century, was reported to have died out. Fenn, "Perfect Equality," 134.

glorification of colonial emancipation, imperial stewardship of freedom, and thanksgiving church services in the colonies. But the era was very different. The postwar weakness of the British Empire, together with the emergence of colonial working-class discontent, resulted in centennial celebrations providing the basis for mobilization around anti-colonial movements. On August I, 1934, UNIA led an Emancipation Celebration march through the "principal thoroughfares" of the Corporate Area of Kingston. In 1938, the Colonial Office received reports of arms shipments arriving with plans for a major rebellion set for the emancipation centennial. This came after major dock worker riots in Falmouth and Kingston in late 1935, sugarcane strikes in early 1938, and strikes by oil field workers in Trinidad. Speakers addressed these crowds, drawing upon past liberation in search of new freedoms from colonial dominion.[7]

There was a similar process during the late 1950s, when future Premier of Trinidad and Tobago Eric Williams would inspire anti-colonial crowds at the "University" of Woodford Square in Port-of-Spain, Trinidad. Today, it is a rundown place. Then, it was a noisy square packed with enthusiastic crowds. There was a direct thread from this anti-colonial discourse through talks by UNIA speakers in the United States to antislavery orations on August First in the post- and ante-emancipation Atlantic world. A few years later, the winds of change swept through the British Caribbean. August First came to commemorate past emancipation and colonial independence day. Meanwhile, African Americans used the centennial of Lincoln's Emancipation Proclamation to make demands in their own national liberation struggle.

At the dawn of the twenty-first century, the epic historical struggle to overthrow Anglo-American slavery seems far removed. Its legacy, however, persists. During the 1990s, Western powers overthrew a powerful dictator in the Balkans, yet proved unwilling to prevent mass slaughter by a group of machete-wielding thugs in eastern Africa. Four decades after winning national independence, Afro-Caribbean people continue to be squeezed between the rock of global financial dictates and the whirlpool of local elites' rhetoric. American, Canadian, and British people of African provenance

7. *Daily Gleaner* (Kingston, Jamaica), July 28, 31, August 2, 1934; Holt, *Problem of Freedom,* 381–86.

continue to bear disproportionate burdens of poverty, poor health, and institutional racism. An academic book is no match for the weight of ages. But it remains important not just to remember August First, but to recognize its commemorative role in political mobilization. It is especially vital that we not overlook the people, ideas, and organizations whose cross-national struggles helped to eventually slay the monster. The power of African-descended people to overthrow slavery and colonialism points to a collective capacity to one day contribute a more humane and decent alternative to the destructive tendencies of the modern world.

Bibliography

ARCHIVES

CORNELL UNIVERSITY, KROCH LIBRARY, RARE BOOKS AND MANUSCRIPTS ROOM,
ITHACA, N.Y.

Samuel J. May Antislavery Pamphlet Collection

Antislavery newspapers

NATIONAL LIBRARY OF SCOTLAND, EDINBURGH, SCOTLAND

Missionary Record of the United Presbyterian Church, vols. 1–12, 1847–56

Andrew Somerville to Henry Highland Garnet, correspondence, 1851–52,
United Presbyterian Church Archives

NATIONAL MUSEUM OF ANTIGUA AND BARBUDA, ST. JOHN'S, ANTIGUA

Emancipation exhibit

NEW COLLEGE LIBRARY OF EDINBURGH, SCOTLAND

Ralph Wardlaw, *The Jubilee: A Sermon Preached in West George Street Chapel, Glasgow,
on Friday, August 1st, 1834, The Memorable Day of Negro Emancipation in the British
Colonies* (Glasgow: A. Fullarton, 1834)

ONTARIO ARCHIVES, TORONTO, CANADA

Antislavery newspapers

Local newspapers

Alvin D. McCurdy Papers

SCHOMBURG CENTER, NEW YORK PUBLIC LIBRARY, NEW YORK

Pamphlets and broadsides

Robin W. Winks Collection

Antislavery newspapers

VASSAR COLLEGE LIBRARIES, POUGHKEEPSIE, N.Y.

Salmon Historical Collection

Duchess County Historical Society Yearbooks

Local newspapers

YALE UNIVERSITY, BEINECKE RARE BOOK AND MANUSCRIPT LIBRARY, NEW HAVEN,
CONN.

Slavery Pamphlets, vols. 50–88

Antislavery newspapers

PRINTED PRIMARY MATERIALS

Anderson, Osborne P. *A Voice from Harper's Ferry*. New York: World View Forum, 2000.

Andrews, William L., ed. *North Carolina Slave Narratives: The Lives of Moses Roper, Lunsford Lane, Moses Grandy, and Thomas H. Jones*. Chapel Hill: University of North Carolina Press, 2003.

Anti-Slavery Society of Canada. *First Annual Report Presented to the Anti-Slavery Society of Canada by its Executive Committee*. Toronto: Brown's Printing Establishment, 1852.

Aptheker, Herbert, ed. *A Documentary History of the Negro People in the United States*. New York: Citadel Press, 1951.

Banks, Robert. *An Oration, Delivered at a Celebration in Detroit of the Abolition of Slavery in the West Indies, Held by Colored Americans, August 1, 1839*. Detroit: Harsha and Bates, 1839.

Barton, Bonnie. *The Bow in the cloud; or, The Negro's memorial: A collection of original contributions, in prose and verse, illustrative of the evils of slavery, and commemorative of its abolition in the British colonies*. London: Jackson and Walford, 1834.

Basker, James G., ed. *Amazing Grace: An Anthology of Poems about Slavery, 1660–1810*. New Haven: Yale University Press, 2002.

Beman, Amos Gerry. *Address Delivered at the Celebration of the West India Emancipation, in Davis Hall, Hudson, New York, on Monday, Aug. 2, 1847*. Troy, N.Y.: J. C. Kneeland and Co. Steam Press, 1847.

Bibb, Henry. *The Life and Adventures of Henry Bibb: An American Slave*. Madison: University of Wisconsin Press, 2001.

————. *Narrative of the Life and Adventures of Henry Bibb: An American Slave, Written by Himself*. Reproduced online: http://docsouth.unc.edu/neh/bibb/menu.html

Bleby, Henry. *Speech of Rev. Henry Bleby, Missionary From Barbados, on the Results of Emancipation in the British West Indies Colonies, delivered at the Celebration of the Massachusetts Anti-Slavery Society held at Island Grove, July 31st, 1858*. Boston: R. F. Wallcut, 1858.

British Parliamentary Papers. *Report of the Select Committee on the Extinction of Slavery Throughout the British Dominions, 1831–1832*. Vol. 2. Shannon: Irish University Press, 1968.

British Parliamentary Papers. *Papers in Explanation of Measures adopted for Giving Effect to the Abolition of Slavery Act, 1835*. Shannon: Irish University Press, 1968.

Brown, William J. *Life of William J. Brown, of Providence, R.I.; With Personal Recollections of Incidents in Rhode Island*. Providence: Angell and Co., 1883.

Carlyle, Thomas. "The Nigger Question." In *Carlyle's Complete Works*. Albany, N.Y.: James B. Lyon and Co., 1887.

Channing, William E. *Dr. Channing's last Address, delivered at Lenox, on the First of August, 1842, the anniversary of emancipation in the British West Indies*. Boston: Oliver Johnson, 1842.

Collins, John A. *The Anti-Slavery Picknick: A Collection of Speeches, Poems, Dialogues and Songs*. Boston: H. W. Williams, 1842.

Cox, Francis A. *History of the Baptist Missionary Society from 1792 to 1842*. 2 vols. London: T. Ward, 1842.

Day, Charles W. *Five Years' Residence in the West Indies*. 2 vols. London: Colburn and Co., 1852.

Dickson, Moses. *Manual of the International Order of Twelve Knights and Daughters of Tabor, containing general laws, regulations, ceremonies, drill, and a Taborian lexicon*. St. Louis, Mo.: A. R. Fleming, 1891.

Douglass, Frederick. *The Frederick Douglass Papers*. Series I, Speeches, Debates, and Interviews, vol. 3. Edited by John W. Blassingame et al. New Haven: Yale University Press, 1985.

Drew, Benjamin. *A North-Side of Slavery. The Refugee: or the Narratives of Fugitive Slaves in Canada Related by Themselves, with an Account of the History and Condition of the Colored Population of Upper Canada*. Boston: J. P. Jewett and Company, 1856. Reproduced online: http://docsouth.unc.edu/neh/drew/menu.html.

Edwards, John P. *The Internationalization of Emancipation Day*. Brooklyn: Caribbean Historical Society, n.d.

Emerson, Ralph W. *An Address delivered in the Court-House in Concord, Massachusetts, on August 1st, 1844: On the Anniversary of the Emancipation*. Boston: James Munroe, 1844.

Faust, Drew Gilpin., ed. *The Ideology of Slavery: Proslavery Thought in the Antebellum South, 1830–1860*. Baton Rouge: Louisiana State University Press, 1981.

Ferguson, Moira. *The History of Mary Prince, A West Indian Slave, Related by Herself*. Ann Arbor: University of Michigan Press, 1998.

Garnet, Henry H. "Eulogy of John Brown, New York City, 1859." In *Let Your Motto Be Resistance: The Life and Thought of Henry Highland Garnet*, edited by Earl Ofari. Boston: Beacon Press, 1972.

Garrison, William L. *West India Emancipation. Speech of William Lloyd Garrison, delivered at Abington, Mass., on the First day of August, 1854*. Boston: American Anti-Slavery Society, 1854.

Levine, Robert S., ed. *Martin R. Delany: A Documentary Reader*. Chapel Hill: University of North Carolina Press, 2003.

Long, Edward. *The History of Jamaica, or, General survey of the ancient and modern state of that Island*. London: T. Lowndes, 1774.

Marshall, Woodville K., ed. *The Colhurst Journal: Journal of a Special Magistrate in the Islands of Barbados and St. Vincent*. Millwood, N.Y.: KTO Press, 1977.

Noonan, Barry, ed. *Blacks in Canada, 1861: Censuses of Ontario, Quebec, and New Brunswick*. Madison: University of Wisconsin Press, 2000.

Pease, Zephaniah W., ed. *The Diary of Samuel Rodman, 1829–1859*. New Bedford, Mass., 1927.

Pennington, James W. C. *The Reasonableness of the Abolition of Slavery at the South: An Address Delivered at Hartford, Connecticut, August 1856*. Hartford, Conn.: Case Tiffany, 1856.

———. *A Text Book of the Origin and History, &c. &c. of the Colored People*. Hartford, Conn.: L. Skinner, 1841.

———. *West Indian Emancipation Address at Newark, August 1, 1839*. Newark: Aaron Guest, 1839.

Phillippo, James Mursell. *Jamaica: Its Past and Present State*. Philadelphia: J. M. Campbell and Co., 1843.

Ripley, C. Peter. ed. *The Black Abolitionist Papers*. 5 vols. Chapel Hill: University of North Carolina Press, 1985–92.

Saunders, Frederick, ed. *Our National Centennial Jubilee: Orations, Addresses, and Poems Delivered on the Fourth of July, 1876 in the Several States of the Union*. New York: E. B. Treat, 1877.

Taylor, Clare. *British and American Abolitionists: An Episode in Transatlantic Understanding*. Edinburgh: Edinburgh University Press, 1974.

Thome, James A. *Emancipation in the West Indies. A Six Months' Tour in Antigua, Barbadoes, and Jamaica in the year 1837*. New York: American Anti-Slavery Society, 1838.

Walker, David. *Appeal to the Colored Citizens of the World*. Edited by Peter P. Hinks. University Park: Penn State University Press, 1996.

Ward, Samuel Ringgold. *Autobiography of a Fugitive Negro: His Anti-Slavery Labours in the United States, Canada and England*. London: John Snow, 1855.

———. *Autobiography of a Fugitive Negro*. New York: Arno Press, 1968.

Watkins, William J. "Our Rights as Men. An Address Delivered in Boston, Before the Legislative Committee on the Militia, February 24, 1853." In *Negro Protest*

Pamphlets: A Compendium, edited by Dorothy Porter, 2–21. New York: Arno Press, 1969.

Woodson, Carter G. *Negro Orators and Their Orations.* Washington, D.C.: Associated Publishers, 1925.

Wright, Richardson. *Revels in Jamaica, 1682–1830.* New York: Dodd, Mead, and Company, 1937; New York: Benjamin Blom, 1969.

NEWSPAPERS

African Repository (Washington, D.C.), 1838–41

Anglo-African (New York City), 1859–61

Anti-Slavery Bugle (Salem, Ohio), 1845–59

Brooklyn Daily Eagle (N.Y.), 1850, 1858, 1859

Chatham Journal (Chatham, Canada), 1842–43

Christian Observer (Philadelphia), 1855

Christian Recorder (Philadelphia), 1862–66

Cleveland Gazette (Cleveland, Ohio), 1887

Colored American (New York City), 1837–41

Crisis (New York City), 1934, 1938

Daily Gleaner (Kingston, Jamaica), 1888, 1934, 1938, 1984, 1988

Daily Globe (Toronto, Canada), 1850–61

Douglass' Monthly (Rochester), 1860–63

Emancipator (New York City), 1836–38

Frederick Douglass' Paper (Rochester), 1851–55

Hamilton Spectator (Hamilton, Canada), 1850–61

Herald of Freedom (Concord, N.H.), 1841–46

Liberator (Boston), 1831–65

London Times (London, U.K.), 1884

Memphis Bulletin (Memphis), 1864

Montreal Star (Montreal), 1963

Nashville Dispatch (Nashville, Tenn.), 1864

National Anti-Slavery Standard (New York City), 1853

National Era (Washington, D.C.), 1847, 1851, 1852

New York Daily Times (New York City), 1852, 1855

New York Daily Tribune (New York City), 1850

New York Semi-Weekly Tribune (New York City), 1856

North Star (Rochester), 1847–50

Pacific Appeal (San Francisco), 1862

Palladium of Liberty (Columbus, Ohio), 1844

Poughkeepsie Daily Eagle (Poughkeepsie, N.Y.), 1848–65

Poughkeepsie News-Telegraph (Poughkeepsie, N.Y.), 1846–48

Port of Spain Gazette (Port of Spain, Trinidad), 1884, 1888

Provincial Freeman (Toronto, Chatham, Canada), 1854–57

Voice of the Fugitive (Sandwich, Canada), 1851–52

Western Cyclone (Nicodemus, Kansas), 1886

SECONDARY BOOKS AND ARTICLES

Aching, Gerard. *Masking and Power: Carnival and Popular Culture in the Caribbean.* Minneapolis: University of Minnesota Press, 2002.

Allen, James S. *Reconstruction: The Battle for Democracy, 1865–1877.* New York: International Publishers, 1937.

Anderson, Jervis. "England in Jamaica: Memories from a Colonial Boyhood." *American Scholar* 69, no. 2 (Spring 2000): 15–30.

Aptheker, Herbert. *Essays in the History of the American Negro.* New York: International Publishers, 1964.

Armstrong, James C., and Nigel A. Worden. "The Slaves, 1652–1834." In *The Shaping of South African Society, 1652–1840,* edited by Richard Elphick and Hermann Giliomee, 109–83. Middletown, Conn.: Wesleyan University Press, 1989.

Ashe, S. A., and Lyon G. Tuler. "Secession, Insurrection of the Negroes, and Northern Incendarism." *Tyler's Quarterly Historical and Genealogical Magazine* (1933).

Austin-Broos, Diane J. "Redefining the Moral Order: Interpretations of Christianity in Postemancipation Jamaica." In *The Meaning of Freedom: Economics, Politics, and Culture after Slavery,* edited by Frank McGlynn and Seymour Drescher, 221–43. Pittsburgh: University of Pittsburgh Press, 1992.

Baraka, Imamu Amiri. *Blues People: Negro Music in White America.* New York: W. Morrow, 1963.

Barker, Anthony J. *Captain Charles Stuart: Anglo-American Abolitionist.* Baton Rouge: Louisiana State University Press, 1986.

Bell, Howard H. "National Negro Conventions of the Middle 1840s: Moral Suasion vs. Political Action." *Journal of Negro History* 42, no. 4 (October 1957): 247–60.

———. "Negroes in California, 1849–1859." *Phylon* 28, no. 2 (1967): 151–60.

Berlin, Ira, et al. *Freedom's Soldiers: The Black Military Experience in the Civil War.* Cambridge: Cambridge University Press, 1998.

———. *Many Thousands Gone: The First Two Centuries of Slavery in North America.* Cambridge, Mass.: Harvard University Press, 1998.

Bernal, Martin. *Black Athena: The Afroasiatic Roots of Classical Civilization.* Vol. I: *The Fabrication of Ancient Greece, 1785–1985.* New Brunswick, N.J.: Rutgers University Press, 1987.

Bilby, Kenneth. "Gumbay, Myal, and the Great House: New Evidence on the Religious Background of Jonkonnu in Jamaica." *African Caribbean Institute of Jamaica Research Review* 4 (1999): 47–70.

Blackburn, Robin. *The Making of New World Slavery: From the Baroque to the Modern, 1492–1800.* London: Verso, 1997.

———. *The Overthrow of Colonial Slavery, 1776–1848.* London: Verso, 1988.

Blackett, R. J. M. *Beating against the Barriers: The Lives of Six Nineteenth-Century Afro-Americans.* Ithaca: Cornell University Press, 1989.

———. *Building an Antislavery Wall: Black Americans in the Atlantic Abolitionist Movement, 1830–1860.* Baton Rouge: Louisiana State University Press, 1983.

———. "'Freedom, or the Martyr's Grave': Black Pittsburgh's Aid to the Fugitive Slave." *Western Pennsylvania Historical Magazine* 61 (1978): 117–34.

Braisted, Todd W. "The Black Pioneers and Others: The Military Role of Black Loyalists in the American War for Independence." In *Moving On: Black Loyalists in the Afro-Atlantic World,* edited by John W. Pulis, 3–38. New York: Garland, 1999.

Bramble, Linda. *Black Fugitive Slaves in Early Canada.* St. Catherines, Ont.: Vanwell Press, 1988.

Brereton, Bridget. "The Birthday of Our Race: A Social History of Emancipation Day in Trinidad, 1838–88." In *Trade, Government and Society in Caribbean History, 1700–1920,* edited by Barry Higman, 69–83. Kingston, Jamaica: Heinemann, 1983.

Brown, Martha A. "Clothing." In *Dictionary of Afro-American Slavery,* edited by Randall M. Miller and John David Smith, 117–21. Westport, Conn.: Greenwood Press, 1997.

Buckley, Roger Norman. *The British Army in the West Indies: Society and the Military in the Revolutionary Age.* Gainesville: University Press of Florida, 1998.

Burke, Ronald K. *Samuel Ringgold Ward, Christian Abolitionist.* New York: Garland, 1995.

Burn, W. L. *Emancipation and Apprenticeship in the British West Indies.* London: J. Cape, 1937.

Cahill, Barry. "The Black Loyalist Myth in Atlantic Canada." *Acadiensis* 29, no. I (Autumn 1999): 76–87.

Campbell, Susan. "Carnival, Calypso, and Class Struggle in Nineteenth Century Trinidad." *History Workshop Journal* 26 (1988): I–27.

Carter, George E., and C. Peter Ripley, et al., eds. *Black Abolitionist Papers, 1830–1865: A Guide to the Microfilm Edition.* New York: Microfilming Corp., 1981.

Cecelski, David S. "Abraham H. Galloway: Wilmington's Lost Prophet and the Rise of Black Radicalism in the American South." In *Time Longer Than Rope: A Century of African American Activism, 1850–1950,* edited by Charles M. Payne and Adam Green. New York: New York University Press, 2003.

Cimprich, John. *Slavery's End in Tennessee, 1861–1865.* University: University of Alabama Press, 1985.

Coles, Howard W. *The Cradle of Freedom: A History of the Negro in Rochester, Western New York and Canada.* Rochester, N.Y.: Oxford University Press, 1943.

Colley, Linda. *Britons: Forging the Nation.* New Haven: Yale University Press, 1992.

Collison, Gary. "'Loyal and Dutiful Subjects of her Gracious Majesty, Queen Victoria': Fugitive Slaves in Montreal, 1850–1866." *Quebec Studies* 19 (1994–95): 59–70.

Coury, Ralph M. "A New Aryanism?" *Mediterranean Quarterly* 5, no. 3 (Summer 1994): 42–56.

Cox, Edward. "From Slavery to Freedom: Emancipation and Apprenticeship in Grenada and St. Vincent, 1834–1838." In *Crossing Boundaries: Comparative History of Black People in the Diaspora,* edited by Darlene Clark Hine and Jacqueline McLeod. Bloomington: Indiana University Press, 1999.

Craton, Michael. *Empire, Enslavement and Freedom in the Caribbean.* Kingston: Ian Randle Publishers, 1997.

———. *Testing the Chains: Resistance to Slavery in the British West Indies.* Ithaca: Cornell University Press, 1982.

Curtin, Philip D. *Two Jamaicas: The Role of Ideas in a Tropical Colony, 1830–1865.* New York: Negro University Press, 1968.

Davis, David Brion. *Challenging the Boundaries of Slavery.* Cambridge, Mass.: Harvard University Press, 2003.

———. *The Problem of Slavery in Western Culture.* Ithaca: Cornell University Press, 1970.

———. *Religion, Moral Values, and Our Heritage of Slavery.* New Haven: Yale University Press, 2001.

Davis, Susan G. *Parades and Power: Street Theatre in Nineteenth-Century Philadelphia.* Philadelphia: Temple University Press, 1986.

De Caro, Louis A., Jr. *"Fire from the Midst of You": A Religious Life of John Brown*. New York: New York University Press, 2002.

Dirks, Robert. *The Black Saturnalia: Conflict and Its Ritual Expression on British West Indian Slave Plantations*. Gainesville: University of Florida Press, 1987.

Dixon, Chris. *African America and Haiti: Emigration and Black Nationalism in the Nineteenth Century*. Westport, Conn.: Greenwood Press, 2000.

Donald, David H., Jean H. Baker, and Michael F. Holt. *The Civil War and Reconstruction*. New York: Norton, 2001.

Dostoyevsky, Fydor. *Crime and Punishment*. New York: Everyman's Library, 1977.

Douglass, R. Alan. *Uppermost Canada: The Western District and the Detroit Frontier, 1800–1850*. Detroit: Wayne State University Press, 2001.

Du Bois, W. E. B. *Black Reconstruction in America, 1860–1880*. New York: Atheneum Press, 1992.

Esedebe, P. Olisanwuche. *Pan-Africanism: The Idea and Movement, 1776–1991*. Washington, D.C.: Howard University Press, 1994.

Fabre, Geneviève. "African-American Commemorative Celebrations in the Nineteenth Century." In *History & Memory in African-American Culture*, edited by Geneviève Fabre and Robert O'Meally, 72–91. New York: Oxford University Press, 1994.

Federal Writers' Project. *Massachusetts: A Guide to Its Places and People*. Boston: Houghton Mifflin, 1937.

Fenn, Elizabeth A. "'A Perfect Equality Seemed to Reign': Slave Society and Jonkonnu." *North Carolina Historical Review* 65, no. 2 (April 1988): 127–53.

Fick, Carolyn E. *The Making of Haiti: The Saint Domingue Revolution from Below*. Knoxville: University of Tennessee Press, 1990.

Figes, Orlando, and Boris Kolonitski. *Interpreting the Russian Revolution: The Language and Symbols of 1917*. New Haven: Yale University Press, 1999.

Findlay, G. G., and W. W. Holdsworth. *The History of the Wesleyan Methodist Missionary Society*. Vol. I. London: Epworth Press, 1922.

Finkelman, Paul, ed. *Articles on American Slavery*. Vol. 6: *Fugitive Slaves*. New York: Garland, 1992.

Fitzgerald, Michael. *The Union League Movement in the Deep South: Politics and Agricultural Change during Reconstruction*. Baton Rouge: Louisiana State University Press, 1989.

———. *Urban Emancipation: Popular Politics in Reconstruction Mobile*. Baton Rouge: Louisiana State University Press, 2002.

Foner, Eric. *Nothing but Freedom: Emancipation and Its Legacy*. Baton Rouge: Louisiana State University Press, 1983.

————. *Who Owns History? Rethinking the Past in a Changing World.* New York: Hill and Wang, 2002.

————. *Reconstruction: America's Unfinished Revolution.* New York: Harper & Row, 1988.

Foster, R. F. *Modern Ireland, 1600–1972.* London: Penguin, 1989.

————. *Paddy and Mr. Punch: Connections in Irish and English History.* London: Penguin, 1993.

Franklin, John Hope, and Loren Schweninger. *Runaway Slaves: Rebels on the Plantation.* New York: Oxford University Press, 1999.

Freehling, William L. *The Road to DisUnion: Secessionists at Bay, 1776–1854.* New York: Oxford University Press, 1990.

Fuke, Richard Paul. *Imperfect Equality: African Americans and the Confines of White Racial Attitudes in Post-Emancipation Maryland.* New York: Fordham University Press, 1999.

Gaspar, David B. *Bondmen & Rebels: A Study of Master-Slave Relations in Antigua.* Baltimore: Johns Hopkins University Press, 1985.

Gaspar, David B., and David P. Geggus. *A Turbulent Time: The French Revolution and the Greater Caribbean.* Bloomington: Indiana University Press, 1997.

Gates, Henry Louis, Jr., and William L. Andrews. *Pioneers of the Black Atlantic: Five Slave Narratives from the Enlightenment 1772–1815.* Washington, D.C.: Civitas, 1998.

Geertz, Clifford. *The Interpretation of Cultures.* New York: Basic Books, 1973.

Geiss, Imanuel. *The Pan-African Movement: A History of Pan-Africanism in America, Europe and Africa.* New York: African Publishing Co., 1974.

Gerber, David A. *Black Ohio and the Color Line, 1860–1915.* Urbana: University of Illinois Press, 1976.

Gibbon, Edward. *The Decline and Fall of the Roman Empire.* One-Volume Abridgment by Dero A. Saunders. London: Penguin, 1982.

Gilje, Paul L. *The Road to Mobocracy: Popular Disorder in New York City, 1763–1834.* Chapel Hill: University of North Carolina Press, 1987.

Gilroy, Paul. *The Black Atlantic: Modernity and Double Consciousness.* Cambridge, Mass.: Harvard University Press, 1993.

Glaude, Eddie S. *Exodus: Religion, Race and Nation in Early 19th Century Black America.* Chicago: University of Chicago Press, 2000.

Glick, Wendell P. "Thoreau and the Herald of Freedom." *New England Quarterly* 22, no. 2 (June 1949): 193–204.

Gomez, Michael A. *Exchanging Our Country Marks: The Transformation of African Identities in the Colonial and Antebellum South.* Chapel Hill: University of North Carolina Press, 1998.

Gravely, William B. "The Dialectic of Double-Consciousness in Black American Freedom Celebrations, 1808–1863." *Journal of Negro History* 67, no. 4 (Winter 1982): 302–17.

Green, William A. *British Slave Emancipation: The Sugar Colonies and the Great Experiment.* New York: Oxford University Press, 1976.

Greenberg, Kenneth S. *The Confessions of Nat Turner and Related Documents.* Boston: Bedford Books, 1996.

Gregg, Robert. *Inside Out, Outside In: Essays in Comparative History.* London: St. Martin's Press, 2000.

Grover, Kathryn. *The Fugitive's Gibraltar: Escaping Slaves and Abolitionism in New Bedford, Massachusetts.* Amherst: University of Massachusetts Press, 2001.

Hahn, Steven. *A Nation under Our Feet: Black Political Struggles in the Rural South from Slavery to the Great Migration.* Cambridge, Mass.: Harvard University Press, 2003.

Hall, Catherine. *Civilizing Subjects: Metropole and Colony in the English Imagination 1830–1867.* Chicago: University of Chicago Press, 2002.

Harding, Vincent. *There Is a River: The Black Struggle for Freedom in America.* New York: Oxford University Press, 1980.

Harris, Joseph E., ed. *Global Dimensions of the African Diaspora.* Washington, D.C.: Howard University Press, 1993.

Harris, Leslie M. *In the Shadow of Slavery: African Americans in New York City, 1626–1863.* Chicago: University of Chicago Press, 2003.

Harris, Tim. *London Crowds in the Reign of Charles II: Propaganda and Politics from the Restoration until the Exclusion Crisis.* Cambridge: Cambridge University Press, 1987.

Harrison, Mark. *Crowds and History: Mass Phenomena in English Towns, 1790–1835.* Cambridge: Cambridge University Press, 1988.

Harrold, Stanley. *Subversives: Antislavery Community in Washington, D.C., 1828–1865.* Baton Rouge: Louisiana State University Press, 2003.

Heuman, Gad. "Riots and Resistance in the Caribbean at the Moment of Freedom." *Slavery and Abolition* 21 (September 2000): 135–49.

Higman, Barry. "Slavery Remembered: The Celebration of Emancipation in Jamaica." *Journal of Caribbean History* 12 (1979): 55–74.

Hill, Daniel G. *The Freedom-Seekers: Blacks in Early Canada.* Agincourt, Canada: Book Society of Canada, 1981.

———. "Negroes in Toronto, 1793–1865." *Ontario History* 55 (1963): 73–91.

Hill, Hilda A. "Henry Bibb, the Colonizer." *Negro History Bulletin* (n.d.): 148.

Hine, Darlene Clark, and Jacqueline McLeod, eds. *Crossing Boundaries: Comparative History of Black People in the Diaspora*. Bloomington: Indiana University Press, 1999.

Hite, Roger W. "Voice of a Fugitive: Henry Bibb and Ante-bellum Black Separatism." *Journal of Black Studies* 4, no. 3 (March 1974): 269–84.

Hobsbawn, Eric, and Terence Ranger, eds. *The Invention of Tradition*. Cambridge: Cambridge University Press, 1996.

Hodges, Graham Russell. *Root and Branch: African Americans in New York and East Jersey, 1613–1863*. Chapel Hill: University of North Carolina Press, 1999.

Holt, Thomas. *The Problem of Freedom: Race, Labor, and Politics in Jamaica and Britain, 1832–1938*. Baltimore: Johns Hopkins University Press, 1992.

Honour, Hugh. *The Image of the Black in Western Art*. 4 vols. Cambridge, Mass.: Harvard University Press, 1989.

Horton, James O. and Lois E. Horton. *Black Bostonians: Family Life and Community Struggle in the Antebellum North*. New York: Holmes & Meier Publishers, 1979.

———. *In Hope of Liberty: Culture, Community and Protest among Northern Blacks, 1700–1860*. New York: Oxford University Press, 1997.

Howe, Stephen. *Afrocentrism: Mythical Pasts and Imagined Homes*. London: Verso, 1998.

Jackson, Debra. "A Cultural Stronghold: The Anglo-African Newspaper and the Black Community of New York." *New York History* 85, no. 4 (Fall 2004): 331–58.

James, C. L. R. *American Civilization*. Oxford: Blackwell Press, 1993.

Jeffrey, Julie Roy. *The Great Silent Army of Abolitionism: Ordinary Women in the Antislavery Movement*. Chapel Hill: University of North Carolina Press, 1998.

Josiah, Barbara P. "After Emancipation: Aspects of Village Life in Guyana, 1869–1911." *Journal of Negro History* 82, no. 1 (Winter 1997): 105–21.

Judd, Dennis. *Empire: The British Imperial Experience from 1765 to the Present*. London: Fontana Press, 1997.

Junne, George H. *The History of Blacks in Canada: A Selectively Annotated Bibliography*. Westport, Conn.: Greenwood Press, 2003.

Kachun, Mitch. *Festivals of Freedom: Memory and Meaning in African American Emancipation Celebrations, 1808–1915*. Amherst: University of Massachusetts Press, 2003.

Kathrada, Ahmed. *Memoirs*. Cape Town: Zebra Press, 2004.

Kerr-Ritchie, Jeffrey R. *Freedpeople in the Tobacco South: Virginia, 1860–1900*. Chapel Hill: University of North Carolina Press, 1999.

———. "Emancipation from *The Communist Manifesto*." *Nature, Society, and Thought* 10, no. 4 (December 1998): 523–38.

————. "Rehearsal for War: Black Militias in the Atlantic World." *Slavery and Abolition* 26, no. 1 (April 2005): 1–33.

Kertzer, David I. *Rituals, Politics, and Power.* New Haven: Yale University Press, 1988.

Lader, Lawrence. *The Bold Brahmins: New England's War against Slavery, 1831–1863.* New York: E. P. Dutton, 1961.

Landon, Fred. "Amherstburg, Terminus of the Underground Railroad." *Journal of Negro History* 10, no. 1 (January 1925): 1–9.

————. "The Anti-Slavery Society of Canada." *Journal of Negro History* 4, no. 1 (January 1919): 33–40.

————. "The Buxton Settlement in Canada." *Journal of Negro History* 3, no. 4 (October 1918): 360–67.

————. "Henry Bibb, a Colonizer." *Journal of Negro History* 5, no. 4 (October 1920): 437–47.

————. "In an Old Ontario Cemetery." *The Dalhousie Review* 5 (January 1926): 523–31.

————. "The Negro Migration to Canada After the Passing of the Fugitive Slave Act." *Journal of Negro History* 5, no. 1 (January 1920): 22–36.

————. "Records Illustrating the Condition of Refugees from Slavery in Upper Canada before 1860." *Journal of Negro History* 13, no. 2 (April 1928): 199–206.

Lindsay, Arnett G. "Diplomatic Relations between the United States and Great Britain Bearing on the Return of Negro Slaves, 1783–1828." *Journal of Negro History* 5, no. 4 (October 1920): 391–401.

Linebaugh, Peter, and Marcus Rediker. *The Many-Headed Hydra: Sailors, Slaves, Commoners, and the Hidden History of the Revolutionary Atlantic.* Boston: Beacon, 2000.

Litwack, Leon. *North of Slavery: The Negro in the Free States, 1790–1860.* Chicago: University of Chicago Press, 1961.

Mahon, John K. *History of the Militia and the National Guard.* New York: Macmillan, 1983.

Marshall, Woodville K. "'We be wise to many more tings': Blacks' Hopes and Expectations of Emancipation." In *Caribbean Freedom: Society and Economy from Emancipation to the Present,* edited by Hilary Beckles and Verene Shepherd, 12–20. Kingston: Ian Randle, 1993.

McDonald, Roderick A. "The Transition from Slavery to Freedom in the British West Indies: The Journal of John Anderson, St. Vincent Special Magistrate, 1836–1839." Presentation, Philadelphia Center for Early American Studies Seminar, 1990.

McFeeley, William S. *Frederick Douglass.* New York: Norton, 1991.

McKay, Claude. *Banjo: A Story without a Plot.* New York: Harcourt, Brace, Jovanovich, 1970.

McKivigan, John R., and Jason H. Silverman. "Monarchical Liberty and Republican Slavery: West Indian Emancipation Celebrations in Upstate New York and Canada West." *Afro-Americans in New York Life and History* 10 (January 1986): 7–18.

McNeil, Lydia. "James G. Barbadoes." In *Encyclopedia of African-American Culture and History,* edited by Jack Salzman, David Lionel Smith, and Cornel West, 1:263. New York: Macmillan References, 1996.

McPherson, James M. *The Negro's Civil War: How American Negroes Felt and Acted during the War for the Union.* New York: Vintage, 1967.

Midgley, Clare. *Women against Slavery: The British Campaigns, 1780–1870.* London: Routledge, 1992.

Morgan, Edmund S. *American Slavery, American Freedom.* New York: Norton, 1975.

Morris, Robert C. *Reading, 'Riting, and Reconstruction: The Education of Freedmen in the South, 1861–1870.* Chicago: University of Chicago Press, 1981.

Muelder, Hermann R. *Fighters for Freedom: The Anti-Slavery Activities of Men and Women Associated with Knox College.* New York: Columbia University Press, 1959.

Mullin, Michael. *Africa in America: Slave Acculturation and Resistance in the American South and the British Caribbean, 1736–1831.* Urbana: University of Illinois Press, 1994.

Murray, Alexander L. "The *Provincial Freeman:* A New Source for the History of the Negro in Canada and the United States." *Journal of Negro History* 44, no. 2 (April 1959): 123–35.

Newman, Simon P. *Parades and the Politics of the Street: Festive Culture in the Early American Republic.* Philadelphia: University of Pennsylvania Press, 1997.

North, Douglass C. *The Economic Growth of the United States, 1790 to 1860.* Englewood Cliffs, N.J.: Prentice-Hall, 1961.

Ofari, Earl. *"Let Your Motto Be Resistance": The Life and Thought of Henry Highland Garnet.* Boston: Beacon Press, 1972.

Ozouf, Mona. *Festivals and the French Revolution.* Cambridge, Mass.: Harvard University Press, 1988.

Palmer, Colin. "Defining and Studying the Modern African Diaspora." *Perspectives* 36, no. 6 (September 1998): 22–25.

Payne, Charles M., and Adam Green, eds. *Time Longer than Rope: A Century of African American Activism, 1850–1950.* New York: New York University Press, 2003.

Pearse, Andrew. "Carnival in Nineteenth Century Trinidad." *Caribbean Quarterly* 4 (1956): 176–93.

Pease, Jane H., and William H. Pease. *Black Utopia: Negro Communal Experiments in America.* Madison: State Historical Society of Wisconsin, 1963.

———. *They Who Would Be Free: Blacks' Search for Freedom, 1830–1861.* New York: Atheneum, 1974.

Phillips, Christopher. *Freedom's Port: The African American Community of Baltimore, 1790–1860.* Urbana: University of Illinois Press, 1997.

Piersen, William Dillon. *Black Yankees: The Development of an Afro-American Subculture in Eighteenth Century New England.* Amherst: University of Massachusetts Press, 1988.

Pulis, John W., ed. *Moving On: Black Loyalists in the Afro-Atlantic World.* New York: Garland, 1999.

Quarles, Benjamin. *Black Abolitionists.* New York: Oxford University Press, 1969.

Quillin, Frank Uriah. *The Color Line in Ohio: A History of Race Prejudice in a Typical Northern State.* 1913: Reprint New York: Negro Universities Press, 1969.

Raboteau, Albert J. *A Fire in the Bones: Reflections on African-American Religious History.* Boston: Beacon Press, 1995.

Rael, Patrick. *Black Identity and Black Protest in the Antebellum North.* Chapel Hill: University of North Carolina Press, 2002.

Reckord, Mary. "The Jamaica Slave Rebellion of 1831." *Past and Present* 40 (July 1968): 108–25.

Reiss, Joao Jose. *Death is a Festival: Funeral Rites and Rebellion in Nineteenth-Century Brazil.* Chapel Hill: University of North Carolina Press, 2003.

Rhodes, Jane. *Mary Ann Shadd Cary: The Black Press and Protest in the Nineteenth Century.* Bloomington: Indiana University Press, 1998.

Rice, C. Duncan. *The Scots Abolitionists, 1833–1861.* Baton Rouge: Louisiana State University Press, 1981.

Richards, Leonard L. *The Slave Power: The Free North and Southern Domination, 1780–1860.* Baton Rouge: Louisiana State University Press, 2000.

Richardson, David, ed. *Abolition and Its Aftermath: The Historical Context, 1790–1916.* London: Frank Cass, 1985.

Riddell, William R. "Interesting Notes on Great Britain and Canada with Respect to the Negro." *Journal of Negro History* 13, no. 2 (April 1928): 185–98.

———. "The Slave in Upper Canada." *Journal of Negro History* 4 (October 1919): 372–95.

Roach, Joseph R. *Cities of the Dead: Circum-Atlantic Performance.* New York: Columbia University Press, 1996.

Rodney, Walter. *A History of the Guyanese Working People, 1881–1905.* Baltimore: Johns Hopkins University Press, 1981.

Rodriguez, Junius P., ed. *The Historical Encyclopedia of World Slavery.* 2 vols. Santa Barbara: ABC-CLIO, 1997.

Ryan, Mary P. *Women in Public: Between Banners and Ballots, 1825–1880.* Baltimore: Johns Hopkins University Press, 1990.

St. G. Walker, James W. *The Black Loyalists: The Search for a Promised Land in Nova Scotia and Sierra Leone, 1783–1870.* New York: Dalhousie University Press, 1976.

Saville, Julie. *The Work of Reconstruction: From Slave to Wage Laborer in South Carolina, 1860–1870.* New York: Cambridge University Press, 1994.

Schappes, Morris U. "Ernestine L. Rose: Her Address on the Anniversary of West Indian Emancipation." *Journal of Negro History* 34, no. 3 (July 1949): 344–55.

Schor, Joel. *Henry Highland Garnet: A Voice of Black Radicalism in the Nineteenth Century.* Westport, Conn.: Greenwood Press, 1977.

Scully, Pamela. *Liberating the Family? Gender and British Slave Emancipation in the Rural Western Cape, South Africa, 1823–1853.* Portsmouth, N.H.: Heinemann, 1997.

Sernett, Milton C. *North Star Country: Upstate New York and the Crusade for African American Freedom.* Syracuse: Syracuse University Press, 2002.

Silverman, Jason H. *Unwelcome Guests: Canada West's Response to American Fugitive Slaves, 1800–1865.* Greenwood, Conn.: Associated Faculty Press, 1985.

———. "The American Fugitive Slave in Canada: Myths and Realities." *Southern Studies* (Fall 1980): 215–27.

Singletary, Otis. *Negro Militia and Reconstruction.* New York: McGraw-Hill, 1963.

Sinha, Manisha. *The Counterevolution of Slavery: Politics and Ideology in Antebellum South Carolina.* Chapel Hill: University of North Carolina, 2000.

Sklar, Kathryn Kish. *Women's Rights Emerges within the Anti-Slavery Movement, 1830–1870: A Brief History with Documents.* Boston: Bedford/St. Martin's, 2000.

StanKlos.com. "Joseph Horace Kimball." *Appleton's Cyclopedia of American Biography.* Reproduced online.

Stauffer, John. "American Responses to British Emancipation: The Problem of Progress," Sisterhood and Slavery: An International Conference, October 25–28, 2001, Gilder Lehrman Center, Yale University.

Sterling, Dorothy. *The Making of an Afro-American: Martin Robison Delany, 1812–1885.* New York: Da Capo Press, 1971.

Stewart, James Brewer. *Holy Warriors: The Abolitionists and American Slavery.* New York: Hill and Wang, 1976.

———. *Wendell Phillips: Liberty's Hero.* Baton Rouge: Louisiana State University Press, 1986.

Stewart, Robert. "A Slandered People—Views on 'Negro Character' in the Mainstream Christian Churches in Post-Emancipation Jamaica." In *Crossing Boundaries: Comparative History of Black People in the Diaspora*, edited by Darlene Clark Hine and Jacqueline McLeod, 179–201. Bloomington: Indiana University Press, 1999.

Stipriaan, Alex Van. "July 1, Emancipation Day in Suriname: A Contested *Lieu de Memoire*, 1863–2003." *New West Indian Guide* 78 (2004): 269–304.

Stouffer, Allen P. *The Light of Nature and the Law of God: Antislavery in Ontario, 1833–1861.* Baton Rouge: Louisiana State University Press, 1992.

Stuckey, Sterling. *Slave Culture: Nationalist Theory and The Foundations of Black America.* New York: Oxford University Press, 1987.

Studley, Marian H. "An 'August First' in 1844." *New England Quarterly* 16 (December 1943): 567–77.

Sullivan-Gonzalez, Douglass, and Charles Reagan Wilson, eds. *The South and the Caribbean.* Jackson: University of Mississippi Press, 2001.

Sweet, Leonard I. "The Fourth of July and Black Americans in the Nineteenth Century: Northern Leadership Opinion within the Context of the Black Experience." *Journal of Negro History* 61, no. 3 (July 1976): 256–75.

Swift, David E. *Black Prophets of Justice: Activist Clergy Before the Civil War.* Baton Rouge: Louisiana State University Press, 1989.

Thompson, E. P. *Customs in Common: Studies in Traditional Popular Culture.* New York: New Press, 1993.

Thornbrough, Emma Lou. *The Negro in Indiana: A Study of a Minority.* Indianapolis: Indiana Historical Bureau, 1957.

Travers, Len. *Celebrating the Fourth: Independence Day and the Rites of Nationalism in the Early Republic.* Amherst: University of Massachusetts Press, 1997.

Turner, Edward R. *The Negro in Pennsylvania: Slavery-Servitude-Freedom, 1639–1861.* New York: Arno Press, 1969.

Turner, Mary. *Slaves and Missionaries: The Disintegration of Jamaican Slave Society, 1787–1834.* Urbana: University of Illinois Press, 1982.

Tyrrell, Ian. "American Exceptionalism in an Age of International History." *American Historical Review* 96 (October 1991): 1031–55.

Waldstreicher, David. *In the Midst of Perpetual Fetes: The Making of American Nationalism, 1776–1820*. Chapel Hill: University of North Carolina Press, 1997.

Walvin, James. *Fruits of Empire: Exotic Produce and British Taste, 1660–1800*. New York: New York University Press, 1997.

———. *Slavery and the Slave Trade: A Short Illustrated History*. Jackson: University of Mississippi Press, 1983.

Warner-Lewis, Maureen. *Central Africa in the Caribbean: Transcending Time, Transforming Cultures*. Kingston: University of West Indies Press, 2003.

White, Richard. "Civil Rights Agitation: Emancipation Days in Central New York in the 1880s." *Journal of Negro History* 78, no. 1 (Winter 1993): 16–24.

Wiggins, William, Jr. *O Freedom! Afro-American Emancipation Celebrations*. Knoxville: University of Tennessee Press, 1987.

Williams, Eric. *Capitalism and Slavery*. London: Andre Deutsch, 1964.

———. *History of the People of Trinidad and Tobago*. Port of Spain, Trinidad: PNM Publishing, 1962.

Williams, George Washington. *A History of the Negro Troops in the War of the Rebellion, 1861–1865*. New York: Harper & Brothers, 1888.

Wilmot, Swithin. "The Politics of Protest in Free Jamaica—The Kingston John Canoe Christmas Riots, 1840 and 1841." *Caribbean Quarterly* 26, nos. 3 and 4 (December 1990): 65–75.

Wilson, Hilary. *Understanding Hieroglyphics: A Complete Introductory Guide*. New York: Barnes and Noble, 1993.

Winks, Robin W. *The Blacks in Canada: A History*. New Haven: Yale University Press, 1971.

Wood, Donald. *Trinidad in Transition: The Years after Slavery*. London: Oxford University Press, 1968.

Wood, Marcus. *Blind Memory: Visual Representations of Slavery in England and America 1780–1865*. New York: Routledge, 2000.

Woodman, Harold D. "Slavery: II Economic Aspects." *Houghton Mifflin Reader's Companion to American History*. http://college.hmco.com/history/readerscomp/reah/html/ah.

Work, Monroe N. "Secret Societies as Factors in the Social and Economical Life of the Negro." In *Democracy in Earnest*, edited by James E. McCulloch. Washington, D.C.: Southern Sociological Congress, 1918.

Yellin, Jean Fagan. "Harriet Ann Jacobs." *Legacy* 5, no. 2 (1988): 55–61.

DISSERTATIONS

Bettelheim, Judith. "The Afro-Jamaican Jonkonnu Festival: Playing the Forces and Operating the Cloth." Ph.D. diss., Princeton University, 1979.

Cooper, Afua Ava Pamela. "Doing Battle in Freedom's Cause: Henry Bibb, Abolitionism, Race Uplift, and Black Manhood, 1842–1854." Ph.D. diss., University of Toronto, 2000.

French, Scott Andrew. "Remembering Nat Turner: The Rebellious Slave in American Thought, 1831 to the Present." Ph.D. diss., University of Virginia, 2000.

Kachun, Mitchell A. "The Faith That the Dark Past Has Taught Us: African-American Commemorations in the North and West and the Construction of a Usable Past, 1808–1915." Ph.D. diss., Cornell University, 1997.

Walton, Jonathan W. "Blacks in Buxton and Chatham, Ontario, 1830–1890: Did the 49th Parallel Make a Difference?" Ph.D. diss., Princeton University, 1979.

Index